The Story of

HULL

South-East View of Hull, by Benjamin Gale, 1798.

The Story of
HULL

Richard Gurnham

PHILLIMORE

First published 2011, this edition 2016

Phillimore & Co. Ltd, an imprint of The History Press
The Mill, Brimscombe Port
Stroud, Gloucestershire, GL5 2QG
www.thehistorypress.co.uk

British Library Cataloguing in Publication Data.
A catalogue record for this book is available from the British Library.

ISBN 978 0 7509 6765 5

Typesetting and origination by The History Press
Printed and bound in Great Britain by
Marston Book Services Ltd, Oxfordshire

Contents

List of Illustrations

Frontispiece: South-East View of Hull, by Benjamin Gale.

Acknowledgements

First I must thank the staff of both my local library in Louth and the Hull History Centre, who always dealt with my inquiries and requests most helpfully. The newly opened History Centre is a considerable asset not only to Hull but also widely beyond the city's bounds which it serves. And, as I hope the final illustration of this book indicates, its striking appearance is yet another architectural asset to this reviving and regenerating city. Our country's library service – now grievously threatened – is of enormous benefit to all communities. I know that this book – like so many others – would not have been possible without the resources and cooperation of the library service.

A very high proportion of the illustrations used in this book come from earlier local histories of the city, all of which are held at the Hull History Centre, and the pictures of bomb damage in the city during the two world wars (illustration 116) are from the Centre's considerable collection of local historical photographs. Copies of other pictures have come from the Ferens Art Gallery (cover, back endpaper, 48 and 64) (many thanks to Collections Curator, Caroline Rhodes) and from friends. Tony Robson, whose family once owned the Moors' & Robson's brewery, let me use his excellent copy of the 16th-century sketch of the town (22). Tony also let me borrow a number of useful sources I might otherwise have missed, read through the last two chapters, and gave me the benefit of his detailed and personal knowledge of the city. Another friend, Mrs Lesley Brown, very kindly lent me her collection of Edwardian Hull postcards, from which illustrations 83, 89, 103, 107 and 112 are taken, and her copy of the 1926 Official Guide to Hull, from which I have taken illustrations 1, 85, 117 and 123.

Thanks are also due to two former colleagues in the History Department of King Edward VI Grammar School, where, until very recently, I worked for 34 years. Robert O'Farrell read through early drafts of the first chapters and helped me considerably in obtaining information for these, and particularly for the town's role in both the Wars of the Roses and the Pilgrimage of Grace. Fellow colleague and former deputy headmaster at the school, Martin Priestley, shared with me his boyhood memories of the city and his enthusiasm for Larkin's poetry, and drew my attention to 'Here', which I have used as a kind of poetic introduction to this book.

Finally, as ever, a big thank-you to members of my family, who have all read chapters of the book and given me the benefit of their wisdom, and especially to my wife, Jeannie, who is always my sternest critic. Jeannie also once again took many of the photographs that appear here.

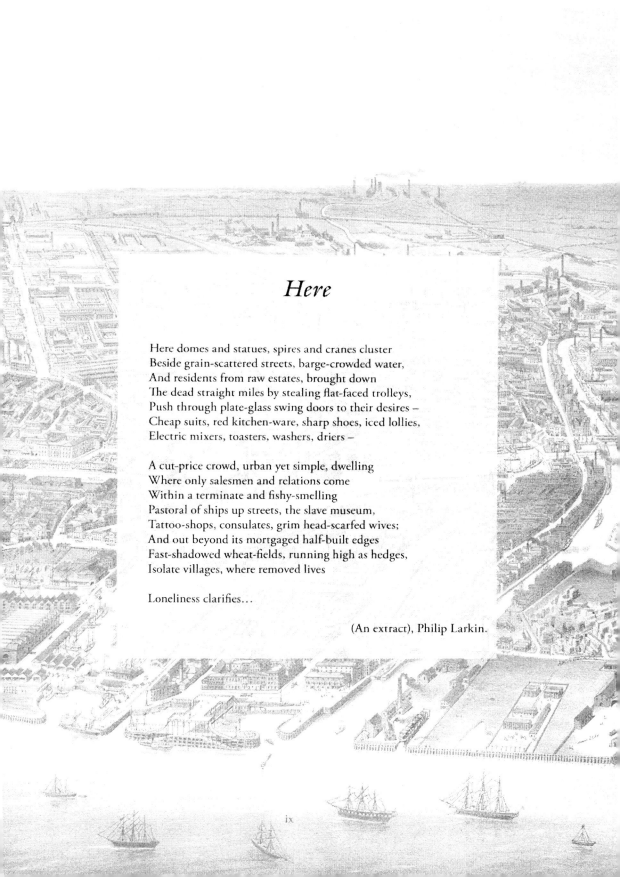

Here

Here domes and statues, spires and cranes cluster
Beside grain-scattered streets, barge-crowded water,
And residents from raw estates, brought down
The dead straight miles by stealing flat-faced trolleys,
Push through plate-glass swing doors to their desires –
Cheap suits, red kitchen-ware, sharp shoes, iced lollies,
Electric mixers, toasters, washers, driers –

A cut-price crowd, urban yet simple, dwelling
Where only salesmen and relations come
Within a terminate and fishy-smelling
Pastoral of ships up streets, the slave museum,
Tattoo-shops, consulates, grim head-scarfed wives;
And out beyond its mortgaged half-built edges
Fast-shadowed wheat-fields, running high as hedges,
Isolate villages, where removed lives

Loneliness clarifies…

(An extract), Philip Larkin.

ONE

The Creation of a Medieval Town

Origins

As we walk down High Street today in the Old Town of Hull, not far from the river from which the town took its name, it is not too difficult to imagine the medieval surveyors of the 13th century, equipped with their long poles, marking out the road and its plots to be sold to enterprising merchants, keen to build their houses and warehouses close to the river. In many respects the old road has hardly changed. It still winds gently as it follows the line of the river, and it is still as narrow in places as ever it was more than 700 years ago.

High Street was originally known as Hull Street and was laid out, along with its adjacent building plots, in the 13th century. This was the nucleus of a town that was to grow quickly in the second half of the century. It was owned and developed by the Cistercian monks of Meaux Abbey, who were keen to have a port from which they could export wool from their rapidly expanding sheep flocks. Before the end of the 13th century it had proved sufficiently successful to attract the attentions of King Edward I, who then acquired and developed it further as a royal port.

But this was not the site of the earliest Hull. The town had been founded by the monks in the second half of the 12th century, but it may have been on a different site, about half a mile to the west, probably close to where Ferensway now runs. Hull was one of many 'new towns' established in England at this time to foster the growth of trade; others included Leeds, Liverpool, Boston and Harwich.[1] This first attempt at town-building by the monks would seem to have been successful but the little town had to be relocated a short distance eastwards following a change in the course of the river Hull. The 'Old Hull', as it would later be known, seems to have gradually

1

become silted up during the 12th and 13th centuries and another channel to the east was created (or at least enlarged), following the course of the river as we know it today. The destruction of the former river course could have resulted from flooding, for in 1253 we are told by the chronicler of the abbey that floods had destroyed much of the abbey's lands, and the chronicler of Louth Abbey, in Lincolnshire, reported that flooding along the banks of the Humber had reached as far inland as Cottingham.[2] This would be the first of many such watery devastations to afflict the town, the latest being in 2007, when, tragically, one man lost his life, millions of pounds of damage was done, and many thousands of people saw their homes wrecked by the flood waters.

The monks had first arrived in the area in 1150, when they had been granted land on which to build their abbey about seven miles to the north of Hull. As a result of numerous gifts they quickly acquired substantial sheep pastures, including the low-lying and ill-drained lands of the hamlet of Myton, beside the river Humber, and where the river Hull flowed into the Humber they established their first new town, which they called Wyke upon Hull. The name Wyke was taken from the Scandinavian *vik*, or creek. The monks took possession of the surrounding lands and began draining and improving them.[3]

The town was probably in existence by about 1180 for before the end of the century it was already a small but flourishing port. It is first mentioned in 1193, when it was used as the collection point for a ransom of wool contributed by a number of monasteries for the release of Richard I from captivity. By this time the export of wool from the abbey's numerous sheep farms was a major part of its trade. Just a few years later, in 1197-9, the Exchequer accounts show that 45 sacks of wool were sold at the port, each sack containing about 200 fleeces, and when King John chose to tax the eastern and south coast ports in 1203-5 Hull was ordered to pay £345, the sixth largest contribution of all the towns assessed, and twice as much as York's contribution.[4]

From 1226 Hull was constantly found in the lists of ports whose officers were addressed by royal officials regarding matters such as the export of wool, the clipping of money and alien merchants. One of the earliest was an order of 5 November 1226 ordering a relaxation of the prohibition against French merchants. The recipient of this instruction was a local landowner, Saer de Sutton, who was addressed as bailiff. In later instructions he is sometimes also referred to as the 'Keeper' of the port.

During Saer de Sutton's period of office Hull would seem to have gained a rather unsavoury reputation for piracy. In 1227 a Spanish ship from San Sebastian was attacked off Sandwich, the merchants on board were killed and the ship was taken to Hull. Here its cargo was plundered and Saer de Sutton and his brothers helped themselves, it was later reported, to six casks of wine. During 1230 it was said that as many as 15 ships had been arrested at Hull by Saer de Sutton and numerous royal mandates had to be sent to the town before their release was secured.

The town's relocation does not seem to have damaged its growth and prosperity. By the 1270s, when customs duties began to be levied on the exports of wool and hides, the town's trade had clearly expanded. During 10 months in 1275-6, 67 cargoes left the port, carrying between them more than 4,000 sacks of wool, 4,700 woolfells and 103 hides. Most years Hull was the third largest wool exporting port in the country, second only to London and Boston. The town was also becoming a major importer of wine. The Exchequer 'pipe rolls' show that wine was being shipped from Hull to York as early as 1204, and wine ships were recorded reaching Hull in the 1220s. By the end of the century the trade was considerable and in 1291 415 tuns of wine were distributed from Hull.[5]

By the 1290s there were about 60 households, or about 300 people, living in Hull, then an area of about 60 acres. The first chapel for the relocated town may only have been built in 1285, on the site now occupied by Holy Trinity Church. Elsewhere, on Monkgate (later Blanket Row and Blackfriargate), a house of Carmelite friars was established in 1289, under the patronage of the Dean of York Minster, Robert of Scarborough, who was keen to assert his interest in the growing town. In 1279 the monks of Meaux Abbey had also acquired the right to hold a weekly market, probably on the site of today's market place, and a 15-day annual fair. The principal street was Hull Street, and here was to be found the house and court of the abbot, and not far away – although the precise location is not known – the abbot's gaol. Hull Street was already where better-off members of the community lived; not only the abbot but also numerous prominent merchants and landowners, such as Sir Geoffrey de Hotham, the highest rent-payer in the town, and Sir Robert de Percy, whose lands, or 'messuage', stretched the whole length of Kirk Lane, from Hull Street to Marketgate (now Market Place). In 1293 about two thirds of the rental was accounted for by the houses and plots in Hull Street and most of the other third by the properties in Marketgate and Monkgate. By this time, other streets had been laid out and building plots marked out, awaiting tenants. Indeed most of the streets shown in the sketch map of the 14th-century town (see fig. 4) already existed at the end of the 13th century.[6]

Edward I's acquisition of the town

Until Charles Frost published his research into the early history of the town in 1827, in his *Notices relative to the Early History of the Town and Port of Hull*, it was believed that Hull had been founded by Edward I, and the town's true early history was completely unknown. Until then it was believed that Hull was a tiny and insignificant hamlet when Edward decided, in a moment of inspired genius, to build a town and port here. The Revd John Tickell, in his *History of the Town and County of Kingston upon Hull*, published in 1798, told his readers that the king was one day hunting with his courtiers in the area when they saw a hare and gave chase:

[It] led them along the delightful banks of the river Hull to the hamlet of Wyke …
[Edward], charmed with the scene before him, viewed with delight the advantageous
situation of this hitherto neglected and obscure corner. He foresaw it might become
subservient both to render the kingdom more secure against foreign invasion, and at
the same time greatly to enforce its commerce. He quickly conceived a thought, worthy
of himself … to erect a fortified town, and make a safe, commodious harbour.[7]

Like all good myths, however, there had to be a grain of truth in the story. Edward
could not found the town because it already existed, but he did purchase it, and it is
probably true that he was persuaded to do this by a combination of economic and strategic
considerations. Edward was in need of a northern port for shipping men and supplies to
his armies and garrisons in the north, and during the first of his wars against the Scots,
soon after his purchase of the town, Hull would play a vital role as a royal supply port.

The idea of buying the town from the Abbot of Meaux was probably first suggested
to Edward by one of his officials, William de Hamelton, who had already had financial
dealings with the abbot, lending substantial sums to the abbey on the security of its
properties in Wyke and Myton.[8] The wool trade's importance to the king cannot be
overstated. Very large sums of money could be raised from both taxes on wool exports
and from loans from the Italian merchants who handled much of the export trade.
Moreover, the king's power to interfere in the trade, including the occasional outright
ban, was a useful weapon in foreign diplomacy.[9] Edward would have been well aware
of the advantages of having his own bailiff present in the port to enforce his will.
Moreover, William de Hamelton was able to negotiate a good price for his master as
the abbey's finances had been mismanaged and were in a fragile state. The manors in
Lincolnshire and Yorkshire which were granted to the abbey in payment for Wyke and
Myton were soon found to fall far short in value, and the abbey chronicler was right
to say that the abbey sold its rights too cheaply.[10]

A rental of the town, made on the king's orders just before he took possession of it,
shows that houses, shops and workshops already lined almost the full length of Hull
Street, and that Marketgate and the eastern end of Monkgate were also nearly fully
built upon. Altogether, 53 plots were occupied, most of them on the east side of the
town, and a considerable degree of plot subdivision had already taken place, with many
of the plots on Hull Street being quite small. The monks had also set aside a field of
about seven acres for a horse fair.[11] To the north of the town, beyond the town ditch,
lay the town's fields, divided into ploughed furlong strips. The 1293 rental shows about
200 acres of ploughed land growing corn.

There was as yet no graveyard in the town. The bodies of those who died in the
little town were buried in the churchyard at Hessle, four miles upriver. Moreover,
there were no roads running to or from the town. Communication with the outside
world was therefore almost exclusively by boat, including the transport of the dead to
Hessle churchyard.

The haven apart, the town's site was far from ideal; not only was the area liable to frequent flooding but it also lacked a ready supply of drinking water. By the late 13th century a dyke had been cut, presumably on the orders of the abbey, to carry fresh water from the village of Anlaby, about three miles to the west. However, any serious flooding meant the dyke could be blocked or polluted and the supply of drinking water interrupted.[12]

Not all the town's first inhabitants enjoyed burgess status; in 1293 some still held their land as villeins and were therefore subject to many limitations on their personal freedom. For some, at least, this was soon to change. On 1 April 1299 Edward I granted his new town its first charter, and under this the town's inhabitants were all made freemen, provided they could contribute to the taxes – the tallage – to the Crown. The townsmen would not yet be self-governing, but the king's representative appointed to govern the town – the warden – had to act in the interests of the burgesses. Moreover, the town was now free from interference by the sheriff. Markets could now be held twice a week, on each Tuesday and Friday, and the annual fair would begin on 26 May and last for 30 days. Instead of an abbot's law court there was now a warden's court, and, as before, a town gaol. There must also have been a gallows nearby for the warden had the power to hang immediately any criminals caught in the act of their crime. The warden, or his deputy, was to live in the town and in 1297 Edward ordered the building of a new manor house, consisting of a hall, chambers and a chapel, surrounded by a protective ditch, with a bridge and gatehouse. This was very probably the manor house later acquired and rebuilt by the town's richest family in the 14th century, the de la Poles, on the site now occupied by the former General Post Office, surrounded by extensive gardens occupying the whole of the north-west corner of the town and running the length of Lowgate (then the northern section of Marketgate).[13]

The king was anxious to ensure that his new acquisition should grow and prosper and the town was charged only £66 13s. 4d. for the charter, whereas one of its local rivals, Ravenser, which received an almost identical charter on the same day, was charged £300. Edward also ordered that a mint and an exchange should be set up in the town in 1300, although the mint seems to

1 *The charter of 1299.*

2   *Silver penny*   3   *A painted metal plaque on Drypool Bridge showing a 13th-century*
coined at Hull.   *merchant ship, with the arms of the town emblazoned on the sail.*

have been closed down again shortly afterwards. In the same year orders were given that the town's streets should be paved with stone. The warden was given the power to raise the money for this by levying a toll on traffic entering the town by land. As part of the settlement of 1293 the king could have a number of roads built across the abbey's lands, and the surveys for these roads were made 10 years later. Three roads, up to 60 feet wide, were made to link the town to Hessle, Beverley and Bilton. Their routes still survive in places today, under their modern successors. As Edward Gillett noted, as a result of the 1303 survey, 'it can be seen that Anlaby and Hessle Roads point straight at the church of Holy Trinity'. If local landowners objected to the new roads, they could expect short shrift from the king. When Sir John de Sutton attempted to stop the townsmen from using the new road to Bilton, where it crossed his lands, Edward I had both him and his brother thrown into prison and only released after they had paid a very substantial fine.[14]

The town's facilities beside the haven were also improved at the Crown's expense. In 1297 a new quay was built, the King's Staithe, with a narrow road running eastwards down to the river Hull from the town centre, with a jetty built of wood and stone at its eastern end. Other quays must also have existed by this time, but more would be built during the 14th century to assist in loading and unloading the ships and weighing the cargoes of wool for tax purposes. While the town remained under the direct control of the king's warden, the Crown maintained both the haven and the banks of the Humber.

With the building of the Bilton Road the burgesses also gained their own ferry service across the river Hull to link the town to the road. They had to wait rather longer, however, to gain permission from the Crown to have their own ferry across the Humber. When permission came, in 1315, it meant a major boost for the town's trade, and ended the dependence on ferries operating from the Lincolnshire coast, particularly from Grimsby and South Ferriby.[15]

The growth of a medieval port

The town did not grow as quickly as the king might have hoped. A rental made in 1320 shows that only 21 plots had been built upon since 1293, and when existing plots had been re-let in 1317 it had been necessary to reduce the rentals on most of the plots considerably. Many of the plots in the more westerly parts of the town were let in 1320 but not yet built upon and the total valuation of the town by this time (£63 4s. 2½d.) was a little less than it had been in 1293. By 1330 the rental had risen to £95 but 30 of the 130 plots were said to be 'in decay' and paying no rent, and a further rental of 1347 showed that, although 166 holdings are listed as tenements, the value of the rents had fallen again to the levels of 1320 (£63 15s. 0¾d.). The first half of the 14th century was a period of only gradual growth for the town, and the street pattern established by 1300 seems to have remained little altered. In the early 1330s, however, shortly after the town gained self-governance, the new mayor and corporation erected a guildhall at the southern end of Marketgate and built 28 shops on either side of the street. But growth remained slow: although almost all the streets listed in the 1347 rental appear also at the beginning of the century, many of the plots were still undeveloped, especially in the western half of the town.[16] On the other hand, the trade of the port appears to have prospered for much of this period, at least up until the outbreak of the Black Death in the summer of 1349, although even this blow would prove to be of a remarkable short duration.

The town's slow growth in these years partly reflects the small share in the profits of trade taken by Hull merchants. In the 13th century and the beginning of the 14th, the port's largest export business, the wool trade, was dominated by Italians, particularly those belonging to the extremely wealthy merchant houses of the Peruzzi and Bardi families, and by Flemish and Brabantine merchants. During the 14th century English merchants played an increasingly important role, but it tended to be York and Beverley merchants, rather than the men of Hull. The costs and risks inherent in the international wool trade were enormous. Piracy and shipwreck were both common hazards and only men of substantial means could undertake the business. Hull, however, did have a few such men. The wealthiest Hull merchant in the first two decades of the 14th century was John Rotenhering, whose house, like those of all Hull's merchants, was on Hull Street, where he had his own staithe running out into the river. The wealthiest local merchants of the 1330s and 1340s were the Pole brothers, Richard and William, who

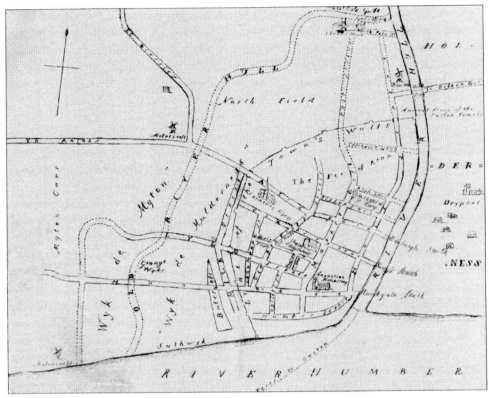

4 *Sketch showing the Hull's main streets and principal buildings in the 14th century.*

had moved to Hull from Ravenser earlier in the century, and by the 1330s the number of wealthy Hull merchants was increasing. In 1337, when William de la Pole helped organise a consortium of wool merchants who would enjoy a monopoly of wool exports, at least 14 were from Beverley, two from York, three or four from Lincolnshire, and possibly as many as six were from Hull, including de la Pole himself.[17]

Throughout the first half of the 14th century the chief goods handled were wool, corn and wine, but there was also a substantial trade in many other goods, particularly in Newcastle coal, timber from Scandinavia and iron from Spain, and during the wars with France and Scotland enormous fortunes could be made by providing the food and drink, weapons and other supplies for the king's armies. Hull maintained its position as the third most important port in the country for the export of wool, and came close to overtaking Boston. Vast quantities of wool from Lincolnshire, Yorkshire and the East Midlands were unloaded at Hull, weighed, taxed, stored and then loaded again onto sea-going vessels. The official figures show that in most years in the early 14th century at least 6,000 sacks left the port; and with smuggling the real figure was somewhat larger. Most of the wool was taken to Flanders, Brabant and Artois to supply the considerable cloth making and finishing industries of the Low Countries.[18]

William de la Pole and his brother Richard were not only the town's wealthiest inhabitants in the 1330s; both also won royal favour and were knighted, and they were among the richest and most spectacularly successful merchants in the country. It is a significant indication of the success of the port in these years that wealth such as theirs could be accumulated in Hull. Indeed, the mutual success of both family and town could be seen in the king's decision in 1331 to allow the town to become self-governing, and for the first mayor to be William de la Pole.

William de la Pole was described by the Meaux chronicler as 'second to no merchant in England'. By 1330 he and his brother had made a very large fortune for themselves in Hull, principally from exporting wool and importing wine. Both had also quickly moved into royal service. Richard became Edward II's butler, responsible for the purchase of wine for the court and an administrator of taxes on wine imports, but after Edward II's murder they befriended and prospered in the service of Edward's widow, Queen Isabella, and her lover, Mortimer. They then moved swiftly to ally themselves with the young Edward III when, in 1330, he took power for himself, executed Mortimer and banished his mother to a comfortable but closely watched retirement. With the outbreak of war against Scotland in 1337, the king needed very large sums of cash and William saw his opportunity to make a speculative 'killing'. In return for promising the king an enormous loan he secured the right to organise a monopoly on the wool exports for that year. Before the end of the year he and his syndicate had overseen the export of 30,000 sacks of wool and a few months later he was able to present Edward III with a loan of £18,000. A grateful king then made William responsible for handling most of his war finance. He became, to quote historian Eileen Power, the 'baron of the exchequer'.[19]

Such eminence could not last long. William was soon out of favour, and was arrested and imprisoned in November 1340, accused of smuggling,; but he had already proved himself to be too valuable to the king to be long in disgrace. Consequently, in May 1342 he was released, and during the next few years he was one of a number of merchants helping put together further syndicates to raise loans for the king in return for the right to farm the customs or collect revenues from other taxes. His brother, Richard, died in 1345 but William lived long enough to see his son, Sir Michael,

5 *Statue of William de la Pole, on the waterfront at Victoria Pier. Originally placed in the town hall, it was moved to its present position in the 1920s.*

6 *Hessle Gate, by Joseph Hargrave.*

7 *North Gate, by Joseph Hargrave.*

become a soldier and courtier. When William died in 1366 his enormous fortune had laid the foundations for the great wealth and power of a new aristocratic dynasty. After his death his son was raised to baronial rank and in 1385 he was created Earl of Suffolk.[20]

The population of the town by the 1320s was probably not above 2,000 but it was by this time important enough to be given the protection of a city wall. Edward II licensed the building of a wall in 1321, and a year later the need for it was made very apparent when a Scottish army descended deep into Yorkshire and camped at High Hunsley, just eight miles west of the town. Fortunately for the town the Scots chose not to attack, but it can be no coincidence that in the same year the king gave his warden permission to raise a murage tax to pay for the building of a wall and four gateways. Excavations have revealed that a very substantial crenellated wall was erected in brick in the next few years, surrounded by a wide moat. Its proportions were impressive. There were 20 rectangular interval towers punctuating the wall, and three of the four gates, commanding the three roads into the town – Hessle Gate, North Gate and Beverley Gate – were defended by barbican towers. The fourth gate, known as the Mamhole, in the south-east corner of the town, facing the Humber, was defended by a single tower. The first mention of the wall does not come until 1339, and it was not completed until the mid-1350s. Four and a half million locally made bricks were used, and this was the most extensive use of brick in medieval England.

Today, the only visible remains of the walls are the foundations of Beverley Gate and some adjoining walling at the west end of Whitefriargate. When completed it enclosed an area of 80 acres.[22]

By 1300 the little chapel that had been built for the town only 15 years earlier was no longer adequate. In 1301 the Archbishop of York gave permission for the chapel to have its own burial ground, and it was probably not long after this that a start was made on building the much larger church of Holy Trinity we see today (although it would officially remain a chapel belonging to the parish of Hessle until 1661). The first step was to build the base of the crossing tower and the transepts. Like the town walls, they were built in brick, constituting the earliest example of the use of brick for a church in England. Both the first stage of the tower and the transepts were completed by about 1320, and together they created a new small chapel which could be used by the townspeople long before any further stages were finished. As early as 1309, John Rotenheryng endowed a chantry in the church, and in 1327 William Skayll requested that he might be buried in the 'new chapel of Holy Trinity'. A chancel was also being built, again in brick, but twenty years later, when the Black Death struck the town, this was still far from completed, and it would not be finished until about 1370.[23]

One of the first to be buried in the chancel was Richard de la Pole, in 1345. He had asked to be buried in the church and his

8   *Beverley Gate.*

9 *Holy Trinity Church: the north transept, one of the first parts of the church to be completed, c.1320.*

tomb, and that of his wife Joan, is believed to be the fine mid-14th-century alabaster effigy in the south choir aisle. It may have once opened into the nearby Broadley Chapel, built originally as the family chapel for the de la Poles. The tomb lies under an ornate 14th-century canopied niche. Nearby, beneath another elaborate niche, is probably the tomb of his son, William Jnr, who died in 1366. There is no effigy but the heraldry depicted on the shields carved on the tomb suggests this is William's resting place.[24]

As the town grew, so did the Carmelite friary established in 1289. In 1307 the king gained the pope's permission to move the Carmelite friary to a new, much more spacious site extending along the south side of Aldgate, which came to be known – as it is still – as Whitefriargate. The royal letter to the pope explained that the existing buildings were no longer adequate for the great number of people who came to the friary 'to hear divine service'.[25] Moreover,

by this time, a second friary, belonging to the Augustinian order, had also been established in the town, on the east side of the market place. It was described early in the 14th century as 'lofty and spacious' and included both its own church and a cemetery, the latter being for the exclusive use of the friars and their lay brothers.[26] The street name Blackfriargate recalls the popular name of the Augustinian friars, always identified by their long black habits, whereas the Carmelites wore white cloaks and scapulars over brown habits. It is unlikely that either friary was welcomed by the local clergy, who saw them as dangerous rivals and a threat to their own incomes and status. They were usually popular with the poor, however, to whom they preached in the streets, and they were famed for their skills as preachers and for their knowledge of the Bible.

A second new church was also soon being built, perhaps partly in competition with the two friaries, a few hundred

10 *Mid-14th-century alabaster effigy of a wealthy merchant in Holy Trinity Church; possibly Sir Richard de la Pole (d. 1345).*

yards to the north of Holy Trinity Church, on Lowgate, the northward extension of the market place. The church of St Mary is first mentioned in 1327 as a chapel of ease, and in 1333 it was still being described as 'newly built'.[27]

The granting of the charter of 1331, making the town an autonomous borough, together with William de la Pole's appointment as the town's first mayor, indicated the influence and favour enjoyed at court by the de la Pole brothers at this time. In confirmation of this, the king ensured that as part of his progress north to join his army in the following year, he and his court paid a visit to the town as the guests of William de la Pole, and were lavishly entertained at the manor house in Lowgate. In recognition of William's services and 'extremely pleased with the reception he had met with', the king then 'knighted his loyal and generous host' before he departed.[28]

A second charter, obtained in 1334, was at least partly a consequence of de la Pole influence. This confirmed the town's status and granted the mayor a special royal seal. All agreements made in the town under the authority of the seal would be protected by law and strictly enforced. From about this time the mayor was to be assisted in the running of the town and in the administration of justice by eight other burgesses elected by the burgesses as a whole, together with two bailiffs and two chamberlains. There was little democracy at work here, however, for the governing body were elected for life, and the mayor was chosen from their number. When a vacancy did occur and an election had to be held, the burgesses had little choice about whom they elected. Only two candidates could be put forward and both had to have the approval of the governing body.[29]

The town had by this time acquired its own law code, governing the behaviour of both the inhabitants of the town and 'foreigners' coming to the town to trade, and a separate code regulating the sale of corn, ale, bread and wine. The regulations concerning the price and quality of bread were detailed and of especial importance to the town's poorer inhabitants, for whom it provided their staple diet. Bakers caught selling underweight bread would be fined for the first two offences but placed in the pillory in the market place if they offended a third time. Similar punishments were specified for brewers who breached the regulations governing the brewing and sale of ale. As this was almost always a woman's occupation, the punishment for a third offence was a little different. Instead of being placed in the pillory, the offending ale-wife would be put in a tumbrel and drawn around the town. Taverns which broke the rules governing the sale of wine could be closed down on the orders of the mayor.[30]

The Black Death

When the Black Death struck Hull in the summer of 1349 the effects were sufficiently severe to persuade the king to remit taxes owing to the Crown four years later. To make matters worse, the rivers Humber, Hull and Ouse had all flooded in the previous winter, devastating both York and Hull, and the town could barely have begun to recover from this when the plague arrived in June or July.[31]

The flooding may also have helped the spread of infection as it drove the rats of the town and neighbourhood from their usual haunts. The causes of the plague were not understood but the chronicler of the Abbey of Meaux had little doubt that God had sent at least two omens of the terrible events. On the Friday before Passion Sunday, he later recalled, the monks of the abbey were violently thrown from their stalls by an earthquake, and a few days before that a pair of Siamese twins had been born in the town.[32]

The only specific reference to the impact of the Black Death on Hull came in 1353, when Edward III explained his reasons for remitting some of the taxation owed by the town. He accepted that the town could simply not pay, and that its plight was genuine:

> considering the waste and destruction which our town of Kingston-on-Hull has suffered, both through the overflow of the waters of the Humber and other causes, and that a great part of the people of the said town have died in the last deadly pestilence which raged in these parts and that the remnants left in the town are so desolate and poverty-stricken.[33]

Just six miles to the north of the town the abbey of Meaux was, according to the chronicler, almost completely destroyed; out of 50 monks and lay brethren only 10 survived. Many of the monks and clergy contracted the disease as a consequence of their responsibility to bury the dead and give the last rites to the laity who were dying of the pestilence. The chronicler noted:

> God's providence ordained at that time that in many places the chaplains were kept alive to the very end of the pestilence in order to bury the dead; but after this burial of the lay folk the chaplains themselves were devoured by the plague, as the others had been before them.[34]

It is thought that about a third of the population of the country died, and in many areas the mortality rate was even higher. The number who died in Hull is not known but ports were especially susceptible. Hull was no dirtier a town than any other at this time, but it is very likely that some of the merchants and sailors coming into the port were carrying the deadly infection. Many may also have died in the flooding, which was extensive and very destructive. It may have been during this flood that almost all of the land immediately to the south of the town walls, facing the Humber, disappeared under the advancing river. Hull would begin to recover in the 1360s and 1370s, but there is no reason to doubt the accuracy of the king's description of the town in 1353: 'desolate and poverty stricken'.[35]

TWO

The Late Medieval Town, 1349-1485

The growth of the cloth trade and the completion of Holy Trinity Church

The city recovered remarkably quickly from the Black Death and in the second half of the 14th century it was probably growing more rapidly than at any time since its acquisition by Edward I. As a principal centre for the export of raw wool, Hull was well placed to become one of the major ports exporting English cloth. The high-quality wool of the sheep bred on the Yorkshire and Lincolnshire Wolds, which had for so long occupied the looms of Flemish and Brabantine weavers, was now being woven for export in England. The cloth industry was long established in the East Riding, and dyes for the trade had been a crucial import into Hull, but large-scale cloth exporting was something new. The number of broadcloths shipped out of Hull rose through the 1360s and 1370s, and from the 1380s, for about sixty years, Hull was one of the most important ports in the country for the export of cloth, in some years second only to London. In good years several thousand cloths were shipped, almost 3,200 in 1424-5, over 6,500 in 1428-9, and over 5,000 in 1437-8. Wool continued to be exported as well up until the 1440s and 1450s, when, like the cloth trade, the wool trade shrank rapidly. Corn and lead were also important exports, while a great variety of foreign goods were imported, particularly from the Baltic, mainly by Hanseatic merchants. Wine remained a great import, for the English had an almost unquenchable thirst for the wines of Gascony, for Rhenish wines, and for the 'sweet wines' of Portugal. English merchants had cloth, wool and corn to sell, and until England lost control of Gascony, towards the end of the Hundred Years War, they could exploit the trade of Bordeaux.[1]

One of the first signs of the town's speedy recovery from the disasters wrought by flooding and plague can still be seen today, in the chancel of Holy Trinity Church,

11 *The nave of Holy Trinity Church, with the exceptionally beautiful late 14th-century marble font in the foreground.*

which was completed in the 1360s. At the time the Black Death struck, only the lower stages of the central tower and the transepts of the church had been completed, even though a beginning had been made to the chancel possibly as early as the 1320s. For many years services had had to be celebrated in a mere fragment of a church. In 1361-2, however, the corporation felt able to raise money 'for the work of the church'. From now on the work went well and the chancel was completed in the next eight or nine years. Like the earlier transepts the builders continued to use locally made brick, but now the style is predominantly 'Decorated', with windows of flowing tracery, whereas in the earlier north and south transepts elements of the 'Early English' style are evident. As Pevsner noted, the east window, with seven lights, 'has a specially fanciful pattern'.[2]

The history of the building of Holy Trinity reflects the history of the town itself. While the completion of the chancel marked the beginning of the recovery of the town, so the building of the nave a few years later occurred during the prosperous years when ever larger quantities of broadcloths were being shipped from the town. Something of the enormous self-confidence of the town's merchants can be glimpsed in the size of the church. A beginning to the nave was made at the eastern end in about 1389 and when it was completed, in about 1425, the church was one of the largest and longest parish churches in the entire country. Due to the nave the church stretches 285 feet, but the style is Perpendicular and brick has been abandoned for the more prestigious stone. Apart from the upper stages of the tower, the church was almost certainly completed when it was consecrated in 1426, and its final glory was the great west front. David and Susan Neave describe it

12 *The choir and great east window of Holy Trinity Church.*

as possessing 'a grandeur that has few parallels in English medieval parish churches, making a fitting climax to this outstanding building.'[3]

Evidence for the town's rapid recovery is also to be found in the poll tax assessment of 1377. Marketgate, which had had relatively few houses on it 30 years earlier, was now becoming quite built up, and Bishop, Salthouse and Chapel Lanes, which had only single plots on them in 1347, were now lined with houses. The poll tax returns recorded 1,557 adult tax payers and 693 households. Both figures suggest a total population of at least three thousand. A number of completely new streets appear in the local corporation records or in the poll tax returns in the 1370s and 1380s, including Fleshmarketgate (later Butchery Street and today part of Queen Street), Listergate and Walker Lane, these last two names suggesting a concentration of textile craftsmen. The western parts of the town were still fairly open, with relatively few houses built on the streets that ran out to the town gates, and very few, if any, beyond the town walls; but at the end of the 14th century both Marketgate and Hull Street were becoming densely populated, as were the smaller streets running between them. Larger, older plots were being subdivided for several houses. More staithes were also built by the richer merchants, running down to the river Hull from their houses on Hull Street.[4]

The 1370s and 1380s were a period of particularly rapid growth and it was at this time that Sir Michael de la Pole, the son of Hull's first mayor, established the Charterhouse, a Carthusian monastery and almshouse just north of the town walls. This was built in 1378, using the land and generous endowments left by his father. The Carthusians were renowned as a particularly austere and reclusive order, and in late 14th-century England they flourished as never before. The house in Hull was one of seven new Carthusian foundations established between 1370 and 1420.[5]

The fortunate survival of a valuation of the 'goods and chattels' to be found in the de la Poles' manor house at the time of Sir Michael's death, in 1389, gives us a description of what must have been the largest and finest house in Hull at that time. Sir Michael, who had been raised to the peerage as the 1st Earl of Suffolk just four years earlier, rebuilt the house in the 1380s. It boasted a tower almost as large as that of Holy Trinity, had three gardens, each with a pond, and two dovecotes. The roof was so enormous that 4,000 tiles were kept ready for repairs. The valuation lists two halls, a chapel and 18 'chambers'. As well as a substantial kitchen and bakehouse there were also two wine cellars, a pantry and a buttery. In later years the house would be popularly known as Suffolk Palace. Moreover, the valuation shows that when the de la Poles were 'at home' and wished to entertain, they could do so on a most impressive scale. The silver plate on which the guests would dine was valued at £95, more than the value of the earl's ship, the *Philip*, at anchor in the haven and valued at £80.[6]

At the beginning of the 15th century most houses were still built in timber, with the laths between the timbers covered with a mixture of mud, sand, lime and cow dung. Brick, however, was increasingly common, especially for higher-status houses;

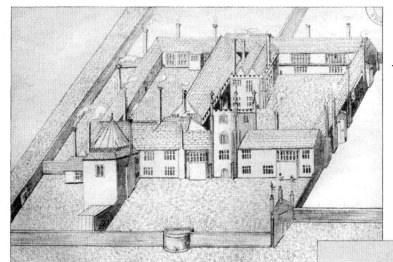

13 *Suffolk Palace, drawn in about 1540, when plans were made to strengthen the fortifications of both the house and the town.*

14 *The last remaining remnant of Suffolk Palace in 1884.*

all the houses owned by the corporation were roofed in tiles rather than thatch. Bricks were sometimes brought downriver from Beverley but most would be made locally. The town's tilery and brickyard lay just outside the town walls near the road to Myton. The Chamberlain's Rolls show that 100,000 bricks or tiles were made there in 1423-4, using brick-clay dug on the site. Very few houses, however, had a chimney. One of the earliest references in the Chamberlain's Rolls to a chimney being repaired dates from 1447-8. At this date most houses, including those of the town's wealthier landowners and merchants, had only a central hearth. The smoke had to escape through a vent in the roof covered by a slatted louvre. During the later decades of the century, more and more houses had chimneys installed, or were completely rebuilt around the chimney, and in the 1480s and 1490s references in the Chamberlain's Rolls to the repairs of chimneys become ever more frequent while those to louvre repairs slowly disappear.[7]

Threats to prosperity: silting and flooding
The continuing growth and prosperity of the town depended very heavily on maintaining the haven and in particular on preventing it from silting up. The dumping of ballast in the haven had long been forbidden, but this was a law too often ignored.

Increasing concerns about the state of the haven prompted the corporation to renew the ancient ban in 1453 and to introduce heavy fines for any caught ignoring it. One effective means adopted by the corporation was to provide a muck-cart to tour the town three times a week, collecting both stable and household refuse. This was taken to the Mamhole gate, in the south-east corner of the town, where it could be dumped instead in the Humber and taken away by the next tide.[8]

Another measure adopted was a ban, first imposed in 1435-6, on the shipmasters' practice of casting their anchors not into the haven, where they might be lost in stormy weather, but rather on the bank itself. The banks of both the Humber and the haven were weak and, if made weaker by a pulling anchor could easily topple into the river, especially when the rivers flooded. In 1461 it was ordered that all ships in the haven unfit to sail be removed to dry land, and in 1462 it was announced that anyone who could dredge up any wreckage, timber, broken anchors or cables from the riverbed was free to keep or sell them. To try to remove the mud banks forming as a result of silting and bank erosion, the men who made their living by supplying ballast to ships were ordered in 1474 to only use mud from these banks when providing ballast to colliers.

The greatest fear was that a major flood would once again totally destroy the haven, and move the river into a new channel altogether, as it seems to have done in 1253. The inhabitants knew there was very little they could do to protect themselves, apart from maintaining the river banks. Relatively serious floods, causing considerable damage to houses and roads, were quite common and the town was sometimes virtually an island reachable only by boat. To try to protect the Holderness road from flooding when the Humber burst its banks, a waterway was dug to the east of the town in the late 1360s, following a very severe spell of flooding in January and February 1365.

Flooding could also cause serious problems for the town's supplies of fresh drinkable water, and as the population grew steadily again in the late 14th century this became an issue of ever greater concern. At high tides, saltwater from the Humber prevented the water from the haven being used, although it was said to be just drinkable at low tide. The town's principal source of fresh water was the 13th-century watercourse bringing spring water from Anlaby, but during serious flooding salty waters broke through its banks and Hull's supplies of fresh water were greatly reduced. Consequently, in 1401 the town undertook a major programme of restoring and protecting the old

15 *No. 5 Scale Lane; a jettied timber-framed house dating from the 15th century. The medieval brickwork of the east-facing wall can be clearly seen. It is now a restaurant.*

watercourse and this seems to have been on the whole successful, for the dike continued to be used throughout the century. When there were exceptional high tides, however, the watercourse could not always be protected. On these occasions drinking water had to be brought down the river Hull by boat, but only the town's richer inhabitants could afford this. The watercourse itself would also frequently overflow and flood the surrounding fields, much to the fury of villagers who lived nearby.

The town in the mid-15th century

Hull in the 1440s was a highly successful port. Merchants were shipping great quantities of wool, cloth and corn from the haven, and importing a considerable amount of wine from Gascony and Portugal, fish from Icelandic waters, and timber and other goods from Scandinavia and the Baltic. Tolls were payable to the town on all goods, imported and exported. The town had grown steadily in the previous 80 years but at the end of the 15th century there would still be much open ground within the town walls.

The drinking water from Anlaby's springs flowed into the town in an open dike, known (confusingly for the modern reader) as the common sewer, and this had to be kept reasonably clean. It was one of the duties of the town's chamberlains, appointed by the corporation, to ensure that any townsman caught polluting the water supply in any way received a fine. Most of the streets seem to have been cobbled since the beginning of the 14th century, and the regular arrival of the muck cart kept them reasonably clean, although occasionally the local court records, the Bench Book, mentions townspeople allowing piles of refuse to accumulate. Fines were also imposed on inhabitants who allowed their pigs to wander through the streets. In an agricultural community so heavily dependent on horses, the dung hill was bound to be a common sight – and smell – but the town was still a good deal cleaner and less unhealthy than it would become in the 18th century, when it became grossly overcrowded.[9]

The charter of 1331 had given the town's governing body considerable power and independence but during the succeeding hundred years this was undermined by the county justices of the peace, whose authority extended into all parts of the East Riding, including the boroughs. In 1440, however, a new charter gave the town the status of a separate county, free from the authority of the county justices, with their powers transferred instead to the mayor and aldermen. A monthly county court would now be held in the town by

16 *Model of a 'cog',
a 15th-century sailing ship.*

the mayor, to hear pleas of all kinds. The Yorkshire justices were now excluded from the town and the mayor and 12 other aldermen would keep the peace in their place. Moreover, the profits of the court would go to the burgesses. A separate royal grant made in the same year gave the mayor the right to have a sword carried before him in all official processions, showing he was the king's representative in the town, and all the aldermen were given the right to wear robes and hoods similar to those worn by the aldermen of London. Another charter, granted by Henry VI in 1447, extended the area of the mayor's and aldermen's authority beyond the town's walls and fields to include the freshwater dike, which became the northern boundary, and 10 local villages: Hessle, North Ferriby, Swanland, Westella, Kirkella, Tranby, Willerby, Wolfreton, Anlaby and Haltemprice.[10]

These two charters and the royal grant of 1440 – so favourable to the town – may have been the consequence of the enormous influence at court enjoyed at this time by William de la Pole, the 4th Earl of Suffolk (and soon to be the 1st Duke), the great-grandson of William de la Pole, the first mayor of Hull and founder of the family's wealth. The Earl of Suffolk had first risen to a position of power and influence during the minority of Henry VI, becoming steward of the royal household in 1433 and shortly afterwards a regular member of the King's Council. By the time Henry came of age, in 1437, Suffolk was one of the most powerful men in the kingdom, enjoying the king's complete confidence. The charters were relatively small favours among the many great gifts lavished by the king on his favourite. In 1437 he became high steward of the duchy of Lancaster, in 1438 chief justice of South Wales, in 1442 he received the reversion of the earldom of Pembroke, in 1444 he was created a marquis, in 1447 he was appointed Lord Great Chamberlain of England, Constable of Dover and Warden of the Cinque Ports, and in 1448 he became a duke.[11]

The judicial and administrative powers of the mayor and aldermen were further extended in 1452 when the town gained the office of deputy to the Admiral of England, Henry, Duke of Exeter. The duke was paid £5 6s. 8d. a year and in return the town gained the right to hold an Admiralty court and to appoint a commissioner who would act as Admiralty judge for the town. The profits of the court were to be shared between the commissioner and the town. The Admiral's powers included the right to search foreign ships coming into the haven and this would later be used to insist that the goods being carried should be offered for sale in Hull first, before proceeding to any neighbouring town.

The lucrative nature of such rights could prompt jealous attentions. In April 1460, Lord Egremont, a member of the powerful Percy family and a friend of the Duke of Exeter, attempted to enter the town with an armed following to claim the rights for himself. The town managed to lock the town gates against him and mustered sufficient forces to dissuade Egremont from attempting an attack from the haven. It also appealed for a judgement on the matter from the Crown, sending messengers equipped with two tuns of wine as a gift to help the King's Council reach the right decision. The Council's power was at this time extremely limited but the corporation was nevertheless glad to gain its blessing. Egremont accepted a face-saving compromise. He was allowed to enter the town but only with a small retinue, and with no more talk of Admiralty rights. Although of little consequence on this occasion, a distribution of substantial gifts to powerful aristocrats, to their servants, and sometimes to the Crown itself, was a frequent and necessary expenditure for the corporation to elicit crucial support when needed.

On a number of occasions the protection of powerful landowners and courtiers proved a licence for lawlessness and violence in the town. In 1464 the mayor, John Green, suffered severe intimidation at the hands of John Neville, Lord Montague, after he had had the temerity to arrest and imprison a group of Montague's servants who had attacked and robbed two ships in the haven, wounded the ships' crews, broken into a house in the town and stolen cloth, and then refused to swear to keep the peace, no doubt well aware of the protection they could expect from their master. Montague was the younger brother of the Earl of Warwick, often known as 'the King-maker', the most powerful man in the country at that time. When he heard of his servants' arrest Montague informed Green that if he came anywhere near his house at Wressle, about 14 miles away, he would either 'lose his head, or else be chopped as small as flesh to pot'.[12]

The Wars of the Roses

The civil wars, which began in the 1450s and continued intermittently for 30 years, were a particularly expensive, troublesome and unhappy time for the town. They served to make a difficult situation worse, for trade was already in decline when the conflict began. The wine trade was badly affected by the loss of Gascony in the wars against France in 1451-3, and the cloth trade shrank from about 1450 as the Hanseatic League stifled export of English cloth to the Baltic. During the 1450s there was only one year in which as many as 3,000 cloths were exported from Hull, and by the 1460s there were rarely more than 1,000 per year leaving the port. London, by contrast, was exporting about 20,000 a year. By 1460 Hull's foreign trade was less than a quarter of its value half a century earlier.[13]

Although the authority of Henry VI's government declined sharply after the victory of the Yorkist faction in the first battle of St Albans, in 1455, and the town's economic problems could be partly blamed on the king's failures in the war against France, the majority of the corporation remained his firm supporters. This was in part due, no doubt, to gratitude for the king's generous treatment of the town in the 1440s, but it may also have reflected anger and resentment felt in the town at the murder, in 1450, of the Duke of Suffolk, which was widely blamed on the Duke of York.[14]

When civil war broke out again, in 1459, the corporation's loyalty to Henry VI and Queen Margaret was not in doubt. Its first concern was to strengthen the town's defences and prepare for a Yorkist siege. The potential strategic importance of the port was well recognised. When the fighting was at its most intense, in September and October 1459, the corporation ordered a tripling of the night watch, from eight men to 24, banned the removal of corn from the town, and called on all townsmen to equip themselves with weapons appropriate to their rank and station. The crisis quickly passed with the defeat of the Yorkist army at Ludlow, in October, and the flight of the Duke of York, his son and their closest allies to Calais a few days afterwards. Eight months later, however, the Duke's son, Edward, Earl of March, and numerous other nobles returned to England with a considerable force, and once more Hull was in danger. On 5 July 1460 news reached the town that the Yorkists had entered London unopposed and were now marching north to confront the king at Northampton. The common bell was rung to summon all burgesses to the guildhall, where it was decided to send 13 men to help the king. It is unlikely that they arrived in time, for the Yorkist forces – 40,000 men led by the Earls of March and Warwick – reached Northampton very quickly and on 10 July defeated the much smaller royal army and captured the king.[15]

Although the Duke of York professed himself anxious for an end to hostilities, the burgesses and aldermen of Hull were right to fear that further warfare was inevitable. While the two factions attempted to reach a compromise in London, whereby the Duke of York swore his loyalty to Henry VI and in return was recognised as his rightful successor, the people of Hull strengthened the town's defences and waited warily. By the end of September about a quarter of the town's men were enlisted as night watchmen and three of the town's four gates were shut and barred both day and night. Only Beverley Gate was opened during the hours of daylight, with a guard on constant lookout duty. The Mamhole entrance was blocked up 'by casting down muck' – a communal activity involving many of the town – and the North Gate's defences were strengthened by digging a ditch inside the walls. The weak point in the town's defences was the unwalled east side, facing the river Hull. To try to plug this gap it was ordered in October that the staithes opening on to the haven must be blocked by gates or bars and in November it was decided to station an armed ship at the jetty and to place archers on each of the staithes. Shortly after this it was also agreed to put a chain across the mouth of the haven so that no ship could enter without approval by the mayor and aldermen.[16]

Although the mayor and corporation, and most of the burgesses, were loyal Lancastrians, it is known that some townsmen, including the son of the mayor, left the town to fight for the Yorkist faction. In October an order was made by the corporation forbidding anyone from leaving the town without permission from the mayor. The corporation's support for the House of Lancaster was also evinced by generous backing for a subscription raised to support Queen Margaret, the effective head of the Lancastrian faction, although this was encouraged by the arrival in the town of a very powerful member of the Lancastrian faction, Henry Percy, Earl of Northumberland.

In November, according to an anonymous London chronicler, Queen Margaret herself arrived in the town and briefly made it her headquarters. She clearly had no doubts about the town's loyalties and presumably had happy memories of her previous visit, 12 years before, when the royal party had stayed with the Duke of Suffolk at his palace in Lowgate. This was almost certainly where she stayed now, sending messages to her most loyal supporters, the Duke of Somerset and the Earl of Devon, to meet her there with their forces and other allies to coordinate their plans with the still loyal northern lords. The king, her husband, may have accepted that their little son should be disinherited and the crown pass instead to York, but she most certainly had not, and so she plotted at Hull how best to destroy the upstart Duke and ensure her son's inheritance. The London chronicler tells us:

> Then the Queen ... sent unto the Duke of Somerset, at that time being in Dorsetshire at the castle of Corfe, and for the Earl of Devonshire ... and prayed them to come to her as hastily as they might, with their tenants as strong in their harness as men of war ... to meet with her at Hull. And this matter was not tarried but full privily i-wrought; and she sent letters unto all her chief officers that they would do the same, and that they should warn all those servants that loved her or purposed to keep and rejoice their office, to wait upon her at Hull by that day as it [was] appointed by her. All these people were gathered and conveyed so privily that they were whole in number of 15,000 ere any man would believe it.[17]

In a series of bitterly fought battles between December 1460 and March 1461 the Duke of York lost his life (at the battle of Wakefield) but his faction emerged triumphant, utterly routing Queen Margaret's forces at Towton on 29 March. Among the many thousands who died in the fighting were the mayor of Hull, Richard Anson, who probably died at Towton, fighting for the Lancastrian cause, and his son, Captain Anson, who died fighting for the Yorkist faction a few months earlier at Wakefield. Anson jnr was captured during the battle and beheaded when the fighting was over, as was his leader, the Duke of York. The heads of both men, along with numerous other Yorkists, were then stuck on spikes placed over Mickle Gate Bar in York. The death of the mayor removed one of the most committed Lancastrians from the corporation of Hull, and a few others chose to resign, making it much easier for the new body to accept the legitimacy of the new king, Edward IV, the former Earl of March and eldest son of the Duke of York.[18]

Not long after the young king's triumph, a deputation led by the mayor travelled to York to pledge their loyalty to their new monarch and to present him with three tuns of wine. Edward was prepared to forgive the town its former support for Henry VI but only at a price. Six ships had to be provided to the king that year and, partly as a consequence of this, the town's finances were badly damaged. The renewal of the town's charter also proved costly, and in the following year another ship had to be fitted out for the king at the town's expense. Then, in 1464, 30 armed men had to be paid for and sent to join the royal army in suppressing a Lancastrian rebellion in the north. To recompense the town for this latter expense, however, it was agreed that the customs payable to the Crown for exports from Hull should be reduced by up to £40 per year for the next 10 years. This concession seems to have been regarded by Edward's government as sufficient compensation for a further demand in 1469, when another 20 fully armed men were called to join the royal army in suppressing a rebellion in Yorkshire. On this occasion, a special tax had to be imposed on the burgesses, causing considerable resentment, and at least one of the burgesses had to be threatened with imprisonment before his assessment was grudgingly accepted.[19]

When, in 1470, Warwick 'the Kingmaker' rebelled against Edward IV and, in alliance with Edward's brother, the Duke of Clarence, forced Edward to flee to the Netherlands, there was little sympathy in the town for the deposed king, and the restoration of Henry VI, released from the Tower of London by Warwick, was welcomed. When Edward IV returned to the country in March 1471, landing on the Yorkshire coast at Ravenser, the corporation refused to open the town's gates to him. The decision partly reflected the region's deep-seated dislike for Edward and the Yorkists, but also well-grounded fear of damage at the hands of his troops. Beverley allowed him entry but York only agreed on the condition that he entered without his army, and made it very clear that he was not welcome.[20]

Later the same year, after successive victories at Barnet and Tewkesbury, Edward succeeded in regaining the throne. With Warwick killed at Barnet, Henry VI murdered and his son, the Prince of Wales, killed at Tewkesbury, Edward was in a firmer position than ever before. After the tumults of the 1460s, the 1470s proved a more settled, peaceful and prosperous period for both the town and the country, but in the 1480s wars and rebellions broke out again.These culminated in the arrival of another rebel army at Milford Haven in 1485, led by an obscure Welsh nobleman who had been in exile in France for many years, Henry Tudor, Earl of Richmond. In September 1481, 13 of Hull's men had to be sent to fight against the Scots, and in 1483, when Richard III summoned forces to join him at Leicester to put down the Duke of Buckingham's rebellion, 14 men were sent from the town, 'arrayed for war'. There is no record, however, of Hull men being sent to fight at Bosworth in August 1485, where Richard III was defeated.[21]

The town at the end of the 15th century

The third quarter of the 15th century was a period of economic decline for the port. The quantities of exported raw wool and cloth fell sharply in the 1450s and 1460s. Cloths did pick up again in the 1470s, and for a number of years 2,000 per year were again being shipped out, but the number was soon again in decline. Consequently the number of merchants and others who sought enrolment as burgesses in the town also fell. Whereas the corporation could expect to raise at least £20 per year in burgess payments at the end of the 14th century, and in the first two decades of the 15th, during the 1460s this income was more than halved, and twice in the 1490s there were no new burgesses at all. The town's receipts from the weigh house and from tolls were also generally much lower in the 1450s and 1460s than earlier in the century, although the improvement in the cloth trade in the 1470s helped at least temporarily to reverse this trend, and in the 1490s they were rising again. The value of property rents also fell sharply during the 1460s and 1470s and only steadied in the 1480s.[22]

It was by no means all 'doom and gloom', however, for there were some more encouraging developments from the 1460s. The coastal trade in bulky goods such as corn and coal became increasingly important in the 1460s and 1470s, and this provided far more local employment than wool and cloth. There was also a prosperous fish trade, especially in 'stockfish' caught off the Icelandic coasts. Raw wool, lead and corn remained important exports (although wool exports were now much lower), and the revival of tolls in the 1470s was due partly to a wide variety of imports from the Scandinavian countries, handled by Hanseatic merchants.[23]

It was also in the mid-15th century that the town's shipmasters established a craft guild for themselves, and between 1465 and 1472 they built a timber-framed and tiled guildhall, together with almshouses and a chapel, on land leased from the Carmelites near the junction of Trinity House Lane and Posterngate, probably close to where the main Trinity House building stands today. The guild had evolved from an earlier, purely religious, guild founded in 1369 in honour of the Holy Trinity. Its members had been drawn from numerous occupations, and its main purpose was to provide candles and masses and ensure a good attendance at the funerals of its members. In 1398 this was still the case, when a 'Second Subscription' was drawn up, showing over 200 members, some of them women; but by the 1450s it seems to have completely changed, and become a guild for shipmasters only. In 1456 24 shipmasters agreed to found a chantry in Holy Trinity Church, and to pay for it from the money raised from the 'lowage and stowage' charges, the payments made for loading goods on the ships' decks and stowing in the hold. This was a guild of relatively wealthy men, and in the 16th century it would greatly extend its powers, obtain a royal charter from Henry VIII, and assume considerable control over the port.[24]

It is impossible to say much about the size of the town's population at the end of the 15th century. It was perhaps no larger than it had been at the beginning of the century, for it was still comfortably housed within its walls and population growth may have been prevented by repeated recurrences of plague; as a port it was particularly susceptible to infection. There is, however, no evidence to support the accounts of some of the town's early historians that the town suffered a series of very serious attacks of the plague in the 1470s.[25]

17 *Trinity House building today, on Trinity Lane. This east-facing front elevation was built in 1753 but the oldest part of the building, on the west side, probably incorporates the original medieval core.*

Hull was an important market centre for the surrounding area, able to boast the usual wide variety of crafts found in towns of similar size. A number of crafts were sufficiently numerous to be able to establish their own guilds. These included the goldsmiths, shoemakers, barbers, chandlers, skinners, weavers, shearmen and fullers. A number of tailors were also to be found, although they do not appear to have established their own guild. The town records concerning resident foreigners in 1481 mention three Scotsmen called 'Berbruer', which suggests beer – as distinct from ale without hops – was being brewed locally. The same records also refer to another foreigner living in the town as simply 'the straw-hat maker' and another has the name Henry Hattmaker.[267]

The cloth industry in the town, as represented by the weavers, shearmen and fullers, was not particularly large. In 1483 two of the town's fullers paid the corporation 6s. 8d. for the right to dry their cloth, after it had been dyed, on the warm, south-facing town wall, between Beverley Gate and North Gate. Another part of the wall

18 *The royal coat of arms, flanked by reclining figures of Neptune and Brittania, above the central doorway of Trinity House.*

was also being used, on the same terms, by some of the town's shearmen, to stretch the cloth on tenters.[27]

The port was an important source of employment for both the townspeople and the surrounding area, offering opportunities especially for unskilled labour, particularly loading and unloading goods from the ships. Work might also be found in ship and boat building and repairing – although on a very small scale – in fish processing, and as mariners; and on the other side of town the brick- and tileworks on Mytongate employed both skilled and unskilled labour. Many would be employed as domestic servants, agricultural labourers and general labourers, and the victualling trades (butchers, bakers, brewers, innkeepers) also employed large numbers. The butchers' stalls were mainly in the flesh-market although by 1492 there was also a butcher's shop under the guildhall.

Fleshmarketgate would also seem to have become, appropriately, the principal 'red-light' district of the town. A brothel is recorded in Whitefriargate in 1450, when Joan Frensshewoman was fined 4d. for keeping a disorderly house there, and the Chamberlain's Rolls record five bawds living in the flesh-market in 1484, one of whom

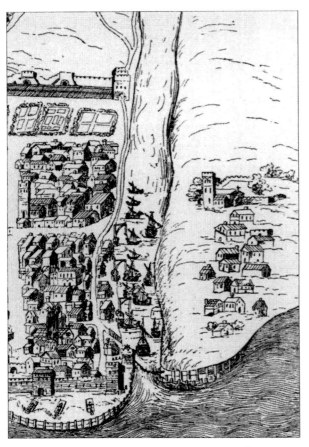

19 *A detail from a map of Hull, drawn about 1540, showing ships loading and unloading on the river Hull.*

had acquired the name 'Frerespowte', meaning a whore particularly popular with friars. Another brothel is recorded in Lowgate, when 'Big Margaret' of Lowgate was fined 2s. for receiving stolen goods, and at least one other was in the Tripett district of the town, just outside the walls at North Gate. One of the bawds mentioned in the Chamberlain's Rolls was simply known as 'Trowlop in Trypett'. The women were occasionally fined, but generally they were left alone by the bench, and at the end of the century the corporation was actually profiting from their work by letting to them a strip of land known as the 'Foreland', between the south wall and the Humber, for £3 6s. 8d. a year.[28]

THREE

The Early Tudor Town, 1485-1558

Economic growth and economic depression

From about 1490 to 1520 the trade of Hull enjoyed a marked revival, becoming the most valuable on the east coast, excepting that of London. For about 30 years, between 50 and 100 ships came into Hull every year. Most of the traffic was with the Low Countries, especially with Antwerp, in spite of fierce competition with London merchants. Hull's chief exports remained wool and West Riding cloth, and a wide variety of European and Asiatic goods were imported. Exports of wool to Calais, in decline at the end of the 15th century, revived from about 1500, and reached their highest point for 30 years in 1508-9. Trade with the Baltic was also of increasing importance, although this was mainly in the hands of Danzig merchants. Cloth, skins and hides were the main exports to the Baltic lands and in return the ships brought back flax, pitch and tar. Hull ships carrying wool to Calais usually returned with wine from Bordeaux; other Hull ships sailed to Spain and Portugal, carrying mainly lead and cloth and returning with wine and oil.

As in previous centuries, the prosperity of the town in the late 15th and early 16th centuries was reflected in church building, for it was now that the great church of the town, Holy Trinity, was given a final splendid embellishment: the last two stages of the tower, built in stone, with two perpendicular windows to each side.[1]

From about 1520, however, the overseas trade of Hull was in decline and the town suffered a deepening depression throughout the 1520s to 1540s. The principal cause was the decision of the Hanseatic merchants, who controlled much of the cloth trade, to abandon Hull for London. Between 1537 and 1542 an average of only two ships a year reached Antwerp from Hull. By 1540 the cloth trade of

20   *The upper stages of the central tower of Holy Trinity Church, as seen from the church roof.*

Hull was only about one-hundredth the size of the London trade.[2]

Another blow to the town in the 1520s was the rapid decline and disappearance of the once most-important Icelandic fish trade. When John Leland visited Hull, in about 1540, he was told (incorrectly) that the town owed its prosperity to this trade, and that the streets were well paved because they used cobbles brought back from Iceland as ballast for the fishing boats. While fishing remained important, and some Hull mariners resorted to privateering, which could be very lucrative, what growth there was in the 1530s and 1540s came mainly from the coastal trade. The export of corn to London and the import of coal from the Fife coalfields of Scotland became of increasing importance. Consequently the number of ships owned in Hull actually increased towards the end of this period, although most were small, suitable only for coastal trade. In 1520 only about twenty ships were owned at Hull, but by 1550 the number had jumped to thirty-five.[3]

The increase in coastal trade could not compensate for the decline in overseas trade, and the town suffered a long period of decline. When the tower and west end of St Mary's Church collapsed in 1518 there was insufficient money to repair it, and much of the church remained in ruins for many decades to come.[4] In 1532, when the corporation applied to Thomas Cromwell, Henry VIII's Master of the Court of Wards, for letters patent securing some of the town's traditional trading privileges, it described the state of the town and its harbour:

> The haven of our town of Kingston-upon-Hull has fallen into great decay by the rage of the sea dashing against the sea walls and embankments erected there to defend it so that the mayor and burgesses are not able to repair the damage done to the haven without help.[5]

The town also suffered in 1537 a return of the plague, the first such outbreak for half a century. Just how serious this attack was is unknown, but in 1551 the town was also badly affected by an outbreak of the sweating sickness. This was a violent and usually fatal inflammatory fever that caused the victim to suffer a fetid perspiration over the whole body.[6]

This decline made the corporation anxious to secure legal backing in 1532 for Hull merchants to be the first to purchase imported goods at the quayside. This was a claim long disputed by rival merchants of York and Beverley but an extremely important one for the town as Hull merchants would able to buy cheaply, sell quickly, and operate with relatively little capital. After assiduous lobbying, an expenditure of £30 in gifts to Cromwell himself and others, the corporation was successful and the official document (virtually a new charter) stated:

> We have granted that no stranger or foreigner to the liberty of the borough shall henceforth buy from any stranger or foreigner within that borough any merchandise or anything else, or sell the same to him, except only in the time when the markets and fairs are held, under pain of forfeiting the merchandise.[7]

This was an important advantage for the town's merchants and any enterpreneurs with a little capital. It was also a major inducement for merchants to purchase burgess rights in the town. In the same year the corporation also tried to boost trade by banning the loading of goods onto other ships if a Hull ship was available. This would have been difficult to enforce, however, and was probably ineffective.[8]

The Reformation

The years of stagnation were also a period of considerable religious turmoil. The town's many trading contacts with the Netherlands and North Germany meant it was one of the first to learn of the ideas of the rebel monk Martin Luther, and its merchants and seamen may have been among the first converts to Protestantism in the country. As early as 1521, the year of Luther's appearance before the Emperor Charles V at the Diet of Worms, Cardinal Wolsey was distressed to learn that the monk's heretical ideas were already circulating in his own diocese of York, and that his books had entered the country through the port of Hull. Prompted by this discovery, he organised in May 1521 a great public burning of every book, sermon or pamphlet written by Luther he was able to lay his hands on.[9]

Nothing more is heard about the spread of heretical ideas in the region until 1527, when a small group of Hull seamen, returning to the port after a long visit to ports in Germany and the Netherlands, were arrested on suspicion of heresy and examined by officials appointed by the Bishop of Lincoln. Their answers suggested some of the men were already acquainted with Luther's views before their visit to Germany and that they deliberately attended a Lutheran service at Bremen. One of them spoke of the popularity of Luther's ideas there and described a service he had attended:

> The people did follow Luther's works, and no masses were said there, but on the Sunday the priest would revest himself and go to the altar, and proceed to nigh the sacring time, and then the priest and all that were in the church, old and young, would sing after their mother tongue, and there was no sacring.[10]

The men seem to have learnt little about Lutheran doctrine, but one man had acquired a copy of William Tyndale's recently published English translation of the New Testament. This was confiscated but only one member of the group seems to have suffered punishment. In 1528 one of the seamen, Robert Robynson, was forced to abjure his heretical opinions and perform prolonged penances in York, in the market place in Hull, and in Holy Trinity Church.[11]

Most of the town's inhabitants at this time, however, were utterly orthodox. The wills of this period continued to make bequests to the churches and friaries, and to pay for obits and dirges to be said by chantry priests to help speed their souls through purgatory. A chantry was founded at St Mary's in 1521, in 1523 the existing guild of St George was incorporated at Holy Trinity Church, and in 1534 the corporation appointed a new chaplain for the Corpus Christi guild in Holy Trinity Church.[12] One historian has commented that 'Holy Trinity in particular must have seemed like a Council Chamber of deceased civic officers and their wives', as so many former members of the town's corporation were buried there.[13] The number of early converts to Protestantism was a very small minority, and the numbers in the surrounding

21   *A drawing of Hull, made in about 1540 for Henry VIII, when plans were being made to strengthen the town's defences.*

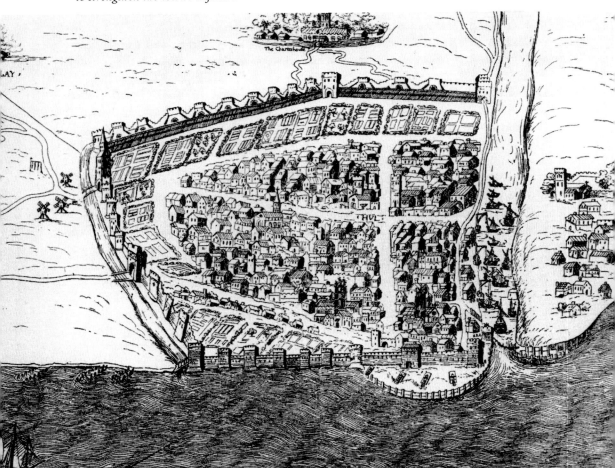

region smaller still. In 1530 the Bishop of Norwich said of his diocese that he thought the gentry and commoners were little affected by heresy, except for 'merchants and such as hath their abiding not far from the sea'.[14] This was probably also true of the East Riding of Yorkshire.

There may, however, have been some support for Lutheran ideas among some of the more educated priests. One local priest, the vicar of North Cave, a village about 12 miles to the west of Hull, preached a sermon in Holy Trinity Church in 1534 which was judged by the ecclesiastical authorities sufficiently heretical as to merit public humiliation. To avoid further, and much more terrible, punishment, he was obliged to make a public recantation of his errors and to walk at the next Sunday service bare-foot and bare-legged in his shirt round Holy Trinity Church, carrying a large faggot to denote that he deserved to be burnt for holding such opinions. He then had to perform the same penance on market day in the market place.[15]

Although the majority in Hull were conservative in their religious views, most were willing to acquiesce in the Henrician breach with Rome. In 1535 the Archdeacon of the East Riding reported that all men in Hull, including the corporation and the monks of the Charterhouse, were in agreement with the king's policies and 'quiet and comfortable' to his pleasure. The corporation did, however, pre-empt the anticipated confiscation of church plate in 1536 by selling it off to meet some of its expenses, including repairs to the church. But later in the same year, most members of the corporation seem to have shown little enthusiasm for the Pilgrimage of Grace, the popular uprising against the dissolution of the monasteries and other changes in the church.

A rebellion against the king's religious policies broke out in the East Riding early in October, encouraged by news of a rebellion in Lincolnshire, where thousands were reported to have marched on the county town demanding changes. By Sunday, 8 October, Beverley was in uproar, rebel leaders had been appointed and contact made with other rebel towns in the county. The corporation of Hull was anxious to remain loyal, and closed its gates on the Beverley rebels, who feared that the king would use Hull's port to move his artillery into the county quickly. A week after the Beverley insurrection a large number of rebels – one account says 9,000 – surrounded the town and put it under a rather ineffective blockade. They were led by a local gentleman, Sir Robert Constable, and the Beverley leader, William Stapleton. Both men attempted to have a moderating influence on their followers, some of whom were keen to launch a violent attack on the town. Stapleton's men wanted to set fire to the ships in the haven by floating barrels of burning pitch down the river Hull. Their motive for this probably had more to do with trading rivalries than questions of religion. Stapleton managed to dissuade his men but was unable to prevent them pulling down a number of windmills just outside Beverley Gate, and although no ships were damaged it was later reported that the rebels had prevented some ships from leaving the port.[16]

Perhaps because of this, and also owing to fear of further violence if the leaders lost control, the corporation decided on 20 October that it would be safer to let the rebels into the town peaceably, on the condition that no one should be forced to take the 'common oath', which could be interpreted as a pledge of loyalty. The corporation had to be sensitive to the views of the town's inhabitants, many of whom sympathised with the rebels and were keen to allow them in. Also, by this time the Lincolnshire rebellion had already petered out, and the Duke of Norfolk was moving north with an army of about 8,000 men. The aldermen seemed to have thought the Yorkshire rebels would also disperse, especially as the initial enthusiasm for the rising was evaporating.

Their gamble paid off, but not as quickly as they may have hoped. A few days after the rebels had entered the town, the Duke of Norfolk reached Doncaster and on the 26th met with Sir Robert Constable and the other leaders, Lord Darcy and Robert Aske, heard their grievances and promised to present them to the king. During the lull that followed, most of the rebels left the town, having inflicted very little damage, and the 'king's party' in the town took the opportunity to expel the remaining leaders. Support for the rebels was still very strong in the town, however, and on 9 November the aldermen again allowed Sir Robert Constable to enter the town with his forces to guard the harbour against royal ships. This time the rebels stayed until the Duke of Norfolk returned to Doncaster, early in December, with vaguely generous proposals and promises of pardons, prompting the rebel army still at Doncaster to disperse. The rebels now finally left Hull and the episode seemed to be over.

However, not everyone trusted the king, and fears that he might yet use Scarborough and Hull to send forces to take revenge on the rebels prompted two men, Sir Francis Bigod of Settrington and John Hallam of Cawkwell Farm, Watton, to hatch a hopelessly ill-conceived plot to seize the two towns. While Bigod and a few followers took control of Scarborough, Hallam and his men would quietly infiltrate Hull on a market day and seize the town. Both efforts failed completely. Hallam and his small band of followers hoped to stir up a rebellion but instead met with hostility or, at best, apathy. On realising their failure they tried to leave but were stopped at one of the gates. The mayor had been tipped off, and he and a small number of armed men, including some members of the corporation, were already looking for him when he was spotted at Beverley Gate. A short fight followed; Hallam was dragged from his horse and overpowered, and he and some of his followers were then quickly tied up and marched back to the town gaol.

The Bigod-Hallam plot gave Henry VIII an excuse to renege on the promises made at Doncaster, and the general pardon granted only a few weeks earlier now acquired a great many exceptions. Altogether about 200 people were put to death for their part in the disturbances across the north. Among them were Hallam and Sir Robert Constable, who were both hanged from Beverley Gate on a market day. It was also decided that Sir Robert should be hanged in chains so that his corpse could be suspended above the people's heads as they entered or left the town for many years to come.

After the arrest of Hallam the mayor received instructions from the king to examine him under torture until a special commission arrived from London to conduct a trial. Constable was tried in London, along with Aske, Darcy, Bigod and others regarded as leaders of the rising. Constable was hanged at Hull, and Aske was returned to York to suffer a similar punishment on York's walls. On 8 July 1537, the Duke of Norfolk wrote to Thomas Cromwell:

> On Frydaye, being market daye at Hull, Sir Robert Constable suifred, and dothe hang above the highest gate of the towne, so trimmed in cheynes, as this berer can shewe you, and I think his boones will hang there this hundrethe yere.

Hallam had been hanged early in February. The two aldermen who had taken part in his arrest were knighted for their services, the town was duly thanked for its loyalty, and no Hull men were excepted from the general pardon.[17]

Although the Pilgrimage of Grace had many different causes, many of those who joined the protests wanted to halt one particular religious change, the closure of the smaller monastic houses, which at the time of the risings was close to completion. In Hull, however, the commissioners who had visited the Charterhouse in May 1536 had been immensely impressed by the piety, good order and usefulness of the house, and had reported to Cromwell that the house should be spared:

> the said prior and brethren are right well favoured and commended by the honest men of Hull and other neighbours thereabouts for their good living and great hospitality by them daily kept ... and that it would please you ... that they might continue in their said house[18]

22 *A detail from the 1540 drawing of Hull, showing the Hessle and Beverley Gates. The windmills which were attacked and damaged by the rebels in 1536 are shown opposite Beverley Gate, and it was on this gate – the principal entry into the town – that Sir Robert Constable was hanged and his body left in chains.*

Cromwell's Court of Augmentations accepted the commissioners' report and the Charterhouse was exempted. The only other religious houses in the town were

23 *The Augustinian friary on Blackfriargate. Although dissolved in 1539, it was not demolished until 1796.*

two small friaries: the Carmelite house of 'Whitefriars' and the Augustinian friary. Unlike the Charterhouse, which had been generously endowed by the de la Pole family, neither of the two friaries possessed any form of wealth except for the plate on their altars, and the few friars still to be found in the town (about 16 altogether) relied almost entirely on the charity of local people. When the visitor-general appointed to suppress the friaries arrived in Hull, in February 1539, the friars quietly surrendered their houses and were released from their vows to seek their fortunes in the secular world.[19]

By the early months of 1539 the decision had been taken to dissolve all remaining religious houses, including those, like the Charterhouse, which had been so recently exempted, and by the end of the year the Carthusian monks had gone, even though only a year before they had paid a 'fine for exemption' to the Court of Augmentations of £233 6s. 8d. When Leland visited the town about a year later, the friaries were empty and deserted and the Charterhouse was a secular hospital. It was still owned by the Crown as confiscated property, but later, in Edward VI's reign, it was granted to the corporation.[20]

Leland also recorded seeing four 'notable' chantry chapels on the south side of Holy Trinity Church, but within a few years of his visit these, too, had gone. Protestantism had no need of chapels devoted to prayers for the dead. There were, in fact, at least ten such chapels in the town in 1547, when the Chantries Act swept them away. Two had been established in St Mary's Church but the rest were either in the side aisles of Holy Trinity or in its precincts. At least three dated from the 14th century. The best endowed was the Alcock chantry in Holy Trinity, founded by Bishop Alcock in the 15th century. The Bishop had also given the grammar school its building and the incumbent of his chantry was master of the school, receiving £10 a year as his salary plus free accommodation in the schoolhouse. Although the chantry was abolished, local protests ensured the grammar school was preserved, as well as the Trinity House hospital, the Charterhouse hospital and two smaller hospitals.[21]

In the same year Edward's regent, the Duke of Somerset, issued injunctions ordering the destruction of all 'shrines'. Protestant activists were chosen to visit every town to enforce the injunctions and during the next 18 months the appearance of virtually every church in the country changed radically. When the visitors, as they were called, arrived in Hull, they ordered the whitewashing of the pictures on the church walls and, rather unusually, smashed the statues in the church themselves, including a huge, three-headed representation of the Holy Trinity. Paintings of the Virgin Mary and the saints were taken out of the church and piled up outside to make a bonfire.[22]

This iconoclasm divided the town. A few protested against the destruction but others welcomed the change. In the next few years, until the death of Edward VI in 1553, the Protestant Reformation proceeded rapidly throughout the country. The injunctions of 1547 banned church processions, instructed all churches to purchase bibles, limited the number of candles that could be burnt in a church and also ordered that every church should possess a copy of Erasmus's *Paraphrases on the Gospels*. Two years later an Act of Uniformity required all services to be conducted in English and every church to use a new English Book of Prayer; a separate Act of Parliament the same year gave priests permission to marry. Another new Prayer Book, issued in 1552, made it clear that the communion service was an act of remembrance that Christ had died to save sinners, rather than a miracle of transubstantiation. The traditional colourful vestments had to be replaced by a plain white surplice, and altars had to be removed from the east end of the church, where it was felt they implied sacrifice and transubstantiation, and moved into the nave, as simply a communion table where the congregation could share the bread and the wine.[23]

Many of these ideas were welcomed in Hull, and this willingness to embrace 'the new learning' was encouraged by the appointment to Hull in about 1550 of the radical Protestant preacher and former Dominican monk John Rough. Rough was a close friend of John Knox, and a fellow Scotsman. He shared with Knox an uncompromising zeal and an absolute certainty in the rightness of his cause. Appointed to a Hull stipend by the Protestant Archbishop of York, Robert Holgate, he is credited by Professor A.G. Dickens with having 'founded the strongly protestant tradition which later marked that port'.[24]

In July 1553, everything changed. With Edward's death and Mary's accession most of the changes in the church would be reversed. Holgate was removed into quiet retirement in London. Rough was also deprived of his living and, like so many other Protestant ministers, fled into exile, though he returned soon afterwards to join the underground Protestant church in London. Here he became 'the chief pastor of the congregation' before being arrested for heresy, thrown into prison, tried and burnt at the stake.[25]

In much of Yorkshire, as in most counties, both Mary's accession and the subsequent return to the 'Old Religion' were greeted with considerable enthusiasm and there were few cases of contempt shown towards either Catholic clergy or restored Catholic ritual. Hull, however, was one of the exceptions. Here, in 1554, a few members of Rough's former congregation made an anonymous protest, taking the reserved sacrament from Holy Trinity Church. Although this was regarded by Catholics as a gross and heretical offence, the perpetrators were never caught.[26]

The building of a royal fortress

One effect of the Pilgrimage of Grace was to remind the townspeople how vulnerable they were to an assault from the haven, and this lesson was not lost on the king. More than four years after the uprising, while Sir Robert Constable's skeleton still swung in its chains, Henry VIII began his progress into the northern counties. He arrived in Hull with his new wife, Katherine Howard, together with a train of courtiers, where he agreed to have plans drawn up for strengthening the town's defences. The first proposal was to turn the de la Pole house into a fortress. This 14th-century mansion had been seized by Henry VII, following the attainder of Edmund de la Pole for treason in 1508, and was being used as the mayor's official residence. The walls and gates were repaired, the gates strengthened with portcullises and cannons, and the moat was scoured and deepened. In the following February, Henry decided to give Hull a completely new fortress close to the mouth of the river Hull. Work began quickly and was completed by the end of 1543. The principal building was erected on the east side of the haven, opposite the Church Lane staithe. The walls were low but 19 feet thick, so that guns fired from enemy ships could do little harm. Two enormous blockhouses were also built, one north and one south of the main building, and these were linked to the central fortress by walls 15 feet thick. Just to the north of the northern blockhouse Henry gave permission to build the first bridge across the haven, very close to the site of the present North Bridge. Most of the stone came from the dissolved Meaux Abbey.[27]

The corporation might have been expected to appreciate the fortress but instead it was viewed as a major threat to the independence of the town. The increased security was welcome enough but not Henry VIII's decision, taken as early as February 1542, to appoint a governor answerable directly to himself and independent of the corporation. Relations between the new governor of the fortress, Michael (later Sir Michael) Stanhope, and the corporation seem to have quickly gone from bad to worse. Stanhope complained to the king's council of the corporation's refusal to cooperate with him and in 1546 two members of the corporation were summoned to London to answer Stanhope's charges. Relations seem to have improved after this and in 1552 the government of Edward VI removed the problem altogether by granting control of the fortress to the corporation. As the Duke of Somerset's brother-in-law, Sir Michael had quickly fallen out of favour when Somerset fell from power and the Duke of Northumberland assumed control of the government. The decision to give the corporation control of so important a fortress was also a very strong indication of the trust shown by Northumberland's government in the loyalty of the town, and in its Protestantism. Now, however, and for many years to come, the problem was the cost of maintenance. The Crown allotted a sum of £50 per year to meet maintenance costs but it was not long before the corporation was complaining bitterly that the true cost of its upkeep was much greater than this.[28]

FOUR

Elizabethan Hull, 1558-1603

The growth of overseas trade

During Elizabeth I's reign, England's international trade grew considerably, and for Hull, as a major port on a great estuary, these were years of expansion and prosperity. Although the plague returned in 1575-6, the population of the town appears to have grown steadily, with about 5,000 to 6,000 people living in Hull by the end of the century.[1]

The inadequacy of the roads compelled everyone to send heavy goods, wherever possible, by sea or river. The coal trade grew particularly rapidly, as demand grew both for domestic use and industry. As early as 1578 it was being said that brewers, dyers, hat-makers and others 'have long since altered their furnaces and fiery places, and turned the same to the use and burning of sea-coal.'[2] By the 1550s the Fife coalfields of Scotland were being overtaken in importance by the Northumberland and Durham coalfields, and by the 1590s 5,000 to 6,000 tons of coal a year were being brought from Newcastle, much of it for re-export.[3]

The fish trade also remained crucial for the town, and was much encouraged by Elizabeth's government, which introduced laws imposing fish days during Lent and on Fridays. Elizabeth's council saw the trade as one of the key nurseries of the country's mariners, from whom it could recruit sailors in times of war. The nature of the trade, however, changed considerably during the century. Fish continued to be imported from East Anglia, the north-east coast and, above all, from the Fife ports of Scotland. From at least the 1570s, Hull's fishermen were venturing into new waters, fishing and trading along the Norwegian coast to Lapland and even beyond, to the harbours of the Kola Peninsula of Russia, much to the annoyance of the Russia Company and the King of Denmark, who seized five Hull ships fishing off Vardö in 1599. This new trade brought Hull men into the whaling industry, and before 1600 seafarers from Hull were participating in whaling off Bear Island and Spitzbergen.[4]

The most important trade, and the foundation of the town's success from the 1560s, was the export of cheap kersey cloth manufactured in the West Riding. Exports rose rapidly, with the Baltic ports becoming the most important market. Large ships of 80 to 100 tons carried kerseys into the Baltic and brought back flax for the growing manufacture of linen and sailcloth canvas, along with other naval stores such as hemp, pitch, tar and timber, imports which greatly increased following the outbreak of war with Spain in 1585. Exports of kerseys reached a peak in 1598-9 and the corporation petitioned the government to be made the staple port for this export.[5]

Hides were also a great export, as was lead, brought to Hull from the Peak District and the Yorkshire Dales, and wine remained a major import from France and Spain. Much trade continued with both Germany and the Netherlands, in spite of competition with London and Hanseatic merchants, and the loss of access to Antwerp following the Dutch revolt against Spanish rule in 1566. Hull exported mainly coarse cloth and lead to the Netherlands and imported a wide variety of goods, including alum, madder and oil for the textile industry, wine and hops, glassware, sugar, rice, ginger and treacle.[6]

Locally grown foodstuffs were also a huge export. The East Riding was a fertile agricultural area and in most years during the reign (until the 1590s) produced a surplus in peas, beans and cereals for export and the London markets. However, in years of bad harvests (and there were many in the 1590s) large quantities of cereals, especially rye, were brought in from the Baltic. Hull merchants were able to make good profits from the trade, especially when prices were high. To prevent prices reaching famine levels in years of bad harvest, the East Riding justices persuaded the Council of the North to ban the export of wheat if its price rose above 10 shillings a quarter and barley and malt if they rose above 6s. 8d. a quarter. Port officials, however, were eminently bribable, and exports continued even in years of dearth and acute hunger. In one particularly bad year, 1569, it was reported that the officials at Hull had allowed the export of 7,000 quarters of corn to Hamburg, Flanders and Newcastle. Local merchants could also use other ports and creeks in the Humber to smuggle out corn when the price was high. It was reported in 1585 that the customs searcher at Hull, John Hewett, would, for 6d. a quarter commission, not only turn a blind eye to such smuggling but actively help to arrange it.[7]

Such corruption meant that much merchandise could also pass through Hull without payment of customs duty to the Crown, and real levels of exports from the port were probably considerably higher than official figures suggested. A common complaint to the Privy Council was that ships evaded customs duties by claiming they were carrying goods up the Ouse or along the Trent, when in reality they were taking them out of the country. The government tried to overcome this problem by insisting that all merchants who claimed to be selling merchandise in English ports must pay a bond to the port officers at Hull, only redeemable on the production of a certificate of sale. This could only be enforced if the port officials were honest, and while John Hewett was in charge there could be little chance of this. In 1586, however, he was replaced as port 'searcher' by Anthony Atkinson, who was determined to stamp out customs evasion and smuggling, and was consequently extremely unpopular with Hull merchants. Atkinson claimed that his predecessor had made at least £1,500 every year out of customs frauds and bribery, and in 1596 he was able to boast that while he had been in charge the customs receipts at Hull had doubled from £1,200 per year to £2,800. Much of this improvement was the result of increasing exports, however, and Atkinson admitted that he had been unable to stamp out all smuggling and customs evasions. His proposed solution to the problem was to restrict all exports to two staithes, which he could properly police, and to close down the private staithes owned by the town's merchants. This, unsurprisingly, was rejected by the corporation, which included many of the town's richer, staithe-owning merchants, as this would 'ruin the town'. Atkinson's powerful enemies finally managed to engineer his disgrace and dismissal in 1602-3, ironically following allegations of fraud and malpractice.[8]

In spite of competition from London and Hanseatic merchants, political upheavals, war against Spain and piracy – so great a problem that Hull seafarers armed ships – the last four decades of the 16th century saw a rapid growth of the town's overseas trade. In terms of the yield in customs duties from foreign trade, Hull was the fifth largest port in the country by 1594-5.

The profits from tolls accruing to the corporation meant it could invest £20 in 1578 in improving the Holderness road. This was partly to answer the complaints of villagers who could not reach the town's weekly markets, as this road was frequently flooded and dangerous. But the corporation's chief concern was to protect the corn trade, which could not thrive if farmers could not get the corn to Hull.[9]

A number of local men were able to make substantial fortunes in these years. Members of the Dalton family particularly prospered in the 1560s and 1570s, and also James Clerkson and John Thornton, who exported lead to the Low Countries. The memorial to Thomas Dalton, who died in 1591, and his two wives, can be seen today in the south choir aisle of Holy Trinity Church.[10] Later, Francis Cherry, a member of the Russia Company but based in Hull, made a considerable fortune trading on the Kola Peninsula, but the town's wealthiest merchant during Elizabeth's reign was William Gee. In 1595, when Gee was recommended to fill a vacancy on the Council of the North, it was said that he had come from Leicestershire 50 years before and so prospered as a merchant of Hull that he had become its most generous benefactor. By 1595 he had spent £300 rebuilding the grammar school, £150 on repairs to Holy Trinity, £200 on a covered corn market, £1,000 on a hospital for 10 of the town's worthy poor, to whom he also made a weekly allowance, and he had also offered the corporation £200 towards the

24 *William Gee, 1568.*

cost of carrying drinking water from the wells in lead pipes rather than in open ditches. He had also been mayor three times and had presented the corporation with numerous fine gifts, particularly silverware, including a salt cellar and 12 apostle spoons.[11]

Hull's aldermen liked to boast that the wealth of their town could be measured by the length and weight of the mayor's gold chain. In 1554 it weighed just under five ounces. It was a gift to the corporation from one of the town's richest former mayors, Sir William Knollys, and was proudly placed on display in the guildhall. By 1571, as a result of further gifts, it had more than doubled in size and weighed more than 11 ounces. One of William Gee's gifts to the corporation was a fine gold chain for the lady mayoress, to be worn when she accompanied her husband to church on Sundays and holy days.[12]

The trading privileges granted to Hull merchants by the charter of 1532 had encouraged some merchants outside the town to purchase burgess status. This brought more income to the corporation, but as early as 1559 these 'foreign' merchants were being resented as interlopers, and it was decided that such outsiders would only be tolerated if their operations brought real benefit to the town. Thus two West Riding cloth merchants, from Halifax and Wakefield respectively, were told in 1559 that they either had to move to Hull or lose their burgess rights, whereas another cloth merchant, who had settled in Antwerp to pursue his export business, was allowed to keep his burgess rights because it was felt that his connections were bringing wealth to the town. By Elizabeth's reign Hull burgess status for a merchant was a privilege to be valued and sought after.[13]

A healthy coastal trade and an ever-expanding international trade helped ensure Hull's markets and shops thrived in these years. By the 1570s large quantities of grain were being sold in Hull, and in 1578 the town was described as the best market for fish in England. In 1582 it received a special royal licence to import herring for distribution inland. It also became the main source of supply for wines and hides, not only for Yorkshire but for much of northern England. A vast range of goods could be purchased in the markets, shops and at the annual fair, including expensive, high-quality goods such as earthen- and lustre-ware pottery from the Continent, Dutch wall-tiles and glass, and fashionable clothing and fine groceries from London. The ancient May fair was replaced in 1598, following a new charter, by a 16-day fair beginning on 16 September. The regulations concerning the fair refer to sellers of mercery wares, groceries, goldsmiths 'and such like', all of whom had to establish their stalls at the north end of the High Street, above Chapel Lane, and pewterers, pedlars, shoemakers, glovers, linen drapers and sellers of wooden wares and hardware, who were to be found on Salthouse Lane. The horse fair was located near the North Gate, and cows and oxen mainly in the Lowgate area, running down to Bishop Lane.[14]

Hull's importance as a port, however, did not stimulate any major growth in manufacturing. In the lists of admissions to burgess rights during the century, the largest groups by far are merchants, mercers and mariners. The growth of the town's population led to an increase in tailors and shoemakers, purveyors of food and drink, and those employed in the building trades, but manufacturing remained on a small scale. The number of shipwrights remained very small until the early 17th century, and almost the only metalworkers in the town were smiths, some of whom were

25 *John Speed's Map of Hull, 1610. This is the earliest published map of the town. The defences on the east bank of the river Hull, erected on the orders of Henry VIII, are clearly shown, together with the first bridge over the river, also ordered by the king.*

employed in ship-repairing. Neither the leather trades nor the textile trades showed any signs of growth, although a handful of weavers were employed in sail-making. The principal group of leatherworkers were probably the glovers, who were one of only four occupations to have their own craft guild at the beginning of the 16th century (along with the weavers, tilers and brewers). The growth in the building trades led to the formation, towards the end of the century, of three new guilds, for carpenters, joiners, and a mixed group of craftsmen comprising bricklayers, tilers, wallers, plasterers and pavers. By this time guilds had also been formed by ropers, bakers and coopers, and nearly a dozen other crafts joined together in 1598 to form another mixed-craft guild, including glaziers, plumbers, goldsmiths and cutlers.[15]

War against Spain and pirates

The last 18 years of Elizabeth's reign were spent at war against Catholic Spain, and for at least a decade before war against that country and its mighty empire had seemed imminent. In 1584, when Spain was poised to defeat the Dutch Protestant rebels, following the fall of Antwerp and the assassination of the rebel leader, William the Silent, the Spanish threat to England seemed great and defence preparations assumed a new urgency. When the men of Hull were mustered that year, however, only 714 reported for training in the use of arms, suggesting many were avoiding the muster. The strengthening of the fortress defences had been undertaken a few years earlier, and in 1585, when war was finally declared, the town's defences were improved by the rebuilding of the mud wall between the North Gate and the haven. Heavy cannon placed on the southern blockhouse commanded the entrance to the haven and guns on the northern blockhouse protected the North Bridge. When the Earl of Leicester led an English army to the Netherlands that year, Hull ships were among the English fleet.[16]

Drake's raid on Cadiz in 1587 delayed the sending of the 'Invincible Armada', but at the beginning of 1588 a large Spanish invasion force was expected. The Duke of Parma's victorious and battle-hardened army in the Netherlands – much more successful than the English forces sent by Elizabeth – were now ready for embarkation to England. Consequently, in February 1588 the corporation issued new orders for the defence of the town. Ten men were put on watch duties every night, each armed with muskets; the gates on the staithes were secured with new iron bolts and a chain was put across the haven each night. The town's store of muskets and armour was checked and put in good repair, and all innkeepers were ordered to report to the aldermen if any strangers – potential 'fifth columnists' – were lodging with them.[17]

The Armada set sail from Lisbon on 8 May, and just a fortnight earlier two ships and a pinnace, manned by 200 of Hull's mariners, sailed out of the port to join the fleet being assembled by Drake and Howard to confront it. During the next few years Hull would also provide ships and men for campaigns in Normandy, supporting the Protestant Henry of Navarre against Spanish forces, in the Azores, Brest, and on the successful Cadiz expedition of 1596. Fears of a Spanish invasion remained, as Philip II was known to be building new armada fleets and still controlled all of the Southern Netherlands (now Belgium). In 1596 it was reported that if an invasion came every householder in Hull was ready with his weapon, and that 40 to 50 men were armed and on watch duty every night.[18]

26 *An Elizabethan pinnace.*

The long war against Spain came to an end shortly after Elizabeth's death, and in it many men from Hull had lost their lives, although far more succumbed to scurvy than were killed by the enemy. The war against piracy, however, was ongoing. During Elizabeth's reign, with trade generally prospering, the threats from piratical attack were greater than ever. When Sir Michael Stanhope had been the governor of the Hull fortress, he had put together a small force consisting of three ships and two small trading vessels to chase off French and Scottish pirates operating off the Yorkshire coast. In Elizabeth's reign the corporation repeatedly adopted this tactic and in 1577 enjoyed its greatest success, when two Hull ships, the *White Hind* and the *Salamon*, assisted by a Newcastle ship, captured an English pirate ship, the *Elizabeth*, plus its entire crew, off the coast of Lincolnshire, near Ingoldmells. The pirate captain and crew were brought back to Hull and put on trial before the mayor and the Earl of Huntingdon, the Lord President of the Council of the North. Three were pardoned and the other 15 hanged. A large crowd gathered to enjoy this unprecedented spectacle, and the hanging of so many pirates was celebrated as a major blow against a grievous enemy, as much hated as any Spanish Catholic.[19]

More expeditions against pirates followed, but none as successful as this, and in the last years of the reign piratical attacks were proving a greater problem than ever. Pirates operating out of Dunkirk were a particular menace in the late 1590s and well into the next century. In December 1598 the appearance of five Dunkirk pirate ships off the coast of Holderness caused widespread panic and during the following spring and summer they so disrupted the coal trade that a shortage of fuel was anticipated for the following winter. At least three Hull ships were captured by the Dunkirk pirates at this time, in spite of the corporation organising armed ships to protect them.[20]

Puritanism and the Church

Although obliged to remain unseen during the five years of Mary Tudor's reign, Protestant sentiment was a powerful force in the town among all classes, but especially among the wealthy and influential merchant families who dominated the corporation. Very shortly after Elizabeth's accession in November 1558 Hull had established a reputation for itself as a centre of Puritanism.[21]

It was not long before the corporation issued an order reminding the townsfolk of the penalties for those who fell into sin. In December 1563 it pronounced:

> we, therefore, the said mayor, aldermen and burgesses, knowing nothing more convenient, needful nor requisite than to redress, supplant or pluck up these great infections and enormities most especially at this present time rearing in this town do with one assent, consent and agreement enact, order and agree that from this present 18th day of December no manner of persons within this town be so hardy as to commit any whoredom, fornication or adultery, nor use nor exercise himself in excessive drinking, riot, dispending his or their time in idleness, wantonness, lightness, scolding or maliciously blaspheming the name of God, to the great provocation of God's wrath against this town, upon pain that everyone offending be punished and made an example of to warn others ... at the discretion of the mayor and the most part of the aldermen.[22]

The influence of Calvin's example of the godly city in Geneva is very evident. No longer would the corporation rent out land beside the south wall for the use of prostitutes. Instead, the improvement in public morals was now seen as one of the corporations' most important responsibilities, and persistent drunks, prostitutes and adulterers could either expect a spell in the town gaol, or possibly a whipping through the town tied to a cart or tumbrel. Alternatively, the justices could sentence miscreants to punishment in the town thew (a small portable pillory) or in the pillory or stocks in the market place, or perhaps the humiliation (usually reserved for women) of being fastened in the cucking stool (a primitive commode) outside their own house, to be pelted by an angry crowd.[23]

Alehouses and inns were viewed as centres of all the devilish sins listed in the proclamation of 1563. Such places were now seen as at best necessary evils that could, they hoped, be controlled. The keeping of an unlicensed alehouse was no longer tolerated and in 1560 the justices arrested a former sheriff, George Shaw, for this. He was fined 20s. and imprisoned for three days in the town gaol.[24] From 1566 onwards the extensive code of town laws concerning alehouses, taverns and inns was read out every year, so that no one could be in any doubt.

To obtain and keep a licence from the justices, both inns and alehouses had to keep at least two beds for travellers. Both had to close at eight o'clock, when the town bell was rung, and after this only those staying could be served drinks. Alcohol could only be served with a meal and servants were not allowed entrance unless on their master's business. A long list of popular games was also forbidden because they encouraged gambling, including bowls, dice, cards and backgammon, and rude jokes and songs were prohibited.[25]

In spite of these regulations, the alehouse and inn remained as popular as ever, and drunkenness became an increasing problem in the town in the 1560s and 1570s. In spite of the sincerity of many of the justices, the regulations could not be enforced. In 1574, when there were 21 brewers in the town, 10 inns and 29 alehouses, the justices made it clear that not only was this too many, but the beer and ale sold was too strong. The justices declared their support for the town's clergy, who used the pulpit to rail against the evils of drink:

> The learned, zealous and godly preachers of the most holy name of God within Kingston-upon-Hull do with one consent most earnestly and vehemently exclaim and cry out against the blasphemy of the most holy name of God, drunkenness, disorder, and infinite other abominable and detestable sins which do abound by reason of the great number of alehouses, the unreasonable and excessive strong ale by brewers there brewed and the continual and disorderly repair of people to these lewd houses. They also do thunder out the manifold, grievous and terrible plagues of God hanging over this town if a speedy reformation be not had.[26]

As the town continued to grow so did the number of alehouses, but the justices – urged on by the town's Puritan clergy – continued to try to limit their number. Noisy, violent and generally disorderly conduct was frequently blamed on excessive drinking, and in the 1590s there were complaints that men were giving up their trades 'to live idly as alehouse keepers'. The truth was that for many poor people there were few other ways of making a living. Nevertheless, it was decided in 1593 that the aldermen would inspect the town's alehouses and alehouse keepers and remove the licences of any they found either unsuitable to run an alehouse or capable of following an 'honest' trade. Whether any licences were removed is not recorded.[27]

Four years later, the justices had the opportunity to close down all the town's alehouses, at least temporarily, when a poor harvest led to an acute shortage of grain and threatened famine conditions. It was ruled they could only open for travellers and any inhabitant of the town caught visiting an alehouse for a drink could expect a week in prison.[28]

Plays and other theatrical performances were also regarded as an encouragement to vice. A puritanical view had been evinced by the corporation as early as 1534, when it had been agreed that corporation funds should not be used to pay the expenses of travelling players, minstrels or jugglers visiting the town, but early in 1573 even the recent Christmas revels were condemned for encouraging lewd behaviour, particularly among young apprentices of the town. Consequently it was ordered that 'henceforth no person shall go a-mumming or disguised in any masquing apparel'. The great achievements in theatre being made in London in the last decades of the century, led by brilliant young playwrights including Marlowe and Shakespeare, meant nothing to the serious-minded and puritanical aldermen of Hull. In 1599, the very year that Shakespeare wrote two of his greatest tragedies, *Hamlet* and *Julius Caesar*, and the Globe theatre was built beside the Thames, the corporation of Hull issued a proclamation declaring that any inhabitant who attended a play put on by travelling players would be fined 2s. 6d., and any who let their house to players would be fined £1. For Hull's Puritans, theatres were little better than brothels.[29]

The corporation's views were those of mainstream Puritanism, sometimes called Foxeian Puritanism. They were not anti-episcopalian and accepted the authority of the Queen as 'Supreme Governor' of the church, and they believed that the godly prince and the godly bishop were essential centrepieces of the godly church. Consequently they were keen to work with the Archbishops of York, most of whom from 1561 could be described as mainstream Puritans. For Archbishop Edmund Grindal, who was sent to York in 1570 by Elizabeth to tackle the problem of recusant Catholics in the diocese, Protestant Hull was a welcome ally. In July 1574 he wrote to the corporation giving his support to their efforts to root out the 'abominable and heinous crimes' of fornication and adultery. The arrest and punishment of offenders for sexual crimes was normally the responsibility of the churchwardens and the church courts but the Archbishop was happy to delegate this responsibility to the justices of Hull. His successor, Archbishop Edwin Sandys, was equally supportive when his backing was sought a few years later. In 1582 he granted the mayor and aldermen an ecclesiastical commission to suppress 'the gross immoralities of the times', again delegating to the magistrates of Hull the powers traditionally exercised by the church court at York, and a similar arrangement was also approved in 1599 by Archbishop Matthew Hutton.[30]

The Protestant sympathies of the corporation had been very evident from the beginning of the reign. Indeed, during Mary's reign, accusations were made by a local merchant that the corporation was opposed to the government's religious policies. Such allegations had to be strongly denied but the corporation was relieved they had not been properly investigated before Mary died. Following Elizabeth's accession the corporation ensured the removal from office of the Marian vicar of Holy Trinity, Thomas Fugall, claiming, among other charges, that he had refused to use the new Protestant prayer book, although ordered to do so by the corporation. The aldermen then sought an unquestionably Protestant minister to replace him. Melchior Smith, who had already made a reputation for himself in Boston as a fiery preacher against sin and popery, was persuaded to take up the post.[31]

Not all of Hull's inhabitants shared the corporation's views, and in the 1570s some were still Catholic. This was certainly the view of Melchior Smith, who was constantly at odds with his parish clerk, William Steade, and with elements of his congregation, whom he regarded as – at best – insufficiently Protestant. In 1571 the parish clerk was removed from office after accusations before an Ecclesiastical

Commission that he had rung the church bells on All Saints' night, although he knew this was against the wishes of the vicar; and the vicar's curate, Simon Pynder, accused him of cutting his sermons short by ringing the bells, playing the organ and altering the church clock. It would seem that while the more puritanical elements of the congregation appreciated Pynder's two-hour sermons, which frequently raged against the sins of the townspeople, others did not. Steade, in his surreptitious campaign against the curate's sermons, represented those who were keen to preserve some of the Old Church.

Smith remained the vicar of Holy Trinity (and its 'parent' parish of Hessle) until 1591 and, with the corporation, he did much to establish and consolidate the town's reputation as a centre of Puritanism. It would seem he was a difficult character and held a number of radical Puritan views, which he tended to express bluntly, and consequently frequently antagonised his parishioners, including members of the corporation. In his first few years at Hull his radicalism soon got him into trouble. In 1564 he was arraigned before the Ecclesiastical Commission and ordered to exercise more discretion in his speech and to wear the correct vestments. A number of his more moderate Protestant parishioners claimed he had preached against vestments, bishops and the nobility, had sometimes worn his hat in church, even during a service, and had also mistreated his wife so badly that the poor woman had on one occasion jumped into the river Hull to escape his beatings. In 1566, at the height of the Vestiarian Controversy, he was in trouble again, and this time the Archbishop of York, Thomas Young, was determined to make an example of Smith, along with a number of other Puritan clergy in his arch-diocese. Smith was threatened with removal from office, and under this pressure he submitted, but the corporation had to ensure he wore the correct clerical vestments and had to write to the Archbishop confirming this.[32]

After this, relations between the vicar and his parishioners seem to have improved. While Smith grudgingly wore his vestments, so an increasing number of his parishioners came to appreciate long sermons. Like most Puritans, Smith regarded preaching as 'the highest and most excellent function of a priest'. In this he was supported by the corporation and by Young's successor at York, Edmund Grindal. In 1573 the latter agreed that Smith should be assisted by the appointment of a lectureship at Holy Trinity, the cost to be shared between the church, the corporation and the townspeople. Not surprisingly, the first lecturer, Grindal's nominee, Griffith Briskin, was a man similar to Smith. He was also soon in trouble with the Ecclesiastical Commissioners, being accused in 1578 and 1581 of omitting those parts of the Prayer Book to which he objected, most probably the sections in the Service of Holy Communion which allowed for ambiguity about whether Christ was physically present in the bread and wine. Briskin remained the town lecturer, giving regular two-hour sermons, until 1598.[33]

The corporation saw it as its duty to reinforce the statutes concerning church attendance. In 1566 it ordered that, as well as being in church on Sundays, at least one member of each household had to be present on Wednesdays, Fridays and holy days, and that during service time on Sundays all shops, ale houses and inns had to be closed. Moreover, it now became a punishable offence to speak ill of the local clergy. In 1574 Grindal wrote to the corporation to ask for its assistance in preventing wickedness and vice, and consequently churchwardens and sidesmen were ordered to visit alehouses and search the streets for absentees from church. At times the Puritanism exhibited by Hull's corporation must have been considerably resented. In 1577, for instance, it was even decided that fines should be introduced for parents who let their children cry during sermons.[34]

Although there were significant numbers of Catholics in the town in 1567 at the time of the Rising of the Northern Earls, very few of Hull's Catholics played any part in it, and the triumph of Protestantism in the town during the next few years seems to have been fairly complete. There were no more than a dozen recusants in the town in 1586 and at the end of the century only two notable families in the district were thought to include recusants: the Ellerkers and the Daltons.[35]

The town's reputation for militant Protestantism may have played a part in the decision of the Lord President of the Council of the North, the Earl of Huntingdon, to use the fortress and blockhouses of Hull from 1575 as a prison for persistent recusants and Catholic priests. Two years later there were 22 prisoners at Hull, and by 1600 about 75, of whom at least 12 died in prison. Many were kept in solitary confinement, some had their ears cut off, and it was later claimed that so little food was given to the prisoners that some may have died of starvation. One prisoner, a Mr Horsley, was said to have survived only on crusts of bread thrown in at the window of the prison. He was not only said to have died of hunger but also to have lain dead so long that when his cell was finally opened rats had eaten much of his corpse.[36]

Plague, poverty and the treatment of the destitute

When plague struck the town in the autumn of 1575 it was seen by many as God's punishment for the sins of the wicked, as foretold only the year before by the corporation when it had warned against 'the manifold, grievous and terrible plagues of God hanging over this town if a speedy reformation be not had'. Measures were taken to isolate the affected areas of the town, which was chiefly in Blackfriargate, close to the port. A fence was erected around the street and watchmen appointed to ensure that no one living in an affected house entered or left the area. The outbreak lasted until the following summer and killed about a hundred people, pushing up the normal number of deaths by about 50 per cent. Had it not been for the precautions taken the situation might have been much worse, although for the inhabitants of Blackfriargate their 'shutting in' condemned many healthy people to a horrible death.[37]

In 1582 the town was struck by a different epidemic, probably influenza, and again there were more than a hundred victims. After this the town enjoyed 20 years free from major epidemics and the population was able to rise steadily, as the rate of baptisms generally exceeded burials by nearly ten per year, and small numbers of country folk came into the town looking for work. This growth received another sharp check in 1602, when plague struck again. Victims were again 'shut in' and pest houses were also built just outside the walls, in Myton Carr, and some of those infected were removed to them. Attempts were also made to exclude from the port all goods and ships from other affected places. In spite of all this, about 200 people died of the infection during 1602 and 1603. As was typical with bubonic plague, the hot summer months were by far the worst, when the plague-carrying fleas multiplied most rapidly. In just three months, between July and September 1602, 98 burials were recorded at Holy Trinity, the great majority victims of the plague.[38]

One long-term effect of the outbreak of 1575-6 was to prompt the corporation to view with much greater concern the movement of poor people into the town from the surrounding countryside, and their cost in poor relief. A poor rate had to be raised to relieve those stricken with the plague and the corporation was now anxious to drive out any beggars and poor not long settled in Hull. Poverty had been a problem in the town in the early Tudor period. The assessment for the subsidy tax of 1525 revealed that two thirds of taxpayers were in the lowest category, of £1 to £4, and scores of other households were too poor to pay any tax at all. In 1559 and 1560 the corporation rounded up beggars and removed them from the town if they refused to find work, and the local orders against vice included injunctions against vagrancy and harbouring vagrants. The saying, first recorded in 1594 but clearly dating from some years before, 'From Hull, Hell, and Halifax, Good Lord deliver us', indicated the ferocious

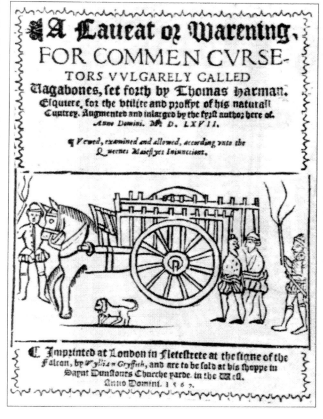

27 *Beggars being whipped and tied to a cart; the title page of Thomas Harman's* A Caveat for Common Cursetors, *1567.*

Ꝁ Stockes to stape sure, and safely detayne,
Lasy lewd Leutterers, that lawes do offend,
Impudent persons, thus punished with payne,
Hardlype for all this, do meanc to amende.

Fetters or Chackels serue to make fast,
Male malefactours, that on mischiefe do muse,
Untyll the learned lawes do quite or do cast,
Such suttle searchers, as all euyll do vse.

28   *Examples of equipment for punishing beggars, 1567.*

treatment vagrants could expect in the town in the late 16th century (with the reference to Halifax being to its frequent use of the gibbet). For Hull's Puritans, poverty and sin were very closely related, and often required similar treatment. Vagrants could generally expect very little sympathy, but a stark distinction was made between the deserving and undeserving poor.[39]

Following the poor law statutes of 1572 and 1576, the corporation could introduce a compulsory poor rate and use the money to provide stocks of material on which the town's able-bodied paupers might be set to work. York had already introduced such a scheme on its own initiative, and similar measures had been operating in London, Norwich and Ipswich for many years. In 1577 the corporation bought a stock of wool and employed two women from Doncaster to teach the unemployed to knit, at first in their own homes, and six years later a fisherman from Great Yarmouth was employed to teach his skills. The knitting school seems to have been developed by the corporation into an institution to give charitable help to the town's pauper children. By the 1590s it had become known as Charity Hall, with Richard Coggishall appointed master and overseer. Children who could not live except by begging were provided with work by Coggishall, spinning yarn for the knitters. The cost was at first met from voluntary contributions, and the townspeople were urged to take the children into their own homes and provide them with meals. Later a compulsory poor rate had to be introduced, but when Coggishall resigned, in 1595, the project was closed down and the corporation tried to find apprenticeships for the children. A few years later it was revived, and seems to have survived throughout the next century.[40]

In times of bad harvests, the corporation attempted to alleviate the situation by restricting grain exports and controlling food prices. In some particularly bad years, such as 1585-6 and 1595-7, the corporation itself bought corn to sell to the poor at a reasonable price. Some help was also provided by private charities, although, by the 1560s, these were mainly controlled by the corporation. Money left in numerous bequests provided food and clothing for some of the town's paupers, and met the cost of apprenticeships and schooling for the fortunate few chosen by the corporation. There was also a number of almshouses, the two largest being Trinity House and Charterhouse, the latter also under the control of the corporation.[41]

The Elizabethan Grammar School

The grammar school, long established immediately to the south of Holy Trinity Church, was also now under the control of the corporation and, having survived the Reformation, flourished in the last few decades of the century. Education had never been so important. For God-fearing wealthy merchants such as William Gee, the grammar school naturally deserved his charity, and in 1583-5 a new and bigger schoolroom was built to the west of the old one, which was then used as the master's house. In 1575 the

29   *The grammar school, built 1583-5. The schoolroom was on the ground floor; the first floor was the merchants' exchange.*

corporation bought reference books for the school, including a 'great dictionary' and Cooper's *Latin Dictionary*, and in 1579 it imposed fees so the master could be assisted by an usher. It also ensured that only graduates were appointed as masters and ushers so that the school was able to establish a high reputation and regularly sent local boys to Cambridge, mainly to be trained for the church. In 1580 it arranged for a new gallery to be built in Holy Trinity Church for the exclusive use of the school.

In spite of the fees, it was not only the sons of the rich who attended. Bright boys from humble backgrounds, the sons of craftsmen and tradesmen, were also educated at the school, having first attended one of the numerous local 'petty' schools. Consequently, the school was able to ensure a degree of social cohesion, and numbers of pupils rose well into the next century.[42]

Today the old grammar school building of the 16th century is a museum, one of very few secular buildings in the city dating from this period. Its external appearance is little altered from William Gee's time: a plain brick two-storey building, four bays wide with brick mullioned and transomed windows. Indeed, Gee's merchant's mark, his initials and the date can still be seen in inset panels on the ground floor, with the town arms on the first floor above.

30   *William Gee's 'merchant's mark' on the north-facing wall of the grammar school.*

FIVE

The Jacobean Town and the Civil War 1603-60

Population and plague

We have seen that, at the time of Queen Elizabeth's death in March 1603, the population of Hull stood between 5,000 and 6,000, having doubled in the previous century despite plague, influenza and the sweating sickness. When the new reign opened, the town was once again suffering from an outbreak of the plague, and during 1603 it claimed another 70 to 80 lives, with the last victims succumbing early in 1604. Not understanding its causes, rumours spread that the disease had been brought by witchcraft, and in September 1604 five local people, Mary Holland, Jennet Wressell, Jennet Butler, Roger Beadneys and John Willerby, were hanged for practising magic. Their guilt was confirmed by the confession of Willerby, possibly after torture. The corporation records claimed he confessed 'many things at his death, accusing many of witchcraft'.[1]

After 1604, there were no more major outbreaks of disease for more than 30 years. Consequently, baptisms regularly outstripped burials in the parish registers and the town enjoyed steady growth. This was not mere good fortune. On a number of occasions during the 1620s the plague raged in other parts of Yorkshire but was kept out of Hull by placing watchmen at the town gates to turn away travellers from areas known to be infected. In 1630 and 1631 men from York were only allowed to enter if they had a certificate from the mayor of York attesting to their good health, and ships arriving in both years from France and London were not allowed to dock in the haven, but had to be unloaded out in the Humber roads. As an additional precaution, the corporation also cancelled the annual fair in 1631. When a visitor from Nottinghamshire was inadvertently allowed in, the house he was staying at, in Whitefriargate, was locked up and all the inhabitants shut in until fear of infection had lifted.

Reports of plague in the county prompted the corporation to reinstate the watchmen at the gates in the summer of 1636, only 18 months after they had been finally stood down, but this time the plague could not be kept out. The summer passed with little incident, but in July 1637 a case of the plague was reported in Mytongate, and it spread across the western side of the town very quickly. Some were shut in but others were removed to pest houses in Myton Carr, and new pest houses were opened to take the growing number of victims. Two men were appointed to look after the sick at the pest houses and bury the dead, and the corporation banned all large gatherings. The daily church services were suspended, schools were closed, the twice-weekly markets were replaced by a temporary market at Drypool, on open land on the far side of the haven. Drinking was restricted, and there could be no festivities to celebrate weddings or baptisms. For about eight weeks it looked as though the outbreak had been confined, and by September no cases had been reported among the larger houses along High Street and beside the haven. The corporation therefore appealed to the Privy Council to lift the ban on trade with the port, which was doing considerable damage to the town. The Privy Council acceded to the request, but it soon became apparent that the corporation had acted too hastily. Very soon the plague had flared up again and was now spreading through the whole town. More pest houses were built, orders were given to remove all pigs and pigsties from the town, fearing that they harboured the infection, begging was banned, and the corporation moved its meetings from the town hall to the castle. More families were shut in, including that of Andrew Marvell Snr, the town lecturer, and the shutting-in period was lengthened and enforced more rigorously. Winter came but the plague continued to rage, and among the victims in December was the mayor, John Ramsden, one of the richest men in Hull. By this time those able to leave the town had done so, including three aldermen, who had to be summoned back to elect a new mayor. By the end of the year about 650 people had died – about an eighth of the population – and it was not until the following spring that the plague finally abated.

The 1637 epidemic was the last great 'visitation' of the plague, but an outbreak of typhus in 1644 may have killed 400, and there were also many casualties of the Civil War. Plague did claim more victims in September and October 1645, despite stringent efforts to keep away travellers and exclude ships from infected areas, but the numbers were mercifully low. Those affected were taken as quickly as possible to the pest houses and orders were issued to clean butchers' shops and stalls. The filthy piles of guts and offal allowed to accumulate on the streets were hot beds of disease, and their removal played a small part in keeping down the mortality rate. Orders were also issued to restrain the movement of dogs, pigs and cattle. The true nature of the disease and its means of transition, in the blood of a flea, would not be known for more than 200 years. The best scientific opinion of the day held that diseases were transmitted in stinking air, 'miasma', emanating particularly from piles of animal and human faeces on uncleansed streets throughout the country. Although the stinking air was a mere symptom of the true problem, any efforts made to clean the streets could only help.

A contemporary pamphlet estimated the population of the town at 7,000 to 8,000 in 1644. This may be too high a figure, given the high mortality rates of the epidemics of 1637 and 1644, together with the casualties of war, and it was perhaps closer to six thousand. During the years of the Commonwealth and Protectorate of the 1650s, Hull was again spared the ravages of disease and the town grew steadily until, in 1660, it was struck once more by another typhus epidemic.[2]

Busy port, fluctuating fortunes

In the plague of 1637 some families were entirely wiped out and numerous families lost at least one or two members. Many also suffered severe financial losses. Gifts of food and money were made by local gentry and, after appeals from the corporation and instructions from the Privy Council, a little money was raised by charity collections throughout the county to assist in meeting the enormous increase in poor relief. In February 1638 it was reported that 2,500 people, almost half the population, were in receipt of help from the overseers.[3]

The suspension of trade caused by the plague had led to bankruptcies and a sudden leap in unemployment, but up to this time the years since Queen Elizabeth's death had been a period mainly of economic growth for the town. The town's principal overseas trade in 1603, the export of Yorkshire kerseys to the Baltic and the import of flax and corn in return, continued to expand in the next 20 years, as did the lucrative whaling industry, although Hull men bringing back large quantities of whale oil caused constant friction with the London-based Russia Company. These years also saw a major expansion in the quantities of timber Hull ships were bringing back from both Norway and the Baltic.

The outbreak of the Thirty Years War, in 1618, did not at first affect the Baltic trade, but in 1626 it seriously disrupted all shipping using Danzig and Elbing, the Hull merchants' two main Baltic ports. Although the trade revived briefly in the 1630s, Hull merchants soon found it impossible to compete with the Dutch carrying trade, and by the early 1640s direct trade between Hull and the Baltic ports was on a much smaller scale. Fortunately this was more than compensated for in the 1620s and 1630s by new opportunities for increasing trade with the ports of North Germany and the Netherlands. Amsterdam and Hamburg now became the principal destinations for Hull ships laden with Yorkshire cloth, and Amsterdam, in particular, also became an important entrepôt from which Baltic corn, timber, flax, pitch and tar could be imported in return. The annual value of Hull's exports of cloth rose from £109,000 in 1609 to £166,000 in 1640, and an increasing proportion of exports from the port were being carried in Hull-built and Hull-owned ships. Moreover, the average size of

Hull ships was becoming ever larger, approximately doubling between 1580 and 1640. By 1626 the port had about 20 ships of over 100 tons, and in 1630 at least one ship of over 300 tons. The disruption of the Civil War in 1642 was a ruinous blow for the port, but during the 1650s the town re-established itself as one of the country's most important links with northern Europe.[4]

The town's coastal trade, which had grown much less rapidly than its overseas trade in Elizabeth's reign, also enjoyed healthy expansion in the first few decades of the new century. Coal from Newcastle and Sunderland was brought into the port in increasing quantities until the 1650s, when the opening of coal mines in Yorkshire and the North Midlands challenged the dominance of the Great Northern Coalfield. Fish imports also remained important, particularly from Great Yarmouth and the Scottish ports. Of the commodities exported from Hull to other English ports, the two most important were lead and foodstuffs, and the largest market for both was London. In 1627-8 it was calculated that 94 per cent of all lead shipped out of Hull was destined for the capital, and as London grew rapidly in the 17th century its demands for Yorkshire corn, butter and cheeses also expanded.

A number of Hull's merchants and shipmasters were able to accumulate substantial fortunes at this time. One of the wealthiest, Alderman Thomas Ferries, was also the town's greatest benefactor. He gave Trinity House the site of the Carmelite friary, founded an almshouse and, at his death in 1631, left money in his will for repairing the North Bridge and the town walls, and for rebuilding the guildhall. A local bricklayer, John Catlyn Snr, carried out the rebuilding of the guildhall between 1634 and 1636.[5]

The approach of Civil War

When, in the spring of 1642, the country began to slip inexorably into Civil War, the people of Hull found themselves at the very heart of the conflict. On 23 April, St George's Day, 1642, the governor of Hull, supported by a majority of the corporation, refused King Charles entry to the town, standing on Beverley Gate to tell the enraged king that his primary responsibility was to parliament. Just three years before, Charles had been welcomed into the town by cheering crowds, had received a silken purse full of gold coins and heard a speech from the mayor pledging the king the town's undying loyalty. During 1642-3, all over England towns and cities had to take sides, and because of its strategic importance the corporation of Hull had to choose earlier than most. From late April 1642 the parliamentary sympathies of the corporation are clear enough, and a crucial factor in deciding this was the Puritanism of its members.[6]

The Puritan dominance of the corporation had survived intact from Elizabeth's time. By this time the moderate Puritan faction in the town had long enjoyed almost a monopoly on the bench, and the anti-Puritan policies of Archbishop Laud in the 1630s served only to entrench Puritanism in the town. In the 1620s many members of the corporation were horrified by the appointment of a conforming High Church Anglican,

Richard Perrott, to the living of Hessle and Hull, and did their utmost to frustrate his efforts to have the organ in Holy Trinity repaired and put back into regular use. To limit his influence the corporation ensured the appointment of a moderate Puritan as the town lecturer in 1625: Andrew Marvell the elder, the father of the poet, who quickly gained considerable respect and authority. Two years later the corporation appointed a fairly militant Puritan, John Gouge, as Perrott's curate, much to the latter's discomfort, and also ensured that another Puritan minister, Anthony Stevenson, was appointed master of the grammar school in 1632. As moderate Puritans, however, the members of the corporation wanted to cooperate with the church authorities and complied when a diocesan commission in 1633 gave orders for both Holy Trinity and St Mary's to be beautified along the lines prescribed by Laud, although for many militants in the town this was quite unacceptable. It also did not protest when the commission supported Perrott in his opposition to the wearing of hats in church, a practice favoured by the more extreme Puritans, and named five men as persistent offenders.[7]

The corporation may have been representative of the majority of the townspeople, but by the 1630s more extreme views were gaining support in the town. Such was the strength of militant Puritanism that an attempt to reinstate daily services using the Prayer Book had to be temporarily abandoned. The services had been introduced by Perrott to popularise the Prayer Book, which the more extreme Puritans regarded with considerable suspicion, but the services had to be suspended during the plague of 1637. When Perrott tried to reintroduce them in 1638 he was blocked by his curate, John Gouge. On this issue, Perrott was supported by the mayor and other moderate Puritans on the corporation, but a large section of the town was now much more radical than the corporation, and supported Gouge. Perrot and the mayor were bluntly warned by Gouge's supporters that if they tried to discipline Gouge there would be uproar. The corporation backed down, but Gouge was forced to conform when he was summoned, in 1639, before the diocesan court of Laud's loyal Archbishop of York, Richard Neile. To the horror of the corporation, Neile's court was determined to crack down on all forms of Puritanism, and it also summoned the moderate town lecturer, Marvell, and ordered him to read more of the Prayer Book liturgy before each of his weekly lectures.

The consequence of all this was a deepening resentment in the town against the king's High Church religious policies. Gouge and Marvell were both popular figures and their humiliation in 1639 would not be quickly forgotten. When Marvell died in 1641 the corporation resisted pressure to appoint as his replacement a Laudian prebendary of York, and chose instead to appoint another moderate Puritan, William Styles. It was probably partly for the same reasons that Gouge now also sought to take revenge against Perrott by complaining to the House of Commons about a sermon the vicar had preached more than two years earlier, on New Year's Day, 1639. The House found against Perrott and he was impeached, but died before the end of the year and the corporation ensured that he was replaced by Styles.[8]

Another event which weakened the king's support in the town concerned the wars against Scotland. At first, the outbreak of war served only to emphasise the town's loyalty to its sovereign. When, in 1638, the danger of invasion prompted expensive repairs to the town's fortifications, and the movement of much of the royal arsenal, or magazine, from the Tower of London to Hull, the cost had at first to be met by the corporation. Though the town could ill afford this so soon after the plague of 1637-8, it seems to have been accepted with little complaint. At this stage there was no hint of disloyalty and in April 1639, when King Charles visited the town to inspect the fortifications and the much-enlarged magazine, the people of Hull thronged the streets to welcome him. Later in the year relations between the corporation and the king's government improved further when the latter agreed to make a grant of £500 towards the cost of recent repairs and replenishment of the magazine.[9]

However, during the following year, opinion seems to have shifted considerably. The strategic importance of Hull, now made all the greater by the shipping of the magazine to the town from London, meant the people of Hull were dragged into the crisis in relations between parliament and monarch developing in the capital. Desperate for cash to fight a second war against the Scots, Charles was finally obliged in April 1640 to bring to an end 11 years of personal rule and to recall parliament. But this proved a disaster as the great majority of MPs had no intention of voting for the taxes until they had first voiced their grievances about the years of personal rule, and on 5 May, after sitting for only three weeks, Charles dissolved the parliament.

Among the MPs elected in April was Sir John Hotham, the long-serving MP for Beverley who was now also governor of the Hull fortress. Hotham was an old enemy of fellow Yorkshireman Sir Thomas Wentworth, who until recently had been Lord Deputy of Ireland but now returned to London and was rapidly becoming the king's chief advisor. As Wentworth's star rose at court, confirmed by his elevation to the Earldom of Strafford, so Hotham's fell, and in August 1640 he was removed from his position at Hull. Strafford, now also High Steward of Hull, had advised the king against Hotham's removal, but this was not generally known, and in Hull it was widely blamed on Strafford and much resented. Hotham had greatly strengthened the town's defences with a strong watch, and had taken command of the local 'trained bands' of part-time gentlemen soldiers.

Strafford angered the town further by sending a regiment of foot soldiers to the town with Hotham's successor, his close friend and ultra-loyalist Sir Thomas Glemham, and ordering the mayor to hand over to Sir Thomas the keys to the city gates. Under Hotham's governorship it had been agreed that no troops would be billeted in the town, but Strafford chose to ignore this, and although the threat of a Scottish invasion passed, Sir Thomas's troops were not withdrawn from the town until the following July. When the king visited Hull again, in September 1640, he was met with a very cool reception.[10]

By this time, however, Strafford's star, too, was beginning to wane quickly. His advice to the king to put together an army without the necessary funds from parliament had proved disastrous when a small, ill-equipped English force was decisively defeated by a much larger Scottish army at the battle of Newburn, on 28 August 1640. Newcastle was then surrendered and the north-eastern counties overrun, and Charles had to recall parliament once again. But now he was in an even weaker position, and to raise the taxes and armies he was obliged to make numerous concessions to both MPs and peers, who met for the first time early in November 1640. Among those MPs who joined the powerful opposition faction, led by John Pym, were Sir John Hotham, again MP for Beverley, and the two Hull MPs, Henry Vane, the son of Sir Henry Vane, one of the king's privy councillors, and Peregrine Pelham, a local merchant, alderman and former sheriff of the town. When, in the following March, Pym and his followers managed to have Strafford charged with treason, two of the earl's most forthright accusers were Hotham and Vane. The latter used his father's Privy Council papers to suggest that Strafford intended to bring an Irish army to England to use against the king's enemies. The evidence

31 *Sir John Hotham in 1621, the year in which he was created a baronet; the portrait was probably commissioned to celebrate the event. The 'background' drawing showing Beverley Gate and King Charles before the walls of Hull was added later.*

was flimsy but Pym succeeded in persuading a majority of MPs to vote for a Bill of Attainder, calling on Charles to sign his friend's death warrant, and, with the king powerless to refuse, the earl was executed on Tower Hill on 11 May 1641.[11]

As relations between king and parliament continued to deteriorate, the question of who should control the magazine became more pressing than ever, and in January 1642 the king appointed the Earl of Newcastle governor of the town. Parliament immediately responded by appointing its own governor, Sir John Hotham, and his son, Captain John Hotham, was despatched to the town immediately. The corporation now found itself in a difficult position, for it had no wish to give offence to either parliament or king, or to take any action which might compromise the rights and freedoms set out in its charters. Fearing for the town's independence, the mayor, Henry Barnard, felt that if there had to be a governor the only suitable choice was himself. Newcastle's commission from the king was therefore not recognised and Captain Hotham was not at first admitted into the town. The great majority of the corporation were, however, on the side of parliament, and when the corporation were threatened with a charge of treason if it did not comply, the captain was allowed to enter, along with some of the trained bands. The corporation was keen to avoid the burdens of again billeting troops in the town, but was forced to do so after the mayor and one of the aldermen were summoned before the Commons.[12]

Parliament now debated how it might safely remove the magazine from Hull back to London, while the king's faction plotted to take the town and gain control of the arms supply for itself. On 22 April 1642 the king's younger son, the eight-year-old James, Duke of York, together with the king's nephew, Karl Ludwig, the exiled Elector-Palatine, and the former governor Sir Thomas Glemham with their respective retinues – a party of about fifty – arrived unofficially in the town and were entertained by the governor and the mayor. Hotham, however, suspected a royalist plot to seize the town, confirmed when he learnt, the following morning, that the king himself was coming to the town later that day to meet his son, accompanied by a troop of cavalry about 300 strong. He immediately called a meeting of the town's aldermen at the *White Hart* inn and, with Pelham's strong support, succeeded in persuading most of those present that his commission from parliament did not allow him to admit the king without parliamentary approval. The drawbridges were raised and the town gates locked. According to one alderman present, the corporation might not have steeled itself to take so dangerous a decision had the young prince James, or members of his party, attended the discussion. How much the royal party knew about this meeting is not clear; the story that they were too busy enjoying the banquet provided in their honour by Trinity House to attend seems unlikely.[13] Hull's defiance of the king would soon come to be seen as one of the last major events in the country's slide into war. Only a little time before, such humiliation of a king of England by one of his own towns would have seemed unthinkable.

Charles and his party arrived at Beverley Gate late on Saturday morning. On finding the gates locked against him a long parley ensued, with Hotham protesting

his loyalty but repeating that he could not admit the king without parliament's approval. This went on until about four o'clock in the afternoon, when the king issued Hotham with an ultimatum, giving him an hour to change his mind. When the king's heralds returned at five o'clock Hotham maintained his defiance, and the heralds thereupon proclaimed him guilty of treason. According to one report, the royal party called on the soldiers on the

32 *All that is left of Beverley Gate today.*

wall and gate to arrest Hotham and throw him into the moat below, and only when they refused to do so did the king and his retinue return sadly to Beverley, where they were joined shortly afterwards by the Duke of York and his party. The following day the royal heralds returned to offer Hotham a final chance of a pardon if he had changed his mind, but again this was politely refused.[14]

Most of the weapons and ammunition stored in the town were now removed on parliament's orders to London, but the strategic importance of the port was still considerable. Charles had made York his temporary headquarters but badly needed to regain control of Hull so that help might be more easily brought in from abroad. His hopes were raised by rumours circulating in June that elements in the town might be willing to surrender it. There were certainly plenty of royalist sympathisers in the town, and relations between the mayor and the Hothams were extremely strained. A force of cavaliers was sent to the town in early July to test its resistance. The town was bombarded and its main water supply was cut, but there was no sign of any treachery, although as a precaution Governor Hotham had the mayor arrested. Shortly before the siege began parliament sent Hotham a force of 2,000 men under Sir John Meldrum to reinforce the garrison; the town's defences were strengthened by the building of bastions outside the gates; heavy guns were placed on both the walls and the forts; and the surrounding area was flooded by the defenders breaking down dykes and river banks.

The siege lasted just three weeks. In an effort to break it, Sir John Meldrum led two sallies from the town, and on the second occasion he managed to force the king's men to retreat from their headquarters at Anlaby and to abandon the attempt to take the town. Consequently, when Charles raised his standard at Nottingham, on 22 August 1642, the parliamentarians' grip on Hull seemed more secure than ever. The rumours of treachery within the town were, however, prescient, and parliament's hold on Hull was soon to be loosened.[15]

The Civil War

In the first few weeks after the raising of the siege, Hotham, with the support of the corporation, consolidated the town's position as a parliamentary stronghold. Damage done to the walls and fortress during the siege was repaired, the regular watch and ward duties on the gates and walls were maintained, and – although in breach of the county's neutrality agreement – Captain Hotham led raids from the town against royalists in the East Riding, as far west as Cawood Castle, and even across the Humber. A number of royalists in the town were arrested and had their property confiscated but only one member of the bench, Alderman James Watkinson, withdrew from the town to join the king. Although relations between Henry Barnard, the mayor, and Sir John Hotham remained extremely strained, Barnard did not resign his position and with his successor, Thomas Raikes, and two other aldermen, formed an inner council to continue the administrative work of the corporation.[16]

Rumours of royalist plots to retake the town persisted, and in late November the most serious plot yet was foiled when a group of royalists managed to enlist in the garrison, planning to blow up one of the gates to allow a royalist force from York through. Sir John had the plotters caught red-handed, while Captain Hotham, together with Sir Thomas Fairfax, successfully intercepted the York royalists on their way to the town.

By this time, Sir John Hotham was a deeply troubled man. He was a conservative country gentleman, proud of his family's ancient lineage, and now very keen to see the war ended. He disagreed strongly with one of the town's MPs, Pelham, once his closest ally in the town but now a member of the 'war party' in the Commons, and, as a local merchant and an alderman with many local connections, a dangerous and influential opponent. He was also at odds with the more radical members of the local clergy, 'the preciser clergy' as he referred to them, and – like many members of the corporation – he was horrified by the growth of Separatist groups in the town, led by Robert Luddington and Philip Nye, who in 1643 established an Independent congregation.

Royalists claimed that acts of defiance and disloyalty, such as Hotham's, had led to attacks on property and the undermining of traditional and long-accepted precepts of deference, order and hierarchical subordination, to which Hotham, and other conservatives, longed to return. During the winter of 1642-3 Sir John privately came to the decision that he wished to defect to the royalists and surrender Hull. One of the very few people to whom Sir John confided his secret was his son, who shared his growing disillusionment with the war. His son later explained how both he and his father, like so many other members of the gentry class, had hoped for a swift end to the war through compromise: 'No man that hath any reasonable share in the commonwealth can desire that either side should be conqueror ... it is too great a temptation to counsels of violence.' He feared that if the war continued, 'the necessitous people of the whole kingdom will presently rise in mighty numbers and ... set up for themselves to the utter ruin of all the nobility and gentry'.[17]

The Hothams' motives were probably a mix of personal jealousies and high principles. An intensely proud man, Sir John was deeply offended when in 1642 the parliamentary leadership appointed Lord Fairfax, and not himself, general of the parliamentary forces in the north, and appointed Lord Fairfax's son, Sir Thomas, lieutenant-general of the horse, under him. He believed these two positions were rightfully his and his son's. After all, no father and son had done more for the parliamentary cause than they.

Sir John's first act of betrayal was to make contact with the commander of the royalist armies in Yorkshire, the Earl of Newcastle, and with the queen, when she landed in Bridlington in February 1643 with munitions from Holland. Captain Hotham was sent to meet the queen and the earl, ostensibly to arrange an exchange of prisoners, but the royalists were shortly afterwards convinced that both father and son were now willing to surrender Hull. But the secret could not be kept, and within a few weeks the Hothams were under suspicion. The parliamentary leadership took the precaution of removing the younger Hotham in April to take a small force to reinforce the garrison at Lincoln and then to assist parliamentary forces besieging Newark. Meanwhile, a Puritan clergyman and relative of the Hothams, John Saltmarsh, whom Sir John completely trusted, was sent to Hull to find out whether the suspicions were justified. Although he had been tipped off by royalist agents that he was under suspicion, it would seem that Sir John opened his heart to his relative. On leaving Hull, Saltmarsh immediately informed his superiors and a plan was quickly drawn up to have both father and son arrested. It had been hoped to keep Captain Hotham in Lincolnshire, where he was arrested for failing to maintain discipline among his forces, but he managed to escape and was back in Hull by late June.

On 28 June a small group of conspirators met to agree the final details of their planned coup. The group included the mayor, Thomas Raikes, a local gentleman, Sir Matthew Boynton, a few members of the corporation, and the captain of the parliamentary ship, the *Hercules*, which was in the Humber. Early the next morning about a hundred men from the *Hercules* landed and took control of the castle and blockhouses, while a party of townsmen and soldiers took control of the walls, gates and magazine. Captain Hotham was arrested but his father escaped through Beverley Gate with some of his bodyguards. He was captured in Beverley and brought back to Hull, and imprisoned with his son on the *Hercules* until both could be taken to London to await trial. They were not put on trial until November 1644, but their guilt was confirmed when letters between them and the Earl of Newcastle were discovered after the royalist defeat at Marston Moor in July 1644. Captain Hotham was executed on Tower Hill on 1 January 1645, and his father the following day.[18]

33 *Sir John Hotham, the governor of Hull.*

34 *Captain Hotham.*

The success of the coup on 29 June was to be of crucial importance for the parliamentary cause in the north of England, for the very next day the parliamentary forces of Lord Fairfax and his son were defeated by the Earl of Newcastle's army at Adwalton Moor, near Bradford, and Hull became the only major centre of parliamentary activity in the north-east of England, and a refuge for all parliamentary forces in the area. By early July both Lord Fairfax and Sir Thomas Fairfax had retreated to Hull with the remnants of their army. Shortly afterwards Lord Fairfax was appointed governor of the town and preparations began to face the expected royalist siege. At the end of August, the Earl of Newcastle began to move northwards again, intent on destroying this last parliamentary bastion in the north-east, and by 2 September his army of 16,000 men were in sight of the town and the second siege of Hull had begun.[19]

For the inhabitants of Hull the next few weeks were among the most terrifying of their lives. From the outset of the siege the royalists poured red-hot cannon balls on to the town from the north to set fire to it. Casualties were remarkably few and serious fires were prevented partly because of the precautions taken by the governor. Householders whose houses were roofed in thatch were ordered to replace them with tile, and every inhabitant was expected to help put out any fires in their part of the town. As in the previous siege a year before, the royalists cut off the town's main source of fresh water and the townspeople had to manage as best they could on the brackish water from wells.

To keep the besieging gunners at a considerable distance from the town, Fairfax had had the earthwork defences outside the walls strengthened, and even the ancient Charterhouse had been virtually demolished so that a new earthwork-defended gun emplacement could be erected on the site. Despite these precautions it became necessary, just a little over a week into the siege, to break the banks and flood the surrounding fields to prevent Newcastle's large army from advancing closer. For many families this meant financial ruin. The town, however, did not starve, for the royalists were unable to prevent parliamentary ships from bringing in supplies. Also, the townspeople were completely united in resisting the royalist army. Tales of the appalling treatment of Beverley's residents by Newcastle's army ensured every inhabitant would endure the hardships of the siege as best they could and give every support to the parliamentary soldiers now stationed in the town.

Conditions for the besiegers were, if anything, worse than those endured by the townspeople. When the royalist MP, Sir Philip Warwick, visited the Earl of Newcastle during the siege he found his army severely depleted by disease. 'Those without were likelier to rot', he believed, 'than those within to starve.' Knowledge of this may have encouraged Fairfax to plan a determined sortie to break the siege, and, according to the account of the Revd John Shawe, 'on 9th September about 400 horse and foot made a sally, and fell upon the royalists at Anlaby'. Fairfax's forces were repulsed, however, and another attempt could not be made until he had received sufficient reinforcements.

Colonel Oliver Cromwell brought in some troops on 26 September, on 5 October Sir John Meldrum arrived with another 400 men, and a few days later Sir William Constable arrived with a further 250 men. By early October 1643 Fairfax was so confident that he had the forces necessary to break the siege that he felt able to release his son and a force of cavalry to assist Cromwell in Lincolnshire. Perhaps fearing another attack, the Earl of Newcastle's army, to quote Shawe again, 'made a desperate assault on the outworks of the enemy, but were met with so much energy that few of their party escaped'. Then, early on 11 October Fairfax ordered Meldrum to lead an attack on the royalist positions to the west of the town, with a force of about 1,500 men. They were at first driven back, but after a second assault, and seven hours of bitter fighting, they succeeded in driving the royalists off and in capturing their guns. The corporation records tell us that the grateful citizens of Hull then brought out refreshments for the victorious soldiers: 'The inhabitants of Hull sent great store of bread and meat, and many gallons of sack and strong beer ... which came very seasonably to them that had been fighting all day.'

On the following day the siege was raised and from this time on, until the Restoration, 12 October was observed as a day of public thanksgiving in the town. Parliament was now able to use the port as a valuable stronghold from which to launch military operations, and as a secure base for the storage of arms and ammunition. Relations between the corporation and both Lord Fairfax and his son, Sir Thomas, who succeeded his father as governor in 1645, were also far more cordial than they had been with Sir John Hotham. The disruption to trade caused by the war meant, however, that the corporation lacked the funds needed to repair the castle and town walls after the siege, and there were complaints that the taxation imposed by parliament on the town in 1644-6, to finance the parliamentary armies in the north, was excessive. Moreover, the imposition of a permanent garrison in 1646 was much resented.[20]

The Interregnum, 1649-1660

The 11 years between the execution of Charles I, in January 1649, and the restoration of his son, Charles II, were marked in Hull, as in many other towns, by bitter religious and political divisions and by an unprecedented degree of central government interference in the public life of the town. The strategic and commercial importance of the town meant that both the parliamentary Commonwealth government of 1649-53, and the Protectorate that followed, were anxious to ensure that the town remained in the 'right' hands. In 1650 the first of a number of dismissals from the corporation began, when John Ramsden was ordered off the bench for refusing to take the oath of allegiance, known as the 'Engagement', to the Commonwealth government. Ramsden was a moderate Puritan with little affection for a government which had abolished the monarchy, the House of Lords and the episcopacy. In 1651 the Council of State, the governing body of the Commonwealth, also dismissed John Barnard and Robert Morton from the Hull bench, and in 1652 a fourth member, Alderman Richard Perkins, was displaced.

These gross abuses of the town's traditional rights and independence, protected by the town's charters, were in each case compounded by the government choosing the replacement for those removed. Also, when the MP Peregrine Pelham became mayor in 1649, the government insisted that Thomas Raikes, a firm parliamentary supporter, should be his deputy. It was recognised that Pelham, as an MP, would probably have little time for his mayoral duties. The town's charter, however, was not altered. There was less interference during the Cromwellian Protectorate, but the wealthy Barnard family was still under suspicion, and the election of Leonard Barnard to an aldermanship in 1656 prompted an investigation by one of Cromwell's much-despised major generals, though Barnard was able to keep his place. Parliament's fears of a possible royalist plot to seize the town diminished after the final defeat of Charles II at the battle of Worcester, and his flight to France, in 1652. In late 1658, however, officers and soldiers stationed at the Hull garrison reported that the former royalist officer Sir Henry Slingsby, who was being held prisoner in the fortress, had attempted to incite rebellion. He was promptly arrested and executed, and his blood-stained shirt can still be seen at Knaresborough Castle.[21]

The religious divisions and controversies that dominated the town during the Civil War and the Interregnum that followed mirrored those of the country generally, but there was personal rivalry and jealousy mixed in as well. The vicar at Holy Trinity at the beginning of the Civil War, William Styles, was a moderate Puritan but an enthusiastic supporter of the parliamentary cause, and he gave his full support to Sir John Hotham's decision to deny the king entry to the town in 1642. He enjoyed the respect and support of most members of the corporation but his position in the town was challenged from 1644 by the appointment to St Mary's of John Shawe, a more militant Puritan. Shawe had first come to the town in 1642 but his more extreme brand of Puritanism had caused repeated clashes with Sir John, and the governor, who regarded him as a dangerous nuisance, had expelled him. Nonetheless, Shawe was an exceptional preacher and on his return to the town quickly won a substantial following, both on the corporation and in the town. Within six months he was appointed town lecturer by the corporation, giving him the right to share the pulpit of Holy Trinity with the more moderate Styles. The two men loathed one another, preached against each other, and Styles publicly disputed whether or not Shawe should preach in Holy Trinity during the principal service of the week, before the mayor and corporation, on Sunday mornings. The corporation managed to negotiate a compromise on this, with Styles obliged to allow Shawe some Sunday mornings. Shawe, however, clearly believed that he should be the dominant voice of the church, and was soon demanding the mastership of the Charterhouse hospital, a post held by Styles, and the chaplaincy of Trinity House, which was vacant. This time, Styles was triumphant. He held on to his Charterhouse position and succeeded in having the moderate John Boatman, a man much closer to his own views, appointed to the Trinity House chaplaincy.[22]

An uneasy truce between Styles and Shawe survived for the next five years, but in 1650 both Styles and Boatman were expelled from their positions when they, like Alderman Ramsden, refused to swear the oath of loyalty to the Commonwealth. Shawe now hoped to succeed Styles as vicar of Holy Trinity with the support of the government. As an ardent Presbyterian, Shawe had, for the previous five years, enthusiastically introduced and enforced in the town the Presbyterian model of church government favoured by the Commonwealth. This meant establishing a strict system of Presbyterian discipline, enforced by the clergy and leading members of the congregation, known as elders. This had made Shawe many enemies, particularly among the more conservative elements, and by 1650 there were enough opposing members of the corporation to block his appointment. Shawe's supporters had him appointed to the Charterhouse vacancy, but he then alienated more members of the corporation by questioning the charity's revenues. The corporation hoped Styles and Boatman might change their minds and take the Engagement oath, so that they could be returned to their positions. When, by 1652, it was clear that this was not to happen, they secured instead the appointment of the moderate minister Henry Hibbert.[23]

Shortly after the removal of Styles from Holy Trinity, at the end of 1650, another dispute came to a head between Presbyterians and Independents. A small congregation of Independents, or Congregationalists, had been established in the town by 1643. During the war their numbers had grown, encouraged by considerable support from parliamentarians, including Henry Ireton and Oliver Cromwell. Unlike the Presbyterians, they had no wish to see the Church of England with its bishops replaced by a Calvinistic system of church organisation modelled on the Scottish kirk. Instead, they preferred individual congregations to remain independent unless, by mutual consent, they chose to form local groupings. The Hull congregation had no support on the corporation, but they found a champion in Colonel Robert Overton, the new deputy governor appointed in 1647 to assist the often-absent Sir Thomas Fairfax, with whom he had fought at the battle of Marston Moor. In 1648 Overton gave the Independents enormous assistance by appointing John Canne to the chaplaincy of the garrison. Canne was a man of considerable learning who had for some years served as pastor to the English Separatists in Amsterdam. He soon became the effective leader of the Independents in Hull, with a sizeable following among both townspeople and soldiers. Following Styles' dismissal, Canne fiercely contested with Shawe to succeed to the vicarage of Holy Trinity. Although the corporation was able to block the appointment of both men, it was not able to stop Canne preaching in the church, as he continued to enjoy Overton's support. Acting on Overton's orders, a group of soldiers, who were members of Canne's congregation, in 1651 built a brick wall across the church, so that they could use the east end of the church while the Presbyterians had the nave. This arrangement continued until 1660, although Canne was removed from the town in 1657, having become increasingly extreme in his beliefs. By this time he had also lost his patron, Overton, who was removed as governor of Hull in 1655, and was then shortly afterwards arrested on the orders of Cromwell and sent to the Tower. Overton had become a member of the sect known as the Fifth Monarchists, who believed the end of the world was at hand. Cromwell suspected that Overton belonged to the more militant wing of the movement, which believed that Cromwell was an agent of the devil who had to be overthrown to allow Christ's kingdom, the Fifth Monarchy, to be established.[24]

Following Cromwell's death, in September 1658, Overton was released from prison and in the following year Cromwell's successor, his son Richard, restored Overton to the governorship of Hull, much to the dismay of the corporation. The elections for Richard Cromwell's parliament suggested that the majority of Hull's burgesses shared the corporation's moderate views. Two republicans were rejected in favour of two well-known local moderates: a former alderman, John Ramsden, who had been dismissed from the bench by the Commonwealth government in 1650, and the poet Andrew Marvell, who had been educated at the grammar school and whose father had been a popular and moderate Puritan town lecturer before his death in 1641. In Hull, as in the country generally, support for republicanism waned rapidly after the death of Cromwell. His son was an ineffective leader, unable to control the numerous factions in the country, and there was a growing fear that the country might drift into anarchy unless the monarchy was restored.

Governor Overton, however, was a convinced republican. Consequently, while the restoration of the monarchy began to be openly discussed as a real possibility, Governor Overton seemed ready to make a stand for the republic. Men suspected of royalist sympathies were rounded up and the garrison told to expect a siege. The town, however, joined with many others in petitioning for a free parliament, which could lead to a restoration of the monarchy. Oblivious to such feelings, Overton made clear his opposition to any such developments, and when General Monck and his army arrived in Yorkshire from Scotland, early in 1660, Overton refused him entry into Hull. Monck's intentions were not yet known, but there were widespread hopes that he would take control of London, end the unpopular government of the so-called Rump Parliament, and restore Charles II to the throne. Overton told Monck that he was banned from Hull because he did not bear 'the image of Christ', but shortly afterwards he was forced to concede to Monck's demands that he hand the town over to Thomas, Lord Fairfax, who had earlier taken control of York and declared his support for Monck. When Monck duly brought the Rump Parliament to an end and fresh elections were called in April, of the town's six candidates, the two republicans came bottom of the poll, and Marvell and Ramsden were returned. Two weeks later, on 11 March 1660, a proclamation declaring Charles II king was read out in the market place, and the general jubilation was accompanied in Hull, as elsewhere, by the prolonged ringing of the church bells and the firing of gun salutes.[25]

SIX

From Restoration to 'Glorious Revolution', 1660-1700

Economic growth and prosperity

The 1640s and early 1650s had been a miserable time for Hull's merchants and those whose livelihoods depended on the fortunes of trade. The Civil War, and Cromwell's subsequent war against the Dutch, had done great harm to England's trade in northern Europe, particularly in the Baltic. The damage, however, was far from permanent and, assisted by the Navigation Laws, which limited the carrying trade of the Dutch considerably, many of Hull's merchants prospered in the next 40 years. The Baltic would become the chief destination for many of Hull's ships, but now the sailors were venturing further eastwards, as far as Riga, to purchase naval stores, their ships were now bigger and more numerous than ever, and the quantities of hemp, flax, iron, tar, pitch and timber which they were bringing back to Hull were greater than ever. The Baltic ports were not good markets for English goods; only lead and a little cloth could be exported, and many Hull ships sailed in ballast to the Baltic. The Dutch, however, were very enthusiastic customers for English cloth. The Yorkshire woollen and worsted industry expanded rapidly in the late 17th century, partly because the merchants of Hull were exporting to Holland very large quantities of Yorkshire kerseys, dozens, cottons and bays. Much lead was shipped to the Low Countries and numerous Hull ships also sailed regularly to France, carrying lead and cloth, and returning with French wines.

Imports of Baltic products, excluding timber, averaged just over 1,000 tons a year in the 1630s, but by the 1690s the yearly average was between 4,000 and 5,000 tons. By 1700, Hull was second only to London as an importer of naval stores, and almost equal to the capital as an importer of building timber and iron. Exports of English cloth through Hull rose by half between 1609 and 1640, to £166,000, and by 1700 average annual cloth exports were worth £340,000. Moreover, most of this was in Hull-owned ships. The Dutch were restricted to carrying only goods – mainly pantiles – from their own territories, while French ships brought wine, particularly from Bordeaux. The most common foreign vessels to be seen in the haven were Norwegian ships carrying timber. The steady growth in Hull-owned ships meant that by 1700 Hull shipowners and merchants possessed between them about 7,600 tons of shipping, or about a hundred vessels, and at least half of these were engaged in foreign trade.[1]

The one area of international trade that did not flourish in these years was the whaling industry. The Dutch proved extremely aggressive competitors and the number of Hull ships taking part consequently declined. Foreign competition also inhibited the local fishing trade, and the great majority of fish landed at the port came from Dutch, Norwegian or Scottish ports, or from other English ports, particularly Great Yarmouth.

Fish, coal and lead remained the principal commodities of Hull's coastal trade. Most of the coal still came from Newcastle and Sunderland, but the Yorkshire coalfield was also beginning to be exploited and a small re-export trade in coal was developed. Derbyshire and Yorkshire lead remained the principal coastal export, and by the 1680s quantities were approximately double those of the 1620s. A great variety of goods were being shipped up and down the coast, with London the principal market for virtually all items, especially foodstuffs, which were second in value only to lead. Ever-increasing quantities of Yorkshire cloth were also being regularly sent down to London, as was Sheffield cutlery, Swedish iron and Yorkshire ironwares. Pilots for shipping in the Humber were provided by Trinity House, which prospered from the fees charged for this service. Until 1677 no lighthouse was built on Spurn Point, and the services of the Trinity House pilots were therefore essential.[2]

By the 1680s a small number of wealthy merchanting houses were emerging specialising in particular commodities. The Moulds and the Maisters, for instance, specialised in iron from Sweden. Henry Maister was the only local merchant trading on a scale comparable to the wealthiest London merchants. Merchants from York, Leeds and London still shipped through Hull, but local merchants controlled an ever-increasing share of both the import and export trades. By 1702 Hull's trade was dominated by a small group of local men, and in that year only seven merchants made more than 40 shipments out of Hull. Two of the seven, William Crowle and John Thornton, between them made more than 160 shipments and handled half of Hull's exports of kerseys. They also, together with a third merchant, Philip Wilkinson, completely dominated the lead export business, handling seven eighths of all the lead exported.[3]

The growing prosperity of Hull from the mid-1650s was reflected in new building, although unfortunately bombing in the Second World War, together with post-war redevelopment, has destroyed much of this. Like many other towns at this time, Hull

35   *Wilberforce House, c.1926.*

enjoyed 'the Great Rebuilding', in which the wealth of the growing 'middling' classes – not only merchants but also lawyers, doctors and clergy – was announced in new and better houses, now of brick rather than half-timbered, and no longer with their gables facing the street, as most earlier houses had done. The best surviving examples from this period are *Ye Olde White Harte*, down a passageway just off Bowlalley Lane; Wilberforce House, built for Hull merchant Hugh Lister, on the High Street in about 1660; and Crowle House, built in 1664 for another wealthy merchant, George Crowle, near to Lister's new house, at 41 High Street, but hidden down an alley and with a mid-19th century frontage.

Crowle and Lister both employed local architect William Catlyn, who was responsible for the rebuilding of the Charterhouse from the 1650s and for Crowle's Hospital in about 1661. His style, sometimes called 'Artisan-Mannerist', was much influenced by Dutch designs, another reminder of the town's close trading links with the Low Countries. Both Wilberforce House

36   *George Crowle's house, as drawn by T.T. Wildridge in the 1880s.*

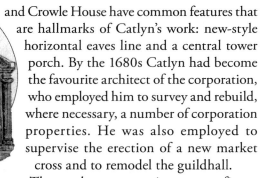

37 *Crowle's Hospital.*

and Crowle House have common features that are hallmarks of Catlyn's work: new-style horizontal eaves line and a central tower porch. By the 1680s Catlyn had become the favourite architect of the corporation, who employed him to survey and rebuild, where necessary, a number of corporation properties. He was also employed to supervise the erection of a new market cross and to remodel the guildhall.

The market cross project was at first a modest one, but by 1680 it had been decided to erect a completely new structure, consisting of a substantial cupola, topped by an octagonal lantern, standing on pillars, with two pairs of arches on a square base, and built in marble. The final cost was £1,700, and the work was completed by local stonemason Richard Roebuck in 1682. It was demolished in 1761 as it was an obstruction to traffic, but fortunately a careful drawing was made of it by local artist J. Hilbert a few years before.[4]

The expansion of trade and shipping began to bring more people into the town. Rapid growth came only in the 18th century, and in 1700 Hull was still contained within its medieval walls. There were, however, fewer empty spaces in the town, and even in the 1660s we know that some householders with large gardens and yards were selling them off for in-fill housing development. This can still be seen behind some properties on the High Street. Behind the house which once belonged to the Pryme family, at No. 52, the frontage has been twice rebuilt since the 1660s, but the in-fill of that period in the garden behind still stands.

Whereas in the middle of the 17th century there were probably about 6,000 people living in the town, there were about 8,000 by the late 1690s. The Hearth Tax assessment of 1673 suggests that even by this time the population had risen to about 7,500, and this is also supported by a religious census taken in 1676, which gives a total of 6,000 adults, or a total population of about eight thousand. The population may have fallen

38 *The Market Cross, completed in 1682.*

during the 1680s, as a result of two serious outbreaks of disease. Thorough quarantine measures meant that the town was able to escape the effects of the plague that devastated much of London and many other towns in the 1660s, but in 1680 annual deaths were doubled to over 520 by a severe attack of ague fever – or malaria. Then, just five years later, an outbreak of typhus killed at least 150, pushing annual mortality up to over four hundred. It is therefore not surprising that the number of tax payers in 1695 (5,759) suggests a population of still only about eight thousand.[5]

Poor relief and poverty

Many of those employed by Hull's merchants and professional classes did not, of course, share much of the wealth enjoyed by their masters and mistresses. When the Hearth Tax assessments were made in 1673 it was found that 261 households, or between 1,200 and 1,300 people, were too poor to pay anything. This underclass, comprising about 15 per cent of the population, included servants, general labourers at the docks and in the brickyards, the casually employed and the unemployed. Life for this class was precarious indeed and for some perpetual hunger and homelessness led naturally to begging, prostitution and petty crime.

The great majority of the poor were not in receipt of any poor relief. In the 1690s only about 200 people were regularly being given 'doles', and of these about 70 were children and the rest adults who were either too old or too sick to work, particularly elderly widows, some of whom were also catered for by the town's almshouses. The able-bodied adult received little sympathy from either the corporation or the parish poor law officials if they were unable to support themselves. Their children could be taken in by Charity Hall and there learn useful skills and hopefully avoid starvation until they could be found apprenticeships, but if the adult poor fell into begging, prostitution or vagrancy, a spell in the House of Correction and a whipping could be expected. The House of Correction had been established on Whitefriargate, close to Charity Hall, in 1620. Vagrants were seen as rogues, lazy and morally degenerate, who had to be punished, and either expelled from the town, if they were not from Hull, or placed in the House of Correction, where they could be set to some unpleasant task.

When civil war broke out in 1642 the House was closed down, but five years later it had to be opened again as the war had prompted large numbers of vagrants to flood into the town and not all could be expelled. Although many in the town prospered following the Restoration, the cost of poor relief did not fall, and by the 1690s there were serious concerns about supporting the deserving poor and running both Charity Hall and the House of Correction. The answer was to open a workhouse which would incorporate both institutions, using the Charity Hall premises. To this end the corporation in 1698 obtained a private Act of Parliament which allowed it to set up a 'Corporation of the Poor', headed by the mayor and aldermen. Poor relief would now be organised on a town-wide basis, and not by the town's two separate parishes, and all beggars would be placed in the new workhouse, which would house more people than the House of Correction. The adult inmates, as well as the pauper children, would learn useful skills to support themselves. For this purpose a woolcomber from Halifax was appointed to teach the paupers.[6]

Churches, chapels and meeting houses
The deep religious divisions in Hull, so evident in the 1650s when a brick partition had been built across Holy Trinity Church, remained just as bitter in the decades following the Restoration. The most controversial figure in 1660, John Shawe, the Presbyterian town lecturer and master of Charterhouse Hospital, seemed to have ensured his survival under the new regime. He was admired for his skills as a preacher in both Hull and York, and claimed in his memoirs to have regularly attracted congregations of about 3,000 to his twice-weekly services at Holy Trinity. Moreover, he had established many useful connections and was appointed a royal chaplain only a few weeks after Charles II's return to the country. Shawe had also been quick to sign the declaration of loyalty to the new king, together with the vicar of Holy Trinity, Henry Hibbert, and the minister at St Mary's, John Bewe. But Shawe's disputes with the former vicar, William Styles, and his militant brand of Presbyterianism had made him many enemies in Hull, not least among members of the corporation. With the king's new government keen to restore the episcopacy and Anglican worship, Shawe's position was clearly in danger. Before the end of the year numerous complaints about Shawe's continuing ministry were reaching London, and early in 1661 he was banned by royal order from preaching in Holy Trinity. Before the end of the year he had also been forced to resign his position at the Charterhouse and leave the town. His old adversary, William Styles, was reinstated as vicar of Hessle and Hull, and his successor, Hibbert, was forced to stand down.

The large and loyal following of John Shawe meant that by the time of his departure there existed in Hull a strong Presbyterian congregation, meeting at first in members' houses but eventually building their own chapel. Under the Act of Uniformity, passed in May 1662, ministers of religion could only continue in office if they subscribed to Anglican liturgy and rituals and accepted the new Book of Common Prayer. The clergy of Holy Trinity and St Mary's did subscribe, but many clergy in the district did not and were subsequently removed, and it was from among these ejected ministers that the Presbyterian congregation in Hull would find leadership. This would also be true of the Independents, who until the Restoration had been able to hold their services at the east end of Holy Trinity, but who were now ejected, and the brick partition behind which they had met was taken down.[7]

A far smaller group of nonconformists in 1660, and one that suffered much more severe persecution, was the Quakers. The first meetings of Quakers in Hull had been established by three families in the late 1650s, and at the time of the Restoration their numbers were still very small. Following the issuing of the Declaration on Ecclesiastical Affairs in October 1660, the Hull magistrates were free to persecute Quakers (and all other nonconformists if they so wished) for 'attendance of conventicles'. Although few in number, to Hull's moderate Puritan magistrates the Quakers appeared to be a dangerous, disloyal and heretical sect, and six Quakers were expelled from the town before the end of the year. When they dared to return they were imprisoned for 15 weeks. Female Quakers arrested at this time were particularly abused by a local mob, which was described later as 'like a company of brutes who had been killing some dog or cat'. In 1661 the Quakers were told that they might meet undisturbed if they held their meetings outside the town. However, when they held their meeting instead across the river Hull in Drypool, they were arrested and imprisoned again. Meetings continued in secret and the Quaker leader, George Fox, recorded in his *Journal* that he addressed a meeting 'near Hull' in 1666. At the end of the century there were only about twenty members in the town, and although the movement would survive, its members and their houses would remain the targets for mob violence as late as the 1770s.[8]

The Independents continued to meet and in 1669 there were 55 members. In that year Richard Astley, a minister ejected from a Lancashire parish, arrived in Hull and became their pastor, and another ejected minister, Mr Thornberry, was reported to be the minister for the Presbyterians. Both congregations knew they had to meet in secrecy to avoid arrest, and this may have inhibited the growth of these churches in the first few years after the Restoration and the withdrawal of religious freedom. In 1672, however, Charles II issued a Declaration of Indulgence which allowed the licensing of preachers and of private houses as places of worship for dissenters. Richard Astley was licensed to preach at the house of John Robinson, a member of his congregation, and another Independent minister, Thomas Oliver, was licensed to preach at a member's house in Newland. For the Presbyterians only one minister was licensed, Joseph Wilson, an ejected minister from Hessle, and two houses were licensed as meeting places, one in Blackfriargate and another in Newland. The lifting on the ban on dissenting services helped both churches recruit new members, although membership figures have only survived for the Independents: during 1671-3 they registered 80 new members.

This freedom, however, was short-lived and in 1673 was withdrawn again. Nevertheless, in 1676 it was estimated there were as many as 500 nonconformists in Holy Trinity parish alone. Alarmed by this, the governor, the Earl of Plymouth, ordered the suppression of all conventicles in the town in late 1682. Presbyterian minister Joseph Wilson had died in 1679 but his successor, Samuel Charles, was arrested in 1683 and imprisoned for six months, and on his release ejected from the town under the terms of the Five Mile Act of 1665. Astley escaped arrest by fleeing the town. Those whose properties were being used as meeting houses were given severe warnings of dire consequences if they dared continue. Neither movement could be extinguished, but for the next few years both Independents and Presbyterians suffered constant harassment if they failed to attend services at Holy Trinity or St Mary's. Relief came only in 1687, when the Catholic James II, keen to restore religious freedom for his fellow Roman Catholics, issued another Declaration of Indulgence. Both Astley and Charles returned and again began winning converts, and following the Toleration Act of 1689 both groups planned to erect purpose-built chapels. Samuel Charles died in 1693 but lived just long enough to see the first Presbyterian church opened in Bowlalley Lane, in 1691/2. Astley was less fortunate, dying in 1696, just two years before his congregation opened their first chapel, in Dagger Lane.[9]

39   *Dagger Lane Chapel.*

By the end of the century both dissenting congregations were well established, with their own chapels. In the first few decades of the new century their numbers would continue to grow, with numerous houses, as well as their chapels, registered as meeting places. Their survival in Charles II's reign had been facilitated partly by the failings of the Anglican clergy in these years, and the congregations of Presbyterians and Independents were swelled in the 1660s to 1680s by men and women dissatisfied with their parish church.

William Styles had died early in 1661 and the corporation took the opportunity to separate the parishes of Hessle and Hull. Styles' successor, Nicholas Anderson, appointed in May 1662, became the first vicar of the new parish of Holy Trinity. A few months earlier the corporation had also appointed a new lecturer for the town, William Ainsworth, who would also hold the mastership of the Charterhouse hospital. Neither appointment proved to be a success. It was not long before the corporation found itself at odds with its new vicar over the size of his stipend, and then complaints began to grow about the poor quality and increasing infrequency of Mr Ainsworth's lectures. Moreover, by 1671 it was clear that the lecturer was too ill to fulfil his duties and later that year he retired, dying shortly afterwards. His replacement, Richard Kitson, was unacceptable to the vicar, who refused to work with him until the governor had to intervene.

Kitson had been the nominee of those parishioners who had petitioned to have Ainsworth removed, so the Revd Anderson's stand against him did not endear the reverend to a large and important section of his congregation. Ten years later there were more complaints from the congregation: Anderson was losing his sight and memory, but refused to resign. The corporation tried to reach an agreement with him over the fulfilment of at least a minimum number of his duties, including preaching, but he was either unwilling or unable to honour the agreement. Eventually, in 1687, a curate was appointed to provide sermons, and this arrangement continued until Anderson died 15 months later, in 1689.

The last decade of the century was a rather happier one for both Anglicans and nonconformists. Anderson's successor at Holy Trinity, Robert Banks, was able to work harmoniously with both his Anglican colleagues and the corporation, while maintaining the support of his congregation. Relations between Anglicans and nonconformists also improved, helped by the new legal status of nonconformity, and both sides were to be found in a new association founded in the town in 1698: the Society for the Reformation of Manners in Kingston upon Hull. The aims of this new group were very much in the tradition of this most Puritan of towns: to promote observance of the Sabbath and to fight against vice.

It was also at this time that a new tower was finally built for St Mary's Church, on Lowgate. It was completed in brick, with stone buttresses and classical windows, in 1697, and replaced the original tower which had fallen down in 1518. As part of the extensive restoration carried out by Sir George Gilbert Scott, in 1861-3, it was encased in ashlar and given new 'Gothic-style' windows and corner turrets.[10]

40 *St Mary's Church, as it appeared after the rebuilding of the tower in 1697.*

One church community which has barely been mentioned yet in this chapter are the Roman Catholics. Catholic priests are known to have been active in the area but the number of Catholic families in Hull was extremely small and only a handful of recusants were ever reported in these years. The Catholic church in Hull was too small for the Romanising policies of James II to be of much assistance, and after reports reached the town that he had fled abroad, in December 1688, following the arrival of the Protestant Prince William of Orange, a happy mob showed their delight by wrecking a house where local Catholics had recently celebrated the mass.[11]

An independent and Puritan town

The strategic importance of Hull, renewed conflict with the Dutch in 1664, and the town's record as a parliamentary garrison throughout the civil wars, meant the new government of the restored monarchy had to ensure the town's security and loyalty. One of the first steps was to appoint the royalist John, Lord Bellasis, as governor, who then undertook a major programme of repairs to the walls, guard houses and fortress. This work would continue intermittently throughout the reign, culminating in 1681 with the decision to completely rebuild the defences east of the river Hull and create a new fortification, called the Citadel. This great triangular fort, covering 30 acres, and surrounded by a wide moat, would not be completed until 1690.[12]

More worrying for the corporation was the government's decision in 1661 to rewrite the town's charter and greatly extend the Crown's powers to interfere in municipal affairs. Those aldermen put on the Hull bench by republican governments were in 1661 removed by the same royal decree that had dismissed John Shawe from his positions. Then, in the same year, the town's new charter reserved to the Crown the future nomination of three important offices: those of high steward, recorder and town clerk.

Further interference soon followed. In 1662 royal commissioners arrived in the town to enforce the Corporations Act, passed by parliament the previous December. This demanded all members of municipal corporations take oaths of allegiance and supremacy, and swear to take communion according to the rites of the Church of England. Most did so but two who did not were immediately dismissed and their places filled not by election but by the commissioners' appointment. A year later the government again interfered by barring Edmund Popple from the bench, following an election, because he too had refused to take the required oaths.[13]

The town was powerless to resist such encroachments on its traditional liberties, but in 1663 it did choose to ignore the advice of the ultra-royalist MP, Colonel Anthony Gilby, that it should remove the town's other MP, the Hull-educated poet Andrew Marvell, for alleged neglect of his duties. Marvell was an object of suspicion for many royalists because he had first served the town as an MP during the Cromwellian Interregnum and (together with fellow poets Milton and Dryden) had been employed as a secretary to the republican government. In the enthusiasm for the king's restoration, the election of 1661 had ensured that few other MPs from the republican era had been able to hold on to their seats. Gilby may also have suspected that Marvell had little liking for the persecution of nonconformists. Marvell, however, enjoyed the confidence of both the majority of the corporation and large numbers of the burgesses, and remained MP until his death in 1678.

In the last few years of his life, Marvell became an important member of the parliamentary opposition to Charles II's pro-French foreign policy, and the consequent resumption of war against the Dutch in 1672. Like many other MPs, he objected to the removal of the penal laws against Roman Catholics in 1672, and to the Romanising policies of the king, particularly following the conversion to Roman Catholicism of the king's brother and heir to the throne, the Duke of York. He voiced his opposition through satirical poetry, usually published anonymously, and, most important of all, through his *Account of the Growth of Popery and Arbitrary Government in England*, published anonymously in 1677. In this work he set out what many people throughout the country, including Hull, had already begun to fear: that a secret conspiracy had been engineered to establish a Roman Catholic despotism in the kingdom with the aid of a French army. This was not too far from the truth, for by the secret treaty of Dover, signed with France in May 1670, Charles had indeed agreed to publicly announce his conversion to Catholicism in return for the promise of financial and military aid from the French king, Louis XIV, should his subjects then rebel against him.[14]

Hull's opposition to government policy was expressed at the by-election following Marvell's death. Again, government interference was much in evidence, but now it was firmly rebuffed. The Duke of Monmouth, the high steward of Hull, nominated a minor official, John

41 *Statue of Andrew Marvell, 1621-78. It was given to the town in 1866 by Councillor John Winship, and stood at first in the town hall. In 1902 the statue was moved to the junction of George Street and Jameson Street, and then in 1922 to the top of Bond Street. Since 1963, it has stood in front of Marvell's old school, the Old Grammar School, on South Church Side.*

Shales, to succeed Marvell, and Shales was also supported by the Duke of York and the Earl of Danby, the leader of the Court party and Lord Treasurer. In spite of such powerful pressure, however, the corporation held firm and instead put forward one of its own, Alderman William Ramsden, who was then duly elected and, like Marvell before him, immediately joined the Whig opposition in the Commons.

Another opportunity to demonstrate independence came just a year later, when a general election was held in February 1679, the first for 18 years. This time, however, the corporation was divided. It rebuffed court insistence that it should re-adopt the royalist ex-MP Colonel Gilby, and a majority of the corporation wished to resist Monmouth's nomination for the other seat, Lemuel Kingdon. The local candidate, Alderman George Crowle, agreed to stand down in Kingdon's favour, no doubt after pressure by representatives of the court. Local feeling against the court was sufficient to persuade another local gentleman of Whig persuasion to stand, and William Gee, whose family had long had close links with the town, agreed to put his name forward. The election was won by Ramsden and Kingdon, but Gee afterwards complained that Kingdon's court supporters had used unfair and illegal pressure on the burgesses to secure his victory. In the second election in the same year Monmouth chose to make no recommendation and the corporation therefore felt under no pressure to support Kingdon's nomination. Consequently he withdrew and the corporation was able to nominate two Whig gentlemen, William Gee and Sir Michael Warton. William Ramsden also stood down, owing to old age and illness, and the two Whigs were elected unopposed.[15]

The events in parliament that year had done nothing to win support for the king in Hull. Charles II had dissolved parliament in May, infuriated by an attempt by Whig politicians to pass an Exclusion Bill, which would have prevented his Roman Catholic brother from succeeding to the throne if he died without a male heir. In Puritan, Protestant Hull, there was very little sympathy for the king's position, and the stories of a wicked Popish Plot to murder Charles and put his brother on the throne, spread in 1678-9 by the notorious Titus Oates, were widely believed, as was the story – much encouraged by Whig politicians – that the Great Fire of London of 1666 had been the work of a French Catholic.[16]

During 1679-84 relations between the corporation and the government of Charles II continued to deteriorate. In 1680 the corporation was divided over whether to dismiss Alderman Daniel Hoare from the bench for failing to take Holy Communion. Under pressure from the Privy Council, which had first raised the issue, the corporation voted seven to three to do its bidding. Two years later the corporation was again divided over the governor's decision to enforce the laws against conventicles, and to close down the local nonconformist meeting houses. Although the local Quaker community had been harshly persecuted, the magistrates of Hull had generally turned a blind eye to the Presbyterian and Independent meeting houses. Indeed, a number of the more Whiggish aldermen were by now strongly in favour of tolerating Presbyterians and Independents, but the majority felt it wiser to support the governor. The continuing crisis in London over the Exclusion Bill also divided the town and exposed the corporation's growing dislike for Charles II's government. At the height of the Exclusion Bill crisis, in the autumn of 1681, a declaration of loyalty to the king was carried by only four votes to three, and in the following June it was decided by seven votes to four not to send an address condemning the Whigs' attempt to exclude the Duke of York from the succession.[17]

Any fears that such demonstrations of political disloyalty might lead to further assaults on municipal independence seemed justified when, in June 1684, the corporation was threatened with a writ of *quo warranto* proceedings. This meant a possible legal challenge to the members of the corporation: a writ calling on them to demonstrate by what warrant they exercised their privileges. The corporation agreed to surrender its charter to the king, but also took the opportunity to press for compensation for the loss of corporation-owned land during the recent building of the Citadel on the east bank. After more than a year of negotiations the charter was returned with one important alteration: the Crown now claimed the right to replace members of the bench at will. Moreover, the Crown insisted on exercising its new rights and, for reasons no longer clear, three aldermen were immediately ordered off the bench, including the mayor at the time the charter was surrendered, Alderman Delacamp. The only good news for the corporation was that it would be compensated for the loss of land to the Citadel, and the maintenance costs of the new fortification would be borne by the government.[18]

By the time the new charter had been received in the town, England had a new monarch. Charles II had been taken ill suddenly and died in February 1685, and his brother, James II, became the first Roman Catholic to succeed to the throne since Mary Tudor. Only a year or two earlier James would not have ascended to the throne without provoking civil war, but now the succession proceeded peacefully, and in Hull, as elsewhere, even with the traditional burst of enthusiasm that normally greeted a new monarch. This may be partly accounted for by a remarkable wave of popular support for the monarchy in the last year of Charles II's reign, as people of all classes came to believe that the Whig politicians had gone too far in their attempts to change the law of succession. Many had come to the conclusion that James II posed less of a threat to the Protestant church than the Whigs had claimed. His heir, his daughter Mary, was after all a devout Protestant, and married to the champion of European Protestantism, Prince William of Orange, who had been for many years at war against the Catholic Louis XIV of France.[19]

The corporation of Hull, however, found the hypocrisy of a loyal greeting a difficult challenge, even though it was at this time anxiously awaiting the return of its charter. In the end it had to be ordered by the governor, the Earl of Plymouth, to rewrite its greeting to include rather more fulsome expressions of enthusiasm. To many, it must have seemed as if the town was now actually being run by the governor and not the corporation. The governor had launched his attack on nonconformists very soon after taking up his post, and he had subsequently also been appointed high steward. Now, under the charter of 1685, he was also made the recorder of the town. He could recommend the removal of aldermen from the bench (and the removals of 1685 could probably not have been made without his approval) and, as he now demonstrated, he could also insist on his nominations for both of the town's two seats in parliament: his relative, Sir Willoughby Hickman, and a local man – but a supporter of the court – John Ramsden. Moreover, in the pro-royalist, anti-Whig atmosphere of 1685, Plymouth could rightly claim the support of the majority of the Hull electorate. Hickman and Ramsden were duly elected and the two Whig candidates, the former MPs Sir Michael Warton and William Gee, were soundly beaten.[20]

For the next three years there was little further interference in the town's liberties, but the king's policy of appointing Roman Catholics to powerful positions in both the army and navy, the inclusion of Roman Catholics in a new Declaration of Indulgence, the appointment of a leading Catholic as Lord Lieutenant of Ireland, and the introduction of the king's Jesuit advisor into the Privy Council, all provoked widespread anger and condemnation.[21] Hull was directly affected by the policy of Catholic appointments, for following the death of Plymouth in 1687 he was replaced as governor by the Roman Catholic Marmaduke Langdale, while the position of high steward was given to another Catholic, Lord Dover. For Hull's very firmly Protestant corporation, there was even worse to come when it was recognised that the king wanted to pack a new parliament with his supporters to repeal the Test Acts of 1673 and 1678, allowing Roman Catholics full civil rights and, in particular, to sit on municipal corporations and become aldermen, and to stand for parliament.[22]

The corporation's disaffection was demonstrated when it was asked by Lord Langdale, in late 1687, whether it would support candidates in the next general election who could be guaranteed to support the king's policies, Hickman and Ramsden having proved a disappointment by opposing the king's policy of granting army commissions to Catholics. Robert Carlile, the mayor, boldly informed Langdale that he and his fellow aldermen would not commit themselves to support candidates who approved of the royal Declaration of Indulgence. Infuriated, Langdale replied with vague threats of very unpleasant consequences for the town's bench if it failed to give its full support to his chosen candidate, Sir John Bradshaw of Risby. By now, Carlile and his colleagues clearly felt they had to make their stand and therefore replied that the election of no one could be guaranteed in advance and their only promise to Langdale was that the election would be 'fair and free according to the laws of the land'.[23]

The dire consequences for this were not long in coming. According to Abraham Pryme, Hull's first historian, writing just a few years later, Langdale encouraged his troops to seek out and assault members of the corporation. At least one member, one of the chamberlains, was said to have been caught by the soldiers and hung upside-down by his heels. In May 1688 court lawyers again began *quo warranto* proceedings against the corporation, forcing it to surrender its charter so that more powers could be taken by the Crown, and then in July the entire corporation was removed by an Order in Council. When the charter was returned to the town, in September, an almost completely new set of councillors and officers were named. The king had been persuaded that his best chance of obtaining a cooperative House of Commons would be to build a coalition of supporters among the municipal corporations, including nonconformists and Anglicans known to be sympathetic to religious toleration. It was hoped the new corporations would then ensure the return of compliant MPs. In Hull this meant the return to the bench of those aldermen who had only recently been dismissed from office, including Daniel Hoare, who now replaced Carlile as mayor, and Delacamp and the other aldermen dismissed in 1685.[24]

By late September, however, the king's priorities had changed. Now his sole concern was mere survival, for William of Orange was planning an imminent invasion. Fears had been growing since early summer and as a result Langdale had been told to strengthen the defences of Hull and prepare for a possible siege. If necessary, he would destroy the dikes and once again flood the surrounding countryside to protect the town. By October James was desperately trying to shore up support among those he had so recently alienated, and as part of this process he issued a royal proclamation on 17 October annulling the charters of 1685 and 1688 and restoring to the town the liberties it had enjoyed before proceedings had begun in 1684. The corporation as it had existed at that time, with Alderman Delacamp as mayor, was therefore reinstated; the corporation nominated by the Crown only a month before stood down; and elections were swiftly organised to fill the gaps caused by those who had died in the previous four years.[25]

However, it was now too late for James II to win back the support he had enjoyed at his accession. His policies had alienated the corporation, the clergy and the burgesses, and the arrival of William of Orange was eagerly awaited. It was rumoured that William might land at Hull, and Langdale had the garrison reinforced with troops supplied by the Duke of Newcastle, the Lord-Lieutenant of Yorkshire. On 5 November William and his motley army of Dutchmen and English and Scottish exiles landed at Torbay, in Devon. Langdale decided to strengthen his hold on the town and garrison by using his reinforcements to arrest his Protestant officers. The plot leaked, however, and the Protestant deputy governor, Captain Lionel Copley, moved quickly to forestall Langdale's scheme. With the support of the mayor, other members of the corporation, his fellow Protestant officers and a few other trusted soldiers and civilians, Copley had Langdale and all his Catholic officers arrested without bloodshed late in the evening of 3 December. With the Citadel secured, he then declared Hull's support for Prince

42 *Gilded equestrian statue of King William III, by Peter Scheemakers, erected in 1734. The king is dressed as a Roman emperor and the inscription on the plinth describes him as 'Our Great Deliverer'. The appropriately named public house can be seen in the background.*

William. York had already been taken by William's supporters a few days before, and with Hull's declaration James had virtually lost the whole of the north of England.[26]

The events of 3 December would be celebrated in Hull for more than a century, becoming known as 'town taking day'. When it was reported, just before Christmas, that King James had fled the country and William of Orange had entered London, there was widespread rejoicing, and the formal address from the corporation to the new joint monarchy of Queen Mary and King William was on this occasion no doubt sincere. The nation, it declared, had been 'miraculously delivered … from those eminent dangers which threatened the perversion of religion and the introduction of tyranny and arbitrary government'. The corporation also welcomed the appointment as governor of Sir John Hotham, the grandson of Sir John Hotham, the Civil War governor. The new governor had landed at Torbay with William, and was a close adherent of the new king, as was the new high steward, the Earl of Kingston.

Two members of the corporation felt that they could not accept the legality of William's accession and were dismissed in August 1689 for refusing to take the new oath of allegiance. For the great majority of the corporation, however, and probably for the townspeople generally, the removal of James II, the accession of William and Mary, and subsequent legislation strengthening the powers of the House of Commons, were all welcome developments, as was the absence of any further attempts to interfere in the town's liberties. The charter of 1665 remained until the municipal reform measures of the 19th century. Half a century later, in 1734, the corporation organised a public subscription to erect an equestrian statue of William III at the south end of the market place, where it still stands today.[27]

SEVEN

The Georgian Town, c.1700-1837

Unprecedented growth in trade and the building of new docks

The growth of industry in the northern and midland counties during the 18th century, together with transport improvements, had a most profound effect on Hull. The little medieval port was transformed into a major town, which by the time of Queen Victoria's accession in 1837 was six times as large as it had been in 1700, possessing three very large docks, and handling imports and exports in volumes unimaginable at the beginning of the 18th century. The town grew well beyond the ancient walls behind which it had sheltered for more than 400 years, but which now disappeared under the new docks. Also, as a result of national legislation, the era ended with the removal of the old corporation, and its replacement by a new, politically very different, governing body.

The growth in trade owed a great deal to the economic success of four areas of Hull's hinterland: the woollen and worsted industries of the West Riding, the iron and steel industries of South Yorkshire, the Lancashire cotton industry and a variety of Midlands industries, particularly in the second half of the century. As road, river and canal communications improved, Hull came to be one of the major ports through which much of their raw materials, food and other requirements could be imported, and from which their finished products could be exported.[1]

The cost of transporting cloth from the West Riding of Yorkshire to Hull was considerably reduced by the development of the Aire and Calder Navigation early in the 18th century, and links were further improved in 1776 by the building of a canal to connect the river Aire to the river Ouse at Selby. In 1834 a railway line linking Leeds to Selby was completed, and six years later the line was extended from Selby to Hull.

43 *Pease Warehouses on the river Hull. The former loading bays can still be clearly seen. The brick arch on the right has the date stone 1745, the one on the left is dated 1760. Joseph Pease, a wealthy Dutch-born merchant, founded Hull's first bank in 1754.*

Better communications between South Yorkshire and Hull – long the chief port for the Swedish iron used by Sheffield cutlers – were achieved early in the 18th century by improvements to the course of the river Don, and a direct link by water was eventually achieved by a long series of waterway improvements connecting the river Humber to Tinsley, near Sheffield, culminating in the completion of the Sheffield-Tinsley canal in 1819.

Similarly, communications with the Midlands industrial areas were enhanced by the improvement of the river Trent and its tributaries, throughout the 18th century, while the completion of the Trent & Mersey Canal in 1777 linked the Trent to Liverpool and the Lancashire cotton towns. A more direct route, across the Pennines, was eventually achieved early in the 19th century by the completion of three canals, the Leeds & Liverpool, the Huddersfield and the Rochdale.[2]

The export of Yorkshire cloth had been extremely important to Hull since medieval times, but the remarkable expansion of the industry in the 18th century meant the scale of Hull's exports also grew rapidly. Between 1700 and 1750 exports varied between 100,000 and 200,000 pieces a year, but by 1768 the number had risen to 307,662, and to 402,857 by 1783. For Manchester merchants Hull also became the chief port for exporting to Europe the products of the expanding cotton factories of Lancashire. In 1758 only 20 cotton pieces are recorded as being exported through Hull, but 10 years later over 8,000 were being shipped out, and the figure had risen to 236,834 by 1783.

The growth of the iron and steel industries of South Yorkshire was also reflected in the expansion in exports of cutlery and other iron wares, particularly in the middle years of the century, and by the growth in exports of tinned iron plates in the second half of the century. In just 25 years, between 1758 and 1783, exports of tinned iron rose from 3,375 pieces a year to over 5,000,000 pieces.

Also spectacular was the growth in earthenware exports through Hull, thanks to the development of inland waterways. In 1737 fewer than 16,000 pieces of earthenware passed through the port, mainly manufactured in Staffordshire and Leeds, but in 1758 almost 450,000 pieces were exported. By 1768 the number had risen to over 1.5 million, and by 1783, incredibly, to over 13 million.

While the variety and scale of exports through Hull continued to increase, their destinations changed very little. Germany and the Netherlands remained the principal markets for exports and imports, and between them accounted for about half the ships leaving Hull. Trade with Germany grew especially quickly in the 1790s, when the number of Hull ships sailing to German ports, more than doubled, from 45 to 104, principally to Bremen and Hamburg. The next most important destination was Russia. At the end of the century about one in seven of all overseas sailings from Hull was to Russia. Trade with other countries was relatively small. At the beginning of the 18th century the Scandinavian countries had been extremely important, with about a third of all Hull ships sailing to Norway and Sweden, but this declined rapidly in the 1740s.

While the exports carried from Hull were mainly manufactured goods of relatively high value, the majority of its imports were raw materials for the industrial hinterland. Imports tended therefore to be greater in volume than exports but lower in value. By the middle of the century Russia had replaced Sweden as the chief source of iron used by the Sheffield steelmakers and cutlers. In 1783 about 8,000 tons were imported, double the quantity in the 1730s. Russia had also become a major source of timber by the 1750s, replacing Norway, and most of the flax and hemp used in the linen and rope industries also came from there. The textile trades of Yorkshire and Lancashire required ever-larger imports of dyestuffs, and these were brought in mainly from the Netherlands and Germany.

Another major import by the end of the century was tobacco, brought in almost exclusively from America. Relatively small quantities at the beginning of the century reached over 400,000lbs per year by the 1740s, and in 1792 they were over 1,000,000lbs. The trade was badly disrupted by the War of Independence but resumed again almost as soon as hostilities ceased. By the middle of the 18th century America had replaced Sweden as the principal source for tar and pitch, but during the War of Independence Hull merchants reverted to their Swedish suppliers and the trade with America was not resumed.

Hull was also an important centre for the coastal trade, providing warehousing and trans-shipment facilities, but throughout the 18th and early 19th centuries little

44 *Blaydes House, built c.1750 for merchant and shipmaster Benjamin Blaydes, at the north end of the High Street (sometimes called 'Little' High Street).*

of this trade was in the hands of Hull merchants and its impact on the town was therefore limited. With the opening up of the South Yorkshire coal pits, imports of coal from Newcastle and Sunderland declined, but a great – and growing – variety of goods continued to be shipped to Hull from London, which in turn received great quantities of Derbyshire lead and foodstuffs of every description.

So throughout the 18th century and beyond, Hull remained one of the major British ports. The tonnage of ships registered in the port rose only gradually between 1702 and 1773, from about 7,000 tons to 20,000, but it then shot up to over 65,000 by 1800, continuing to grow in the new century, to 72,000 in 1829. By the 1830s it was the sixth largest port in the country in terms of registered tonnage, behind London, Newcastle, Liverpool, Sunderland and Whitehaven, and its foreign trade was greater than that of either Newcastle or Whitehaven.

Germany and the Netherlands remained the principal markets for Hull's exports throughout the first four decades of the 19th century, and the Baltic the principal

45 *View of Hull from the South East, 1745, by Buck.*

source of imported raw materials. Until the last years of this period, the nature of these goods changed little, although raw wool became increasingly important to meet the voracious demands of the West Riding wool and worsted industry. In the 1830s, Lancashire cotton-twist became the greatest single export, while wheat became the greatest import, as Britain's farmers could no longer produce enough to feed the growing population of Hull's hinterland.

The early 19th century also saw a remarkable expansion of the Hull whaling industry. Hull sailors had been pioneers of this most dangerous trade at the end of the 16th century but it had died out in the town during the latter half of the 17th century. Heavy duties on imported whale oil imposed in the 1760s, however, encouraged a revival and by 1790 about 24 ships were sailing every year to Greenland's whale-fishing waters. Briefly, between 1815 and the early 1830s, the industry boomed, and in 1820 Hull sent 59 ships to Greenland. On average, almost 5,000 tuns of oil were being produced each year in the 1820s, rendered down from the whale blubber to be used in both domestic and street lighting, to cure leather, and in soap and paint manufacture. Whale bones were also much in demand from corset makers, and the ambergris, extracted from the intestines, was sold to perfume makers. At this time more than 2,000 men were employed in the industry. But northern whales were being hunted to extinction, and by 1835 the industry was in decline.

As in the 17th century, the great majority of Hull's merchants throughout the 18th and early 19th centuries operated on a very small scale. Most made less than

46 *The Maister House, High Street. The Maisters were among the wealthiest and most successful of Hull merchant families in the 17th and 18th centuries. The family home was burnt down in 1743 in a fire that also took the lives of Mrs Henry Maister, her baby son, and two female servants. The house seen today was built on the same site later that year. Its exterior appearance is rather plain but the magnificent staircase (which is open to the public) has been described by John Markham as 'one of the glories of Hull'.*

10 shipments a year, and some made only one or two. Trade, and to some extent the town, was dominated by a handful of wealthy merchant houses able to make 40 or more shipments every year. It was these businesses which owned private staithes. The 'small man' had to find what space he could on the very restricted public wharfs, and opportunities for rapid growth of business were for this reason alone extremely limited.

As trade increased during the 18th century, the wharfage facilities beside the river Hull became inadequate, and the case for building a new, larger quay open to all merchants was by the 1770s quite compelling. The corporation was also under pressure from the Commissioners of Customs to establish a new dock with sufficient space to establish a proper Legal Quay. As a result, a private Hull Dock Act was obtained from parliament in 1774, and the Hull Dock Company was created, with power to raise up to £80,000 in shares and a commitment to build a new dock for the town. The Citadel on the east bank of the river Hull prevented development of this area but the company was able to build an enormous new dock, designed by John Grundy, immediately to the north of the town, on the site of the old town wall and the adjacent town ditch, approachable from the old haven. Ten acres in area, and capable of accommodating 100 square-rigged vessels, this was the second largest dock ever built in the country. The enterprise was ambitious but proved a great financial success. The shares were sold at £250 each and within a few years of the dock opening the shareholders were receiving handsome dividends. Construction began in 1775, it was completed in less than four years, and the first ship sailed in from the haven in September 1778.[3]

So rapid was the growth of trade in this last quarter of the century that there were soon calls for the company to build another dock, but disputes over its location prevented a second private Act of Parliament until 1802. Work began on a new dock on the west side of the town, between the Hessle and Myton gates, the next year, and one of the first steps was again the removal of a substantial portion of the medieval wall and ditch. The new dock would have the advantage of direct access from the river Humber, and cover about six acres, but it would take six years to complete, cost over £230,000, and at first prove to be not nearly as profitable as its predecessor. Such was the demand from Hull's merchants, however, that as soon as trade recovered in the 1820s, after the Napoleonic Wars, proposals were made for a third dock, to link the Humber Dock, as the new dock was called, with the 'Old Dock'. Work on this 'Junction Dock' began in 1827 and was completed in 1829, at a cost of £165,000. Covering about 6½ acres, its construction meant the destruction of the last remains of the medieval wall and ditch, whose course, like the Old Dock and the Humber Dock, it approximately followed. Many merchants believed that the company and the corporation had reacted too slowly in building new docks, and complaints about the inadequacy of the docks, the high charges imposed on ships, and the failure to maintain the haven were frequently heard in the 1830s, but there would be no further improvement in the port's facilities until another Act of Parliament was obtained in 1844.[4]

New industries and new roads

At the beginning of the 18th century Hull could boast of no large-scale manufacturing industries other than shipbuilding. As a result of the growth in trade, however, not only did the town's shipbuilding industry expand considerably, but new raw material processing and refining industries also developed. Together with the building of the new docks and the consequent disappearance of the old town walls, the new industries completely changed the character of the town and drew in a vastly increased population.

One of the most rapidly growing industries was oil-seed extraction. Oil mills are reported in the town as early as the 16th century, but large-scale production can be

47 *The First Dock, later known as Queen's Dock, showing the entrance from the river Hull, with the early dock office on the right.*

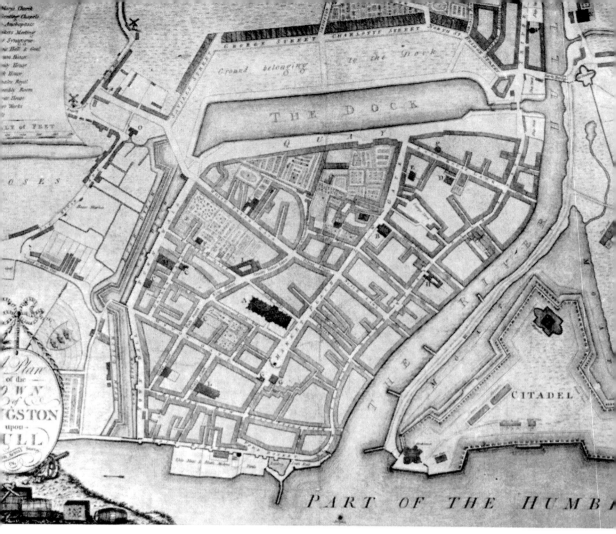

48 *Thew's plan of Hull of 1784.*

dated to the 1740s, when Joseph Pease set up a mill on the corner of Lowgate and
Salthouse Lane. The increasing demand in the second half of the century for linseed
oil in the cloth, paint and soap industries meant more mills were soon established.
By the end of the century oil-crushing mills in the town were being powered by
wind, horse and steam, and there were three windmills and a steam-powered mill in
one street alone, on Wincolmlee, north of the new dock beside the river Hull. As a
result, cattle cake exports and linseed imports shot up, the latter from less than 2,000
bushels in 1725 to almost 19,000 by 1758 and over 66,000 by 1783.

The growth of the oil-extracting industry encouraged the development of paint
manufacturing, white-lead making (an important constituent of white paint) and
an oil-milling machinery industry. Hull was well placed to develop other processing
industries, such as the extraction of whale oil, sugar refining and soap manufacture.

The latter two were described as 'considerable manufactories' in John Craggs' *Guide* of 1817 and a map of Hull drawn the following year shows the wide range of industries now to be found. There were 11 corn mills, two sugar houses, two oil mills, a whiting mill, two lead mills, a glue manufactory, a soap works, a foundry, an engine manufactory, six roperies and a wool spinning and sail cloth factory, mostly situated close to the river Hull, to the north of the town.[5]

The largest industry in the town was still shipbuilding. At the end of the 18th century Hull built more ships than any other port besides London. Most were relatively small ships, the average size being only 127 tons, and in terms of total tonnage Hull ranked fifth or sixth in the 1790s, behind London, Newcastle, Liverpool, Sunderland and even Whitby. Some large ships were built, however, particularly naval vessels for the Admiralty, which were often well over 1,000 tons. The first steam packet was also built in Hull, in a yard off Wincolmlee, in 1796.

The demands of the new industries, together with the popular market days, meant that by the 1740s there was a dire need to improve Hull's roads. These improvements came slowly, even though local flooding often made the roads into the town impassable. The first turnpike was the road from Hull to Beverley, opened in 1744, and two other local turnpikes opened the following year, one from Anlaby a few miles to the west of the town, and the other from Hedon, to the east of the town, taking a circuitous route through Preston, Wyton and Bilton, before entering the town by the North Bridge. The road from Hessle and Ferriby was not turnpiked until 1825 and there was no direct road from Hessle until 1833. The growth in local traffic meant that the old North Bridge was in regular need of repair, and in 1787 it was replaced by a new, more substantial, four-arched stone bridge, but this too had to be rebuilt in 1831.[6]

The turnpike roads carried the mail service, passenger-coach services, and carrier services to and from Hull. A mail coach service from York was established in 1788. Three years later the town's first directory, produced by a local bookseller, Robert Battle, reported that the mail coach set off from the *Cross Keys* in the market place every afternoon at three o'clock, and would reach York at nine o'clock, stopping at Beverley and Weighton. It returned the same night, leaving York at midnight and arriving back in Hull at six o'clock in the morning. The fare was 12s. By the end of the 18th century there was also a twice-daily passenger-coach service to York and services to Bridlington and Scarborough, while a daily ferry service enabled passengers for London to catch the coach at Barton, on the Lincolnshire coast. In 1811 the services to York were improved and an alternative route to London, via Doncaster, was established, reaching the capital in 36 hours. The last years before the arrival of the railway were golden ones for coach travel, with services running on an occasional basis as far as Sunderland, Newcastle and Liverpool, and three coaches running every day to Beverley and four to Scarborough. The late 18th and early 19th centuries also saw a major increase in the number of carriers serving the town. Battle's directory of 1791 lists 48 carriers serving a wide area, including a number of north Lincolnshire towns, and by 1851 there were 160, using 30 different inns.

The chief coaching inns in the 1790s were the *Cross Keys* and the *Reindeer*, both of which stood in the market place, together with the *Moor's*, in the street known as 'The Land of Green Ginger', and *Welburn's* in Lowgate. The *Cross Keys* and the *Reindeer* were still important in the 1830s but much of the trade had gone to the *Victoria Tavern* on Queen Street, to the *Bull and Sun* on Mytongate, and the *Black Horse* on Carr Lane. The *Bull and Sun* was also an important base for many of the carriers. Battle's 1791 directory only lists three other inns offering this service: the *Blue Bell* in the market place, the *Coach and Horses* in Whitefriargate, and the *King's Head* in Mytongate, but within a few years there would be many more.[7]

Population growth and the expansion of the town

As trade and industry developed during the 18th century, the population of the town grew, as increasing numbers from the surrounding rural communities came in search of employment. High death rates caused by disease and insanitary conditions meant that in the first half of the century the town's growth was due entirely to migration. By 1750 the population of the 'county of Hull' plus the village of Sculcoates had risen by more than 50 per cent, to about 12,700, since the beginning of the century. In the second half of the century, as the pace of economic growth quickened, the rate of migration increased, and the birth rate also began to regularly outstrip the death rate. Consequently, the town and its immediate hinterland now grew faster than ever, by approximately 50 per cent between 1750 and 1780 and then equally quickly between 1780 and the first census of 1801, when the combined population of Hull and Sculcoates stood at 27,609 people. When the census was taken in 1831, 32,958 people were recorded in the municipal borough and 10 years later, the population had leapt to over 65,000, after boundary changes in 1837.[8]

Until the 1770s the growth of the town was sufficiently modest to be contained within its medieval walls and gates. When Defoe visited Hull in 1726 he found the town already overcrowded:

> The town is exceeding close built, and should a fire ever be its fate, it might suffer deeply on that account; 'tis extraordinarily populous, even to an inconvenience, leaving really no room to extend itself by buildings.[9]

The first substantial suburbs to be developed outside the Old Town came only after the removal of the northern walls and the opening of the first dock in 1778. Thew's plan of Hull of 1784 shows a fashionable suburb along the north side of the dock on George Street, whose residents two years later included the mayor. Many of these houses were bombed during the Second World War, but among the survivals are

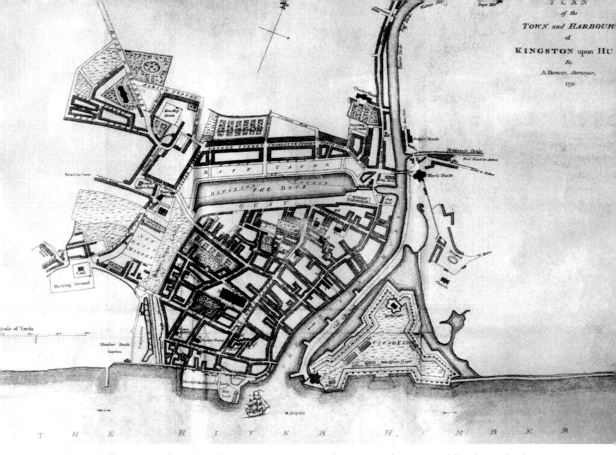

PLAN
of the
TOWN and HARBOUR
of
KINGSTON upon HU
By
A.Bower, Surveyor,
1791.

49   *Hull in 1791, from the plan by A. Bower. The first stages of a new middle-class suburb are already beginning to appear to the north of the dock, along the new streets laid out by the Dock Company.*

some of the earliest and grandest examples. These three-storey houses built in brick with stone dressings were built in about 1782 in the section of George Street then known as Charlotte Street, and the largest have frontages of five bays. Some of the houses still retain their original staircases and decorated plaster ceilings.[10]

This first estate, planned and laid out by the Dock Company, was designed for the town's merchant and professional classes. One man who quickly saw the opportunity for investment was the banker and industrialist J.R. Pease, who had nine houses built on Charlotte Street, and chose to keep one for himself as his town house. It was soon followed by further small estate developments immediately to the north of Charlotte Street and George Street, owned by some of the town's wealthiest inhabitants. By 1801 the estates of Joseph Sykes, Alderman John Jarratt, and tobacco manufacturer Richard Baker had all been laid out, many of the streets had been built upon, and their owners are still commemorated in the street names today. Other very similar small estates had been laid out by 1801, a little further to the north, between Prospect Street and the river Hull, but these were not built upon until the 1820s and 1830s.[11]

50 *Nos 83-5 George Street (formerly Charlotte Street), built 1782; today the last survivors of a once very elegant terrace.*

The last decades of the 18th century saw the merchants and professionals leaving the High Street. Some of the wealthiest built themselves country residences in nearby villages; some moved into the fine houses being built in the new 'Northern Suburb', but new attractive streets were also being laid out from the 1770s in the Old Town itself. The fine row of three-storey terraced housing built by Joseph Page on Prince Street in the 1770s can still be seen, and the city's most complete Georgian street, Parliament Street, also survives. It was built in 1796, linking Whitefriargate to the new dock.

During the 1780s and 1790s a far less salubrious working-class suburb was emerging to the west of the Old Town, in the area near the Beast Market, which had been moved out to Waterhouse Lane in 1782, and near the new three-storey prison built in 1785 on nearby Myton Place. Another large area of working-class housing was also spreading to the north-west of the Old Town, on the western side of Prospect Street, and similar housing was also beginning to appear further north, along the banks of the river Hull. The most rapid development of working-class housing did not come until the first decades of the new century, when a myriad of small streets and courts appeared in all these areas, as can be seen from the plan of the town in 1835.[12]

Poverty and the Poor Law

Throughout the 18th century, before the growth of these suburbs, Hull's poorer inhabitants mainly lived in small two-storey cottages in little courtyards, referred to as terraces, running back from the main streets of the Old Town and usually approached through a tunnel. At the time of the first census, in March 1801, conditions were extremely overcrowded. Many of the cottages were only one-up, one-down and the average number of families per house was 1.7, which was even higher than in Manchester and Liverpool (1.5 in both). This was partly due to older, larger houses being occupied by numerous families, but it also reflects the poverty of the town's seamen, labourers and industrial workers. Wages were invariably low and uncertain, and many impoverished families could only hope to find the rent for their homes, however small, by letting out a room to a yet more desperate family.[13] The consequences of appalling housing conditions, and particularly the lack of either effective sanitation or clean water supplies, were seen in the very high death rates.

The most numerous section of the working classes was the seamen. They were paid by the month and rates varied according to the destination. Those sailing to Russia, Sweden, Prussia and elsewhere in the Baltic in 1768 were paid £1 8s. 0d. a month, while those undertaking voyages to America, the West Indies and further south received £1 5s. 0d. a month. Crews on coastal sailings were paid by the voyage, with sailings to Newcastle or Sunderland for coal, for instance, paying £1 15s. 0d. During the winter months, when the Baltic was frozen and trade impossible, many seamen were entirely without work, and so the paucity of income was as much a problem as the infrequency of payment. Many families lived permanently in debt to local shopkeepers.[14]

From left to right:

51 *Jarratt Street Terrace today. This was the first part of John Jarratt's estate to be developed, a little later than Albion Street. Kingston Square, which it faces, was originally called Jarratt Square.*

52 *Prince Street today.*

53 *Albion Street Terrace, 1794-6, as it appears today. This was the first part of Richard Baker's estate to be developed.*

54   *Parliament Street today.*

As the population of the town grew, so did the number of paupers and the cost of poor relief. The Corporation of the Poor, set up in 1698 and headed by the mayor and aldermen, enforced the Settlement Laws vigorously in an attempt to minimise the burden of poor rates. Any paupers caught begging who could not prove their right of settlement in Hull were expelled, sometimes after a whipping and a brief sojourn in the House of Correction. In 1718 constables were ordered by the Corporation of the Poor 'to examine in their several wards, what strangers were come in, who might be chargeable, give an account of their names, and summon them to appear at the Town Hall'.[15]

In a further effort to keep down poor relief, and to discourage the able-bodied poor from applying, outdoor relief for the able-bodied was stopped in 1728. From now on relief would only be available in the workhouse, or Charity Hall (as it was still locally known), which stood next door to the House of Correction in Whitefriargate, having been rebuilt in 1702. Until 1728 the inmates of the workhouse were mainly orphaned children who were given a basic education, taught to spin wool, and found an apprenticeship. Now, however, they had to share the workhouse with adult paupers, and 'their unrestricted association with beggars, debauchees, and harlots was an acknowledged evil'. In 1743, when Archbishop Herring asked for details of the workhouse as part of his visitation, it contained 20 men, 48 women, 23 boys, 42 girls and 11 babies. In 1790 lunatics were also transferred to the workhouse from the House of Correction.[16]

The number of paupers with a legitimate settlement in Hull continued to rise throughout the century, and never more sharply than in the 1780s and 1790s. In these years the population of the town was increasing rapidly, but high unemployment levels caused by the war with France plus poor harvests reduced unprecedented numbers to pauperism. Outdoor relief had to be given again and

55   *The new prison, Myton Place, c.1789.*

the poor rate assessments leapt. Whereas in 1779 they stood at £1,404 (itself a record), by 1789 they had more than doubled to £3,275, and in 1798 they stood at £8,320. The workhouse could only accommodate about 270 paupers and in the 1790s it was in most years completely full. According to the Revd John Tickell, in his *History of Hull* (1798), there were 276 paupers in the workhouse in 1792 and another 1,000 were receiving outdoor relief. As many as possible of the workhouse inmates were spinning wool but the money raised by this was always grossly inadequate and the workhouse had to be maintained by poor rates and charitable contributions. Tickell tells us, 'the value of their labour amounts to little more than one hundred pounds per annum'. Renewed efforts were made to drive out of the town any who could not prove their right to relief, and in 1794-5 166 families were expelled from the town.[17]

The poor of Hull were made desperate by hunger during the 1790s, and food riots broke out in 1795. Anticipating trouble, the bench had authorised a relief committee

56   *Plan of Hull, 1835.*

57   *The workhouse, rebuilt 1702.*

to buy up cereals to sell at subsidised prices to the poor, but nothing like enough was purchased and in August bakers found themselves obliged to raise their prices, already at starvation levels. Women who had gone to the market to buy flour showed their despair by breaking windows, and the riot was only stopped after the arrival of the Surrey Militia, who were being kept in readiness at the Citadel garrison. The bench dared not employ local men for such duties in case they showed sympathy for the rioters. The women, and numerous boys who joined in the window-smashing, were easily dispersed and apparently without injury, but special constables were now sworn in to be the first line of defence should trouble break out again.[18]

By increasing the poor rate assessment to an unheard-of level, over £5,600, the bench managed to get through the following winter without serious trouble, but food prices remained very high and a great many of the town's poor were literally starving. When flour prices went up yet again, in May, this was quite sufficient to set off another bout of violence. A baker who had put up his prices was chased to his house, where the angry crowd began smashing his windows and terrorising the poor man until the Nottinghamshire Militia arrived from the Citadel and two of the magistrates read out the Riot Act. The mob dispersed but the next day there was further, and more extensive rioting, as the wholly unsympathetic editor of the *Hull Advertiser* explained:

> The next day being market day the mob again assembled in the market place and different parts of the town and compelled the butchers and country people to part with meat, butter, poultry, eggs etc. at prices of their own fixing, besides wasting great quantities by throwing them about the streets in the most wanton manner. They then went to the place where the market boats land and there committed similar depredations on the property of people who bring provisions from Lincolnshire etc.

The militia was again able to restore order fairly swiftly and the leaders of the riot were arrested. It was recognised by most members of the town's ruling elite that the suffering of the poorer classes was genuine and that more help must be given. The poor rate assessments therefore rose in 1797 to £6,760, and again the next year to £8,320. In the winter of 1799 a committee for the relief of the poor was established, and a temporary soup kitchen was set up near the House of Correction 'for the convenience of serving the poor with soup or other such provisions as the committee may judge proper for them.' The corporation also granted an additional 20 guineas towards providing 'cheap food for the necessitous poor'.[19]

Many of the town's middle classes resented these constant increases. Although there was little fall in the number of starving people in the town, it was felt necessary in 1800 to cut the poor rates substantially and therefore to find every possible means of cutting the costs of the workhouse. The editor of the *Hull Advertiser* was a keen supporter of such economy and gleefully announced in January 1800 that the poor rates had been 'lowered by one half and the imposters on the charity detected and exposed', by which he presumably meant those who could not prove they had a right of settlement in Hull had been expelled. Just how Thomas Thompson, the governor of the workhouse, managed to cut his budget so drastically is not explained, but he did so and some of the grateful ratepayers, those who were members of the Grocers' Company, decided in August to spend £50 to present him with an inscribed silver plate. The dedication thanked the 'governor of the poor of this town for his meritorious and valuable services rendered to the inhabitants by introducing a system of economy and industry into the workhouse'. We can only assume that Thompson managed to make conditions in the workhouse so unpleasant that even the most desperately hungry family would not apply to enter.[20]

Widespread severe hunger during 1799-1800 was almost certainly why so many of the very young and elderly succumbed to a serious intestinal epidemic in 1800, which pushed up mortality rates sharply, but the anger of the poor did not erupt into violence again for two more years. A small fall in wheat prices in the summer of 1800 probably helped the situation, and fear of the militia was also a restraining factor. Following the agreement of the Peace of Amiens in 1802, the troops were withdrawn from the town, and when some food prices were put up at a Saturday market in July that year violence broke out again. Stalls were overturned, the butchers' shops were looted, and when the magistrates arrived to read the Riot Act without troops to protect them, the crowd chased them back to the town hall. While the mayor and aldermen cowered in an inner room, the crowd vented their anger first by smashing every window in the building, and then by breaking into the kitchen and doing as much damage as they could.[21]

A fairly novel way of trying to help the poor was to club together to buy or erect windmills so that grain could be milled as a non-profit-making venture. Two mills were built near Hull for this purpose, one in 1795 on the south side of Holderness Road, and another in 1800 on Dansom Lane, just outside the town. But in the face of high wholesale cereal prices success was limited. Attempts by working people to form trade unions to force their employers to pay higher wages were suppressed speedily. To meet the challenge of trade unionism, the Combination Laws were rushed through parliament in 1799, and two of the first to be caught by these new measures were a pair of Hull shoemakers. The two men were tried at York assizes in February 1800 for conspiring to form an illegal combination and were sent to Newgate Prison to serve a nine-month sentence.[22]

The return of troops to the town following the resumption of war against the French in 1803 helped keep the peace. So nervous was the bench, however, that when troops had to be sent from Hull to assist in dealing with Luddite violence in Huddersfield, in 1812, replacement troops had to be brought immediately from Sheffield. The *Hull Rockingham* reported that it had not been thought 'expedient to leave Hull without military'.

There would be no more food riots in the town after 1802 but this is no indication of improving living standards. Although food prices came down in the 1820s, the conditions endured by Hull's poor did not improve before the middle of the century. The new working-class suburbs of the 1820s and 1830s were no improvement on the cramped hovels of the Old Town. Not only did speculative builders squeeze as many houses into as small an area as possible, but there was no thought of how clean water or adequate sanitation might be provided. Water continued to be drawn from the river Hull, although it was recognised as a grossly polluted source, and removal of human excreta and other noxious waste was still the responsibility of the 'night soil men', small contractors who only visited the houses irregularly and took the waste to nearby dumps, known as 'muck garths', not far from the new suburbs. These were left to decompose in the open air, surrounded by houses. Some were enormous – one was said to cover an area of about three acres – and they were often used as a play area by children.[24]

In such conditions the cholera epidemic of 1832 found numerous victims among the poor of Hull. When this water-borne disease first reached the town, in April, it struck first in the Wincolmlee district, one of the relatively new working-class suburbs that had grown up around the oil mills and shipyards north of the Old Town, close to the river Hull. From here it spread to the equally squalid housing of Hull's new north-west suburbs. In reporting the progress of the disease, Dr James Alderson noted that this was an area of many lodging houses, tramps, Irish labourers and paupers. The death rate was particularly high in Bellamy Square, which on one side was bounded by pigsties. The last deaths from cholera were reported in early September 1832, by which time the disease had killed 270 people. During its progress, subscriptions were raised to help provide food and clothing for poor families stricken with the disease. Many children were orphaned and many families reduced to destitution.[25]

The appalling overcrowding in many of the poorer areas of the town was commented upon a few years later in a paper presented to the British Association by James Wood in 1841: 'There are courts, and courts of a very peculiar construction, a court within a court and then another court within that.' Wood also reported that in one house, possibly a cheap lodging house, he had found as many as a hundred people, and all 'of the worst description'.[26]

To meet the growing demand, the old workhouse on Whitefriargate was considerably extended in the early 19th century, and in 1833 serious consideration was given to building a new one, with architects invited to submit designs, though the old building would survive until 1852. Its administration was at first little affected by the Poor Law Amendment Act in 1834. The body responsible for the workhouse and the poor rate, the Corporation of the Poor, was formally made subject to the Poor Law Commissioners in London but in practice it was left for many years free from outside interference. The surrounding parishes were affected rather more directly by the 1834 Act. Until this time Drypool, Sculcoates, Sutton and Marfleet all had their own workhouses, but in 1837 all became part of a new Sculcoates Poor Law Union, closely supervised by the London Commissioners.[27]

Not all the needy were forced into the workhouse. Numerous charities and almshouses continued to play an important role throughout the 18th and early 19th centuries. The largest almshouse, the Charterhouse hospital, was rebuilt in 1778-80 and later extended to accommodate more than 50 pensioners. The old Trinity Almshouse was rebuilt in 1753 and several new almshouses were built in the late 18th and early 19th centuries. Trinity House provided help for elderly seamen and their widows and children, and in 1742 it introduced a compulsory insurance scheme for all seamen, making a levy of 6d. per month on their wages. According to Tickell, this fund meant that 'a great number of decayed seamen, their widows, and children, who otherwise would have no claim on the guild, obtain a comfortable relief'.[28]

Many families drew on the help of the friendly societies to which they belonged. The town's first such society was set up in 1726 and a 'Sailors' Society' was said to

58   *The Charterhouse Hospital, 1793.*

59   *The General Infirmary, Prospect Street.*

be in existence by about 1730. By 1796 there were 25
friendly societies in Hull and by 1812 nearly eighty.
During the early 19th century a number of the societies
joined 'lodges' or 'orders', such as the Oddfellows'
lodge, a branch of which was established in the town
in about 1811.[29]

There was also some improvement, from the late
18th century, in medical help available to the poor.
The Hull General Infirmary was opened on Prospect
Street in 1782 for patients unable to pay for their
treatment, and a dispensary for the poor was opened
in 1814. Both institutions relied mainly on charity and
on doctors willing to give their time freely, but also
received some financial help from the corporation. One
doctor whose support for the infirmary was particularly
important, Dr John Alderson, was awarded the freedom
of the town by the corporation in 1813 in recognition
of his work, and in 1833 – four years after his death
– a statue was erected in his honour at the entrance

60   *Statue of Dr John Alderson today.*

to the infirmary. The Infirmary was demolished in 1972 and the site is now occupied by the Prospect Shopping Centre, but, most fittingly, the statue of Dr Alderson stands today instead in the forecourt of the present Royal Infirmary, on Anlaby Road.[30]

Leisure

For many of the poor, the principal means of escape from the hardships of life was provided by the gin shops, alehouses and inns. At the beginning of the 18th century it was said that in the market place, and in the streets leading from it, alehouses were as ubiquitous as shops. Here one could enjoy not only a drink – and Hull was famous for the strength of its beers – but also a game of skittles or cards and a smoke. Some of the inns also had a cock pit, and cockfighting remained a very popular entertainment until the early 19th century. Puppet shows were also very popular. Hadley tells us that in 1741 'Mr Scott … exhibited his puppet-shew with great applause'. There were also public executions to be watched on Myton Carr, until the last hanging there in 1778, and some found amusement at the expense of unfortunate women placed in the cucking stool. This was an ancient punishment 'for the benefit of scolds and unquiet women'. In 1731 the old cucking stool was in need of replacement and the corporation ordered a new one to be placed at South End, the most southerly part of High Street, close to the Humber bank. The week-long Hull Fair in the autumn was also an opportunity for leisure and fun appreciated by all classes, and in the 18th century it ceased to be a general fair and became a pleasure fair.[31]

The town's wealthier inhabitants had a rather wider choice of amusements. Horse racing was well established in the town by the middle of the 18th century, and during the general election of 1768 one of the town's MPs seeking re-election, William Weddell, was asked by a number of Hull merchants to cease his support for the local races because they disliked the 'great idleness and disorder' the races caused. Weddell had been in the habit of contributing prize money for the races, but under this pressure he now agreed to end the practice. The strong puritanical element among the town's elite, such a powerful force in 16th- and 17th-century Hull, was still very much alive and may well explain why horse-racing never developed as successfully in Hull as in many other similar-sized towns. Its success depended on the patronage of the wealthy, but the merchants who complained to Weddell felt that too many of their working people were being drawn to the races, and the gambling and heavy drinking associated with them would also have been much deplored, to say nothing of the pick-pockets and prostitutes.[32]

Rather less controversial gentlemanly pleasures were later recalled by the anti-slavery campaigner and local MP William Wilberforce, born in Hull in 1759. As a young man in the 1770s, he saw Hull as 'one of the gayest places out of London. The theatre, balls, large supper and card parties were the delight of the principal merchants and their families'.[33]

61 *The Theatre Royal, Humber Street, opened 1810.*

The theatre to which he referred was the Theatre Royal, on Finkle Street, built in 1768 by actor-manager Tate Wilkinson to replace his earlier playhouse, the New Theatre, on Lowgate. The Theatre Royal was said to have a 'piazza' at the front and separate entrances for each section of the house. Inside, the walls were lined with boxes linked by a gallery. Below was the pit, much frequented, Wilkinson later recalled, by 'seafaring persons'. The season ran from October to January, and under Wilkinson the theatre was a success, with pantomimes particularly popular. John Kemble began his career as part of Wilkinson's company and even the great Mrs Siddons appeared in Hull for a week in 1786, although the cost of promoting her season considerably reduced the profits that year. By the time Wilkinson's son took over the theatre in 1803, it was in sad decline, the stage too small for the elaborate melodramas by then in fashion. The *Hull Rockingham* described it in 1809 – the year it closed – as 'dirty, ill-lighted, and incommodious'. John Wilkinson opened a new, much larger theatre on Humber Street in 1810, also called the Theatre Royal. It contained three tiers of boxes, two galleries and a pit, with accommodation for 1,700, and a stage 54 feet deep. A domed ceiling was supported by a circle of groined arches and the boxes were lined with scarlet cloth. Wilkinson was unable to fill it, however, and his attempts to run summer seasons were an expensive failure. He retired in 1814 and his successors also failed to make it a financial success, and in 1859, when it was destroyed by a fire, one local newspaper commented that 'latterly the managements have changed almost yearly' and 'the prestige of the property has lamentably decreased'.[34]

During the 1820s and 1830s the Theatre Royal faced competition from two smaller theatres, the Minor Theatre (as it was first called, in 1826), on the corner of Humber Street and Queen Street, and the Adelphi, on the corner of Wellington Street and Queen Street, which was converted from a circus and opened in about 1831. Like the Theatre Royal, both theatres struggled to remain solvent, and the Minor Theatre – whose name changed at least six times in 10 years – was demolished in 1836. These years, as we will see shortly, saw the enormous growth of Methodism, and it is likely that this new Puritanism among the lower middle classes and skilled workers played no small part in the decline of theatre-going.[35]

The balls and card parties to which Wilberforce referred were mainly held at the Assembly Rooms on Dagger Lane, built in 1752. Before this assemblies were held in the upper room of the grammar school, but this had long been unsuitable. One of the largest balls staged in the Dagger Lane rooms was in November 1788, to celebrate the centenary of the 'Glorious Revolution'. These were occasions to be seen, for the urban merchant families to mix with country gentry families and members of the 'higher' professions, the doctors and the clergy, for gossip and match-making, and, for the younger participants, for romance. The editor of the *Hull Packet* could barely contain his enthusiasm in reporting the Centenary Ball in 1788: 'Such an assembly of beauty and brilliancy had never before shone forth in these rooms.' Less formal dining and card parties were organised by local clubs, such as the *George*, whose minute book for 1784-1813 has survived. Its members met every Saturday evening to gamble at cards.[36]

As the town's wealthier classes expanded, larger premises for balls and concerts were needed. In 1823 a house was acquired for the purpose in North Street (today the easterly section of George Street), but this soon proved inadequate and at a public meeting in 1827 it was agreed that new assembly rooms were needed to accommodate balls, concerts and lectures. The prospectus for the new building announced that shares could be purchased for £25 each and regretted that 'the Mechanics' Institute can erect a building for their objects while the gentlemen of the town do not possess a place to meet in worthy of its rank and opulence'. By 1830 the foundation stone for a building so worthy had been laid, on the corner of Jarratt Street and Kingston Square; it was completed in 1834 and still stands today, now the New Theatre. It is indeed a grand building, designed by Hull's principal architect, Charles Mountain Jnr (as was the ill-fated Theatre Royal on Humber Street), and built of stuccoed brick in the Greek Revival style, with a five-bay frontage and a portico of Ionic columns. When first opened it offered a ballroom (known as the Music Room) 91 feet long, 41 feet wide and 40 feet high, together with a separate dining room, drawing room and lecture hall. It had barely been opened before there were complaints about the high rents charged for its use, and as a result the Victoria Rooms were opened in 1837, to provide a smaller-scale, less expensive suite of assembly rooms, on the site of the former Minor Theatre, on Queen Street.[37]

From the late 18th century some of the town's more cerebral middle classes started a subscription library as well as literary and scientific societies. The library was founded in 1775, housed in a rented room. The admission fee was at first one guinea and the annual membership fee 12s. The earliest known literary or scientific society was established in 1792, formed by a local doctor, Dr Moyes, and some friends, who began meeting that year in one of the member's houses in Lowgate 'for the purpose of literary information'. Like many similar small groups that followed it, it enjoyed only a short life, and nothing is heard of it after 1797. The subscription library, however, was a considerable success, and in 1801 it moved to larger premises in Parliament Street. At the same time it was decided to substantially increase both the admission fee and the annual subscription, and both were further increased in 1817

62 *The Assembly Rooms, or Public Rooms, Kingston Square, built 1830-4; this engraving was made just after the building had been completed.*

with no loss of membership. In 1801 it also began an evening discussion group for its members but, according to local historian Charles Frost in 1830, these meetings had to be soon discontinued as 'the harmony of its proceedings was interrupted', owing to 'unfortunate differences, which took place among a few individuals'. Between 1803 and 1809 a select literary society met weekly in the winter months, and in 1804 and 1805 there were weekly meetings (again only in the winter months) of the Scientific Society, at which scientific experiments were demonstrated. In 1807 a second subscription library, known as the 'New Subscription Library', was set up in the market place. This enjoyed much success, aiming to attract younger middle-class

63 *The market place; from an aquatint by T. Malton, 1780.*

64 *The market place, looking south, by W. Carroll, 1796.*

readers. By 1826 it was known as the Lyceum Library and had moved to Parliament Street, and in 1835 it moved again, to St John's Street. By this time it had a stock of 4,400 books.

Both libraries would survive throughout the 19th century, as would the Hull Literary and Philosophical Society, formed in 1822, primarily as a result of a meeting called to raise funds to buy the 'Hyde Collection' of 'natural and artificial rarities'. The collection became the nucleus of the society's museum, which it subsequently considerably expanded. Meetings were then held monthly, and later fortnightly, mainly to hear lectures on scientific subjects. It met first in the reading room of the New Exchange building off Lowgate, but in 1829 it moved to rooms in the subscription library, and in 1831 into the brand new (and not yet completed) Assembly Rooms on Jarratt Street. For many decades to come, its membership continued to grow, despite from 1826 its considerable annual membership fee of £1 5s.[38]

Churches and chapels

When, in 1834, a census was organised to discover the numbers regularly attending a church or chapel, the statistics were most revealing. For Anglicans the results were alarming for they showed that the Church of England had lost the loyalty of the great majority of the town's rapidly expanding population. Only about 6,400 people were attending an Anglican Sunday service and there were not more than 1,200 regular Anglican communicants, and possibly less than eight hundred. This was in spite of an evangelical revival in the church from the late 18th century which had led to the building of a number of new churches, in addition to the ancient churches of Holy Trinity and

65 *Holy Trinity Church from the south-east in the late 18th century.*

66 *Holy Trinity Church from the south-east today.*

St Mary, to serve the new suburbs to the west and north of the Old Town.

For nonconformists, on the other hand, and particularly for the Methodists, the findings were a triumph, for approximately twice as many people were now attending a nonconformist service as were attending an Anglican service. At the beginning of the 18th century there had been just two little nonconformist chapels in the town, a Presbyterian chapel in Bowlalley Lane and an Independent chapel in Dagger Lane, both then only very recently opened. Now, however, there were 23 nonconformist churches and chapels, with a combined Sunday attendance of about 12,000 and over 4,000 regular communicants, and a Roman Catholic church with about 450 attending regularly on Sundays.

The most successful of the nonconformist churches were the Methodists. By 1834 there were seven Wesleyan churches in the town, one Primitive Methodist chapel, an Independent Methodist chapel and one New Connexion Methodist chapel, which together boasted about 6,800 weekly attendants. The Independents could also be pleased about their progress. At the time of Archbishop Herring's visitation in 1743 there had been about 200 attending an Independent service in the Dagger Lane chapel, but as Hull had grown so had their church, and now there were six Independent chapels and over 3,000 regularly attending on Sundays. The Baptists formed a rather smaller group, with only about 1,000 regular adherents attending three chapels, but their church had been completely absent from the town in the early years of the 18th century and only about 60 Baptists were attending Sunday services in 1743, meeting in the tower of the semi-derelict Pole family manor house in Lowgate.[39]

Disappointing for both Anglicans and nonconformists alike was the revelation that about half the town's population was attending no place of religious worship at all, at least not on a regular basis, particularly those at the bottom of the social scale. The Primitive Methodists enjoyed some success after establishing their first chapel in Mill Street in 1819, in the heart of the slums of the new north-west working-class suburb. Their congregation doubled in its first year, inspired in no small measure by the indefatigable and charismatic William Clowes. He was a former local pottery worker who had returned to the town that year as a missionary, determined to bring his stirring brand of Christianity to the poorest of the poor. Before the end of the year he and his followers had opened a second meeting place among the shipyards and oil mills of Wincolmlee, and by the mid-century four more chapels had been taken over or built, and Hull had become an important centre for Primitive Methodism. At the time of the 1834 census there were said to be 1,000 regularly attending their services, and there were about 2,200 when the national religious census was taken in 1851.[40]

In Hull, as in other large towns by the 1830s, the majority of those who regularly attended either an Anglican or nonconformist church had probably written off the poorest sections of society as immoral heathens, immune to the appeals of Christianity. The most successful of the new churches, the Wesleyan Methodists, drew their support mainly from the middle classes, the lower middle classes and the skilled working class.

The Wesleyan Church had grown rapidly since its foundation in the town in the mid-18th century. The first meetings were held in 1746 in a private house in the Back

Ropery, in the southern-most part of the Old Town, beside the Humber. Wesley himself did not visit the town until 1752, when he preached to a large crowd in Myton Carr, but the meeting ended in disorder and he was chased back into the town by a mob. His followers did not establish their first chapel until 1761, when

67 *The St Charles Borromeo Roman Catholic Church, opened on Jarratt Street in 1829, the same year that the Catholic Emancipation Act was passed, giving Roman Catholics equal civil rights.*

68 *Salem Independent Chapel,*
opened 1833 on Cogan Street.

69 *Wesley Methodist Chape*
Humber Street, opened 1833

they moved into the manor house tower premises recently vacated by the Baptists, but from this time their numbers grew rapidly, and in 1772 the congregation moved into a larger chapel in Manor Alley. When Wesley visited that year (his seventh visit since 1752) he described the new chapel as 'extremely well finished, and, upon the whole, one of the prettiest preaching-houses in England'. In 1786 the congregation had outgrown this chapel and built a yet larger one in George Yard, on the site of a former theatre, which was no doubt seen as a fitting metaphor for the triumph of godliness over sin. Wesley preached here in 1788 and again in 1790, when he made his final (17th) visit to the town. It was during the next half-century, as the town was growing most rapidly, that the Wesleyans enjoyed even greater success, opening 15 new chapels between 1804 and 1842.[41]

Although a great many Anglicans strongly disliked John Wesley and his movement, there were many others in the Church of England who shared his evangelising passion that all men and women, however poor, had souls to be saved. For William Wilberforce it was this belief that caused him to dedicate his life to the abolition of slavery. Hull's one outstanding Anglican minister of the 18th century, the Revd Joseph Milner, who was appointed master of the grammar school in 1767 and Holy Trinity lecturer the following year, was similarly motivated. His sermons were often at variance to those of the vicar and this led to charges of Methodism and 'enthusiasm', and it was probably owing to Milner that John Wesley was invited to preach in Holy Trinity during his visits to the town in 1786 and 1788. Milner only became vicar at Holy Trinity shortly before his death, in 1797, but he had a considerable influence on many

70 *The recently opened George Yard Chapel,*
built 1786, shortly before this engraving was made.

71 *Waltham Street Methodist Chapel,*
opened 1815.

in the town, including some of his pupils.
One was Dr John Alderson, whose work
for the poor and for the Hull General Infirmary was at least partly inspired by evangelical zeal. Another was the Revd Thomas
Dykes, who succeeded Milner as the leader
of evangelicalism in the town. Encouraged
by Milner, Dykes managed to have the first
post-Reformation Anglican church built in
the town, dedicated, appropriately, to St John
the Evangelist, in St John Street (now part
of Queen Victoria Square), close to the new
middle-class 'Northern Suburb' but also not
far from the new working-class areas west of
the Old Town. It was consecrated in 1791 and
opened the following year. It was a modest
little church, a Georgian preaching-house in

72 *St John's Church, built 1790-2.*

73 *Christ Church, Worship Street, built 1822.*

74 *The Wilberforce Monument, erected 1834-5, and St John's Church. Boats moored in the adjacent Junction Dock (later Prince's Dock) can be seen in the foreground.*

red brick with stone dressings, but Dykes had to sink his own fortune in the venture and overcome considerable opposition from the corporation, who feared a possible loss of income for Holy Trinity. Building problems also had to be overcome. The church was built partly on the old town moat and when it was decided to extend the church, in 1803, by adding a chancel and tower, the costs proved much greater than expected to strengthen the foundations. Dykes was the first incumbent and remained at St John's for more than fifty years.[42]

In 1822 a second new church, Christ Church, was opened on Worship Street to serve the middle-class 'Northern Suburb', and its first incumbent, John King, was a strong evangelical. In the same year the medieval church of St Peter, in the rapidly growing working-class suburb of Drypool, east of the river Hull, was rebuilt, but the first new Anglican church to be built in the heart of a working-class area was not opened until 1831, when St James's, in St James's Square, Myton, was consecrated. Dykes was again the moving spirit behind this and since 1819 he had been holding services in a school in the same area. Also, in 1828 he had opened a church specifically for the town's seamen in Prince's Dock Street, the Mariners' Church, occupying a former Independent chapel. The only other new church built before 1837 was St John the Evangelist, in Clough Street, Newland, which was consecrated in 1833.[43]

Schooldays

At the beginning of the 18th century the majority of poor children, and particularly poor girls, received no education at all. In 1700 a poor child's best hope of acquiring the ability to read or write was to be taken into the workhouse. The vicar of Holy Trinity, the Revd Robert Banks, who was a keen supporter of the Society for the Promotion of Christian Knowledge, had by this time taken control of the provision of education for pauper children in the town, and he ensured that the 40 or so boys and girls in the workhouse were decently clothed, taught the catechism of the Church of England, and taught to both read and write, as well as to spin wool, before being found suitable apprenticeships.[44]

75 *Statue of William Wilberforce (1884) in the forecourt of Wilberforce House, High Street, where he was born in 1759. Wilberforce attended the local grammar school, served as MP for Hull (1780-4) and dedicated his life to the abolition of slavery.*

Outside the workhouse, however, only a very few boys were given the same opportunity. In 1729 another vicar of Holy Trinity (and also a keen SPCK correspondent), the Revd William Mason, founded a society of tradesmen described by an historian of the SPCK as 'eminent for its religious zeal, and especially its well-ordered charity in respect of poor people's children'. In 1730 Mason and his society opened the Vicar's School in Vicar Lane to teach 20 poor children reading, writing and Christianity. In 1792 the school was rebuilt by the Revd Thomas Clarke, Wilberforce's brother-in-law, and the number of pupils increased to sixty. It was at first supported from subscriptions and from a collection taken at an annual sermon in Holy Trinity, but from 1813 a fee of 1s. per quarter was introduced.[45]

At about the same time, Trinity House began paying a private teacher of navigation to instruct the sons of poor members, to ensure Hull shipowners received a sufficient supply of trained apprentices. As the port grew, it became necessary to open a marine school. This opened in Trinity House Lane, in 1787, in a new building adjoining the chapel. Thirty-six boys aged 10 to 13, chosen by the elder brethren, were given a uniform and taught navigation, arithmetic, writing, accounts, and 'practical religion'.

The first charity school established specifically for poor girls opened in 1755, in a house in Salthouse Lane, given by Alderman William Cogan, who also set up a trust fund from which the salary of the mistress would be paid. Twenty girls would be admitted at the age of 10, chosen by the trustees. The parents had to be judged as orderly people 'who would not sell ale or spirituous liquors or receive weekly allowances or ask alms, or let their children beg'. The girls were given a uniform and would stay at the school for three years, but reading and writing would not be part of their education. Instead they were 'taught to knit, sew, wash and get up linen, to wash rooms, and other housework to fit them for useful servants'. The school gradually took on more girls as its income increased and from 1760 it was supplying dowries for former pupils to help them find husbands. It would survive, little altered, for almost 200 years, closing finally in 1950.[46]

By the early 1780s the need to provide some sort of education for the great number of the town's children whom the charity schools were not admitting had long been apparent to men like Joseph Milner, and in 1786 he and a group of other like-minded evangelicals came together to open four Sunday schools. The original proposal was to open eight Sunday schools for girls as well as boys. This met considerable opposition and girls from poor families were instead offered only spinning schools, three of which were opened in 1786. One particularly hostile critic of Sunday schools, and especially Sunday schools for girls, was the local historian George Hadley. In his history of the town, first published just two years later, he explains that the schools were proposed 'in order to check the progress of vice and profaneness, and to rescue poor children of both sexes from ignorance and dissoluteness'. He applauded the aims but regarded spinning schools as a much better solution to the problem, and the proposed Sunday schools are described as a 'preposterous institution, replete with folly, indolence, fanaticism and mischief'. Hadley, like many others at this time, regarded the education of the poor as a threat to the social fabric and the peace of the realm:

> The working poor are by far the most numerous class of people, and when kept in due subordination, they compose the riches of the nation. But there is a degree of ignorance necessary to keep them so, and to make them either useful to others or happy in themselves.

In spite of such attitudes, the first nondenominational subscription day school for poor children was set up in 1787 in Carr Street, Sculcoates. The first day school in Hull was opened in Salthouse Lane in 1809, a 'Lancastrian' school for boys, based on the principles of education as laid down by Joseph Lancaster, who visited the school himself shortly afterwards. Two years later it was followed by a similar school for girls, built next door.[47]

Interdenominational cooperation would be short-lived. In 1819 both the Anglican and nonconformist churches in the town set up rival denominational Sunday schools and further similar initiatives followed in the 1820s and 1830s. In 1835 the nonconformist Sunday School Union opened 16 schools, run by 500 voluntary teachers and educating approximately 2,620 children. The Anglicans were unable to match this, and could claim only 1,200 children attending their Sunday schools but, with greater financial resources, they were ahead in the provision of day schools in the 1830s.

In 1818, the Sculcoates school was reorganised under the patronage of the recently established Anglican body, the National Society for the Education of the Poor in the Principles of the Established Church, and in 1825 all children attending had to be regular members of St Mary's Church in Sculcoates. Also in 1825 the trustees of the two Lancastrian schools on Salthouse Lane affiliated to the National Society, and these too became church schools, closely tied to St Mary's in Lowgate. An Anglican infants' school opened in Eastcheap in 1826, with the support of numerous local clergy, and two years later the trustees of the Salthouse Road schools opened another Anglican infants' school in the High Street. In 1828 an Anglican national school was opened on Church Street, in Drypool, by the Revd Henry Venn, and in 1832 the Revd John King opened the Christ Church National School next to his recently opened church in Sculcoates. The Drypool school was a two-storey building; boys were educated on the ground floor and girls on the first floor, and in 1833 there were said to be 420 children enrolled.

In the 1820s nonconformist parents who wished to avoid sending their children to a church day school had to make do with private 'dame' schools, which often charged only 2d. or 3d. a week, supplemented by one of their own Sunday schools. However, a nonsectarian school opened in 1833, the Dock Green British School, affiliated to the 'British Society', which was dedicated to promoting nonsectarian schools and was soon heavily supported by nonconformists. A second British School opened in

1838, the Holderness Ward School, in Dansom Lane. It was paid for from public subscriptions, the great majority from nonconformists. One other, completely unique, nondenominational school had opened in 1831. This was the Hull Savings Bank School, on Waltham Street, but until 1841 this only admitted the children of those who had deposits with the bank.[48]

In spite of all this activity, the great majority of Hull's poorer children were still, in the late 1830s, receiving either no education at all or at best attending only a Sunday School. The day schools for poor children, supported mainly by subscriptions, and from 1833 by very limited government grants, could rarely afford to employ more than two teachers, and had to rely heavily on the services of the older and brighter pupils, who were often employed as unpaid 'monitors' to help maintain discipline and educate the younger children. In 1838 the Salthouse Road Church Schools were reporting an average attendance of 250 boys and 125 girls, and the Sculcoates National School had 170 boys and 60 girls. The earliest records for the two British schools come from the 1840s: in 1841 330 children were attending the Dock Green School and in 1844 there were 140 enrolled in the Holderness Ward School.

For the poorest children, those in the workhouse, the provision of education deteriorated during the 18th century. There were usually at least 80 children in the workhouse in the 1790s but in 1799 it was reported that their only teacher was a drunken pauper. The boys were usually sent to sea but the girls were harder to place and in 1800 as many as 40 were apprenticed to linen mills in Otley.

76 *The Mechanics' Institute, Charlotte Street, 1825.*

The lack of an elementary education for many working people was addressed by the setting up of the Mechanics' Institute in 1825. The leading promoters were Dr Alderson, the Unitarian minister, the Revd George Lee, and the vicar of Holy Trinity, the Revd J.H. Bromby. Their initiative helped working men gain a better education but also improved the relationships between the social classes. The Institute taught reading, writing and grammar and aimed to achieve 'the instruction of its members, at a cheap rate, in the principles of their respective arts, and in the various branches of useful knowledge'. A library was soon established as an essential part of the Institute, charging lower fees than the subscription libraries, and in 1838 it was said to have 2,000 books, but no novels, romances, 'controversial divinity' books or politics were allowed.[49]

For the sons of better-off families the grammar school was the only provider of a secondary education at the beginning of the 18th century, but growing dissatisfaction with its strictly classical curriculum led to it losing its monopoly by the second half of the century, when other private academies offered a wider and more commercial curriculum. One of the most successful was Benjamin Snowden's Mercantile Academy in Blanket Row, established before 1790 and still flourishing in the late 1830s. It appealed to the middle classes because, as well as academic subjects, it also provided courses for boys 'intended for the accounting house or counter' and 'practical mathematics, particularly navigation and surveying'. From the 1790s advertisements in the local newspapers informed the public of seminaries for girls, such as Miss Benison's seminary in Bond Street, and Miss Thompson's in Blanket Row. They offered English grammar, writing, geography, French, dancing, music, needlework and drawing, usually with the assistance of 'the most approved masters'.

The grammar school eventually widened its curriculum, but its success depended heavily on the character of the master in charge. Under the Revd G.J. Davies (1811-24) the school flourished, with 60 boys attending in 1818, but under his successor, the Revd William Wilson, the numbers enrolling fell to between 20 and 30, and when Wilson died in 1836 the school closed completely for almost two years.[50]

A revolution in local government

As the Georgian era came to an end so did the system of local government under which the town had been governed since the 14th century. Under the terms of the Municipal Corporations Act in 1834, the old unelected corporation was swept away and elections were held for a new body of 42 councillors, elected by the town's ratepayers. Not one of the former 12 aldermen was elected to the new body, and almost every winning candidate belonged to the reform party. The aldermen of the old corporation had been members of the long-established merchant class; the new councillors were mainly shopkeepers.[51]

This decisive rejection of the former governing body reflected the dissatisfaction in the town regarding the corporation, the lack of democratic elections, the secrecy

surrounding much of its work, the borough finances, and, in recent years, the failure
to provide adequate policing. Some of these criticisms had then been given further
weight by the parliamentary commissioners who in 1833 came to Hull to investigate
the corporation's handling of borough affairs, in preparation for 1834 Act, and also
by the Reform Bill controversy of 1831-2, which had put the issues of representation,
accountability and voting rights in the forefront of public discussion.[52]

Moreover, in Hull theses criticisms were whipped up by a campaign led by James
Acland, a journalist who had recently moved to the town from Bristol. Acland was a
radical, a passionate supporter of reform, and a virulent critic of the old corporation
in Hull. He was also an effective orator, propagandist and self-publicist. Shortly after
his arrival in 1831 his campaign against the old corporation created a state of political
agitation such as Hull had never seen before. According to the commissioners who later
investigated the corporation, 'from August 1831 until November 1832 the public peace
in the town was constantly broken by the assemblage of mobs, and by the committal
of the most daring and outrageous acts of violence.'[53]

Acland criticised the old corporation vehemently both in his weekly journal, the
Hull Portfolio, and at nightly meetings, and 'persons going about their ordinary business
were frequently molested and assaulted by the mob'. Although his criticisms were
often grossly exaggerated or even libellous, he certainly managed to demonstrate the
corporation's failure to police the town. On one occasion an official of the corporation
was seized and brought before Acland, and only released after the intervention of a
solicitor, who was then hissed through the streets on Acland's instructions. As part of
his campaign against the corporation's market tolls he set up his own stall, in front
of the statue of William III, selling his journal but refusing to pay the stallage toll,
and persuaded some other market stall holders to also refuse payment. Acland was
surrounded by a large crowd of his supporters who ensured the constables would not
dare arrest him or remove his stall. Emboldened by this success, he went on to lead a
march over the town bridges, again refusing to pay tolls, and demonstrated against the
charges of the Humber ferry by chartering his own steamboat to carry passengers at a
cheaper rate. This led to a court case in March 1832, and although a sympathetic jury
imposed only a derisory fine of one farthing, he was unable to pay the court costs and
was subsequently imprisoned in November. Before this, however, he stirred up a further
riot in September by standing in the borough elections as a chamberlain candidate,
even though he was not a burgess of the town. Special constables were sworn in to
keep order but were attacked by a large crowd of Acland's supporters. The cavalry had
to be brought in to restore the peace, and Acland was again arrested. Once he was in
prison, however, he was quickly forgotten, although he would later enjoy a career as
an Anti-Corn Law League campaigner and as a Liberal party agent.[54]

EIGHT

Victorian and Edwardian Hull, 1837-1914

Following boundary changes in 1837, the population of the parliamentary borough in 1841 was 65,670; within 30 years, and after another boundary change, it had almost doubled to 123,408, and in 1901 it had reached 239,517, by which time it had been officially granted the title and status of a city. At the time of the last pre-war census, in 1911, the city's population stood at 275,486, which meant Hull was larger in 1911 than it is today, 100 years later.[1] The economic changes which made this remarkable growth possible were due to the creation of new industries, the development of the railway, the continuing expansion and improvement in the town's dock facilities, and the rapid growth of the shipping industry.

New and old industries

Linseed oil crushing and paint manufacturing remained major employers throughout the century, along with shipbuilding, with over 1,700 men listed as either shipbuilders or shipwrights in 1891. The brewing industry also expanded, although a series of take-overs and amalgamations meant that by the end of the century the industry was dominated by just two firms, the Hull Brewery Company and Moors' and Robson's. When Edward Robson merged his firm with that of Henry and Charles Moor, in 1888, the two firms owned between them 71 public houses, and by 1890 the newly formed Hull Brewery Company owned 160 licensed premises.

The most important new industries, in terms of numbers employed, were the glue and starch works founded in 1840 by the Quaker Isaac Reckitt, which would later be enormously expanded and diversified by his son, Sir James Reckitt; trawler fishing,

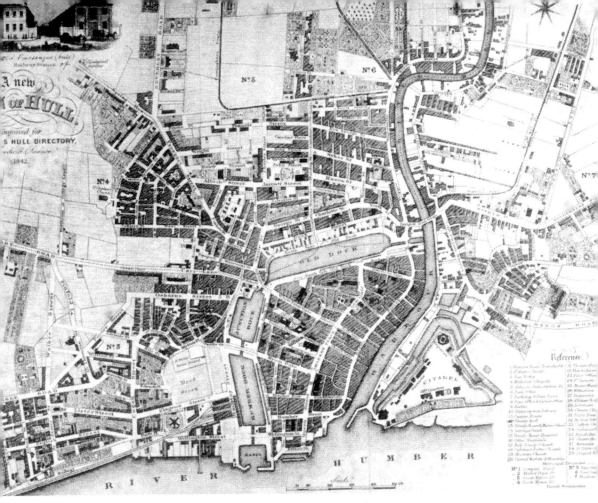

77   *Plan of Hull, 1842, by Goodwill and Lawson.*

which developed from the 1840s; corn milling, which was transformed by technological developments in the 1880s; and cotton spinning and weaving, which flourished in the 1830s and 1840s but had gone again before the end of the century.

The substantial quantities of cotton yarn exported from Hull made it a natural site for a cotton mill, even though it was far from Lancashire, the centre of the industry. The first mill established was the Hull Flax and Cotton Mill, which opened on the north-east edge of the Groves district in 1836. During the boom year of 1845, a second mill opened, the Kingston Cotton Mill, a little further up the river Hull, in Cumberland Street. Both were large-scale enterprises. The 1851 census recorded 971 men and 1,247 women employed in the industry, and 10 years later the numbers were only a little less: 735 men and 1,179 women. However, both firms were struggling to survive. They were equipped with the most modern machinery, and their workforces consisted mainly of migrants from the Lancashire textile towns, but they were managed by local businessmen who lacked the necessary knowledge of market conditions. The Hull Flax and Cotton Mill went into liquidation in 1857, was reconstituted in 1860, and then finally closed in 1866. The Kingston Cotton Mill also struggled to compete with its Lancashire rivals but survived until 1894.[2]

Corn milling proved more successful and by the end of the century was one of the most important industries in the town. Yet in 1831 there were only a dozen corn millers in the town, each employing no more than two or three men and boys. By 1851 there were 30 mills but all were still very small scale, employing only 105 men and boys between them. In the 1870s and 1880s, however, the industry was transformed by steam milling and, even more importantly, roller-grinding rather than stone-grinding. The first roller-mill in Hull, Alexandra Mill, was opened by Joseph Rank in 1885, beside the newly opened Alexandra Dock. It was immediately successful and in 1891 Rank opened another, much larger, mill, Clarence Mill, beside the river Hull. Rank recognised that the whiter flour produced by the new roller-mill method was extremely saleable. Clarence Mill soon had to be enlarged further, and from 1904 Rank began opening mills in London and South Wales. The growth of the industry made Hull a centre for the import of foreign grain. Relatively low dock dues and competitive railway rates also made Hull an attractive port for the import of grain for transport elsewhere

78 *Plan of Hull, 1867, by Goodwill and Lawson.*

79 *Kingston Cotton Mill, Cumberland Street,*
from an engraving by Archibald and Stoole.

in the country, and whereas in 1870 39,050 tons were imported, by 1911 imports had reached 885,000 tons.[3]

The town's docks and railway were important factors in the rise of the fishing industry from the 1840s. In 1841 only four men and boys were employed in the industry but 10 years later the number had jumped to 313, and in the decades that followed the industry continued to grow. In 1863 Hull had 270 fishing smacks, by the 1870s there were over 400, and by the census of 1881 1,578 men and boys worked in the industry. The introduction of steam trawlers in the 1880s led to economies in crews and the censuses after 1881 do not include men at sea. Nevertheless, the industry continued to employ 1,500 fishermen or more up to the outbreak of the First World War. For every fisherman employed by the late 19th century, there were three people employed in various ancillary trades. Fish-curing and processing were particularly important. By 1898 there were 55 smoke-houses in Hull, dealing with herrings, cod and haddock. Ice manufacturing was also a rapidly growing industry. Until the 1890s almost all the ice needed to preserve fish was imported from Norway, but by 1913 three local ice manufacturers were between them producing over 75,000 tons of ice a year and only about 6,000 tons were imported. There were at least three cod-liver oil manufacturers in the town, and *Kelly's Directory* for this year also lists five fish manure manufacturers. At the time of the outbreak of the First World War there were about 6,000 employed in the industry, more than in any other industry in the town.

Conditions on the fishing boats, especially during bad weather, were very dangerous. Boys as young as 12 were apprenticed to the skippers, often drawn from the local workhouses. They were usually poorly fed and clothed, and frequently had nowhere to live between voyages. Accidents, physical abuse and harsh punishments were commonplace. Some poor apprentice boys did not survive the beatings, and in 1882 Otto Brand, the skipper and part-owner of the *Rising Sun* fishing smack, was found guilty of the murder of 14-year-old William Pepper, and in the same year Edward Wheatfield, a mate on another boat, was found guilty of murdering an apprentice, and the two men were hanged at Leeds.

The fishing industry was brought to the town by fishermen from Ramsgate and Brixham who moved to Hull, with their boats, in about 1844, and in 1851 most were to be found living in Humber Street and in the alleys and courts of the Old Town, while their boats crowded into a corner of the Humber Dock. It would only be later in the century, after the opening of new fish docks to the west of the town, that the industry came to be focused on the Hessle Road area. Of the 313 men and boys listed in 1851, almost all give either Ramsgate or Brixham as their place of birth – they had been attracted to the town by the discovery in 1843 of an extremely productive fishing ground, known as the 'Great Silver Pit', on Dogger Bank, just 50 miles from Hull.[4]

Railways, docks and shipping

The first railway line opened on 1 July 1840, running from Hull to Selby, where it joined the line to Leeds and thus connected Hull to the West Riding. In the first week alone it carried more than 4,500 passengers. By 1844 it had brought Hull within 12½ hours of London, and faster trains in 1849 cut the journey to 10 hours. The first station was opened facing the Humber Dock on the newly laid-out Railway Street, but two years after the completion of a branch line to Bridlington in 1846, a new, larger station opened in a more central position on Paragon Street, with the old terminus becoming a goods station. By this time the Hull & Selby Railway Company had agreed to lease their two lines to George Hudson's York & North Midland line. Hudson lavished considerable expenditure on the new station and its adjoining hotel, the *Station Hotel*, later renamed

the *Royal Station Hotel* after Queen Victoria's visit in 1854. Both station and hotel were built on a grand scale in ashlar stone and in an Italian Renaissance style, complete with Doric columns in the booking hall, Doric porticos and pedimented windows to the first floor. Although a fire destroyed the hotel's interior in October 1990, the original exterior of both station and hotel survive, and the reconstruction of the hotel interior, completed in 1992, is a faithful copy of the original.[5]

80 *Paragon Station today.*

In the same year, Hudson's newly acquired line faced competition from another company. In 1848 the Manchester, Sheffield & Lincolnshire Railway reached Hull by way of the New Holland ferry and, with the opening of the Great Northern line to Peterborough in 1850, the time to London via the ferry was cut to seven hours.

More lines were opened in the 1850s and 1860s. The 3¼-mile Victoria Dock Railway opened in 1853, encircling the town to link the new (1850) Victoria Dock with the other docks. This was one of the first suburban passenger lines in the country, but this was not successful and the service was withdrawn after only 14 months.

In 1854 the Hull & Holderness line opened, linking Hull to Withernsea, which the promoter, Alderman Anthony Bannister, a Hull coal merchant and shipowner, hoped to develop as a seaside resort. Bannister was a larger-than-life entrepreneur who prided himself on his coarse manners, broad Yorkshire accent, and ability to get things done. Although Withernsea never became as fashionable as Bannister hoped, he was the creator of the modern town that thousands of Hull residents came to appreciate, particularly at weekends and Bank Holidays. In 1864 another Hull businessman, Joseph Wade, a timber merchant, completed a line to Hornsea, which he also planned to develop as a popular resort. Hornsea was already a rather refined spa town much visited by the upper and middle classes but with the coming of the railway its character changed. On August Bank Holiday in 1911 it was reported that 20 excursion trains left for Hornsea and that another 18 took 'their trainload of pleasure seekers' to Withernsea.[6]

Local businessmen protested vehemently in the 1870s that the North Eastern Railway Company, which had absorbed the Hull & Selby line in 1872, and enjoyed a monopoly north of the Humber, was setting its freight charges too high. There were also demands for a new, deep-water dock to the east of the town with new railway

81   *The* Royal Hotel *today; the name was changed when British Rail sold the hotel.*

82 *The Victoria Pier, c.1906; the view from the pier looking west. The New Holland paddle-steamer waits at the pier for its passengers, while, in the background, another ship waits to enter the Humber Dock.*

83 *The Humber Ferry Booking Office, built 1880. This was often called the only railway station in England never to see a train. The ferry service closed in 1981 when the Humber Bridge opened.*

facilities. To avoid further reliance on the North Eastern, by now thoroughly distrusted in the town, plans were put forward for a line through the Yorkshire Wolds linking the new dock to the greatly expanding South Yorkshire coalfield. The consequence was the opening in 1885 of both the Alexandra Dock and the Hull, Barnsley & West Riding Junction Railway (or H.B.W.R.J.), five years after the joint projects had been launched with a capital of £4,000,000.[7]

Following the completion of the Junction Dock in 1829 (renamed Prince's Dock after the royal visit in 1854), the Dock Company resisted pressure to risk further heavy investment for 17 years but then, within 40 years, five more docks were built. The Railway Dock was completed in 1846, opening out of the west side of the Humber Dock, close to the railway terminus in Kingston Street, and the Victoria Dock opened to the east of the Citadel in 1850, and was extended when the long-disused Citadel was demolished in 1864. Then, between 1869 and 1883 a string of three new docks opened along the western foreshore: the Albert Dock (1869), the William Wright Dock (1880) and, a little further west, the St Andrew's Dock (1883) which replaced the Albert Dock as the principal fish dock for the town and helped consolidate the fishing industry along the nearby Hessle Road. Trawler-owners had persistently complained of overcrowding in the Albert Dock and needed land near the docks to build fish-curing works, to compete with the rival port of Grimsby, where the local railway company had provided a separate fish dock in 1856. When the Alexandra Dock was opened to the east of the town in 1885, covering 46 acres, it was larger and deeper than any previous dock built in the port, accommodating the largest ships, and was equipped with the coal hoists needed for the loading of large quantities of Barnsley coal.[8]

Competition between the H.B.W.R.J. and the North Eastern forced down freight charges as hoped, and the new independent Alexandra Dock had a similar effect on the dock charges levied by the Dock Company. This, however, was ruinous for both dock companies and the H.B.W.R.J., and in 1893 the North Eastern was able to buy the Hull docks cheaply while the H.B.W.R.J. (later to be known as the 'Hull & Barnsley Railway') only avoided bankruptcy by reaching a tacit understanding on freight charges with the larger company. All this was to the great regret of Hull Corporation, which had invested heavily in both.[9]

The town's merchants and shipowners benefitted considerably from the eight-year price war, and although charges rose again after 1893, their interests continued to be served by further investment in the port. St Andrew's Dock was extended in 1897, the Riverside Quay opened in 1907, and in 1914 the town's largest dock yet was completed, the King George Dock, which covered 53 acres to the east of the Alexandra Dock.[10]

In some respects the shipping of Hull changed little between the 1830s and the 1910s, remaining centred on the Baltic and northern Europe. In 1913 two thirds of the total tonnage arriving at the port came from Russia, Scandinavia, Denmark, Germany, Holland, Belgium and France.

84 *An aerial view of St Andrew's Dock, c.1920; by this time the dock had been extended to the west. The fish train can be seen coming into the platform alongside the dock.*

85 *An aerial view of the Alexandra Dock, with Riverside Pier, c.1920.*

But in almost every other respect the industry was transformed in these years. The numbers of men employed grew considerably. The census of 1891 recorded just over 4,000 seamen living in the town, and almost as many dock labourers. The total tonnage of ships had grown enormously, and the great majority by 1913 were no longer sailing ships but steamships, which proved ideal for the Baltic trade, being much better able to navigate the Sound between Denmark and Sweden. The tonnage of shipping entering Hull approximately doubled between the early 1830s and 1860, to a little over 700,000 tons, and by 1913 it had reached 4,705,000 tons. Moreover, the number of large ships using the port also grew as the size of Hull's docks increased and the range of facilities improved. In the 1870s a ship of 3,000 or 3,500 tons was considered large but by 1891 some ships entering the port were over 10,000 tons and 19 ships built that year for Hull shipowners were over 5,000 tons. By the 1870s Hull was the third largest port in the country, behind London and Liverpool, and it would remain so until the outbreak of the First World War.[11]

The most successful of the Hull shipping companies in this period was the firm of Thomas Wilson & Sons. In the 1850s it established regular sailings to a number of Baltic ports; in the 1870s it began sailings also to Trieste, Constantinople and Odessa; and by 1885 it was advertising weekly sailings to New York and fortnightly ones to Boston. It frequently undercut its competitors and drove a number of Hull's older firms out of business. It also benefitted from the growth in emigration from Scandinavia, Russia and Eastern Europe to Britain and – in much greater numbers – to the United States, which developed from the 1870s. By the 1890s over half of these countries' emigrants to America passed through Hull. Most were simply looking for a better life, but many were Jews escaping from persecution in Tsarist Russia. By cooperation with the rail companies and Liverpool shipping companies, the Wilson Line transported emigrants to Hull, then by rail to Liverpool and from there to America. In Hull they were escorted by the police through the streets

86 *Statue of an immigrant family, arriving in Hull, en route for Liverpool and America. The statue is by Neil Hadlock and was commissioned by the Trek Foundation of America. It was erected at Humber Quays in 2001. It is estimated that about 2,200,000 people passed through Hull and other Humber ports to America between 1836 and 1914.*

in lines, direct from the docks to the railway station, where a waiting room and platform in the far corner of the station were kept especially for the migrants due to fear of infectious diseases. The waiting room survives today as the *Tiger's Rest* public house.[12]

Hull also gained from the progressive exploitation of the South Yorkshire coalfield, especially as deeper borings discovered new seams nearer to the coast. There were borings near Doncaster between 1900 and 1905, and Thorne colliery, only 37 miles from Hull, began production in 1910. A direct rail link between Hull and Doncaster had been completed in 1869, followed by the 'Hull & Barnsley' line in 1885. In 1913 4,500,000 tons of coal was shipped from Hull.[13]

Public Health and Housing

As the population of the town grew rapidly the problems of sanitation, water supplies and overcrowding multiplied. Most of the growth was outside the 'Old Town', in the working-class areas already grossly overcrowded by the 1830s. The most rapid expansion up to the 1870s was to the west of the town, particularly in South Myton, on either side of Hessle Road, which grew from 15,000 in 1831 to 54,000 in 1871. In the next few years this area would become an almost separate suburb of fishermen and their families. Rapid growth was also to be found to the north of the town, in the area between Beverley Road and the river Hull, among the cotton mills, oil mills and shipbuilding yards, while across the river, Drypool, a small parish of only about 1,800 in 1831, grew to over 12,000 by 1871. This growth continued up to the outbreak of the First World War, and the majority of those moving in to the town – from Ireland or abroad, but mostly from the surrounding countryside – were poor families attracted by the prospect of work.[14]

Improvements in public health and housing in the 1830s and 1840s were made difficult by the variety of administrative bodies. The corporation had direct responsibility for water supply, but drainage was until 1851 the responsibility of Sculcoates and the Hull and Myton Commissioners, and neither body had responsibility for Drypool. Moreover, the Public Health Act of 1848 ensured that those charged with the levying of rates continued to be chosen by a middle-class electorate, and this would prove to be an even bigger obstacle to reform.

In the autumn of 1847 a fearful epidemic of cholera was raging in Russia, one of the town's most important trading partners, and it was then that a local sanitary committee drew up the first thorough report on the town's public health. First, the difficulties of providing an adequate system of drainage were described. The town suffered from having a series of open agricultural drains cutting through it, and, because of its position on low-lying land, sewage could not be made to flow swiftly into the Humber without spending a considerable sum on deep sewers and powerful pumps. Up to this time the rate payers had not been keen on such expenditure and consequently the sewage system consisted of a series of short sewers emptying into open land drains, which in turn flowed into the river Hull. During the high spring tides the poorer areas, close to the river, could be flooded with the sewage.[15]

The supply of clean water was the second challenge. The spring water from Anlaby, which had supplied the town since the 13th century, was insufficient, and in 1842 a new waterworks was built at Stoneferry, on the river Hull, to pump water from the river. The works were completed in 1845 but, to avoid expense for the rate payers, the water was not drawn sufficiently high upriver to avoid pollution at high tide. The water-borne nature of some diseases, including cholera, was not yet recognised, but many in the town, including some doctors on the sanitary committee, were still rightly concerned about this development.

Another major health hazard identified was 'scavenging', which employed about 300 men and boys in collecting the town's 'night soil' (waste from privies and cess pools). The collections were irregular and resulted in enormous 'muck-garths', close to the housing of the poor. The committee also drew attention to the overcrowded churchyards of both St Mary and Holy Trinity, although this was being tackled. A cemetery company formed in 1846 had opened a new cemetery in Spring Bank in 1847.

Fears of the cholera epidemic grew in 1848 when it reached Hamburg, from which many ships came regularly to Hull, and in September two sailors on a steamship from Hamburg docked in Hull were suffering from the disease. At first nothing more happened, but then, during the following summer, many hundreds of Hull's poorer inhabitants were stricken and mortality rates shot up. The disease reached its peak in the first three weeks of September, when 500 died every week. Altogether, 1,834 died of cholera in Hull, the highest mortality rate in the country. As E.F. Collins, the editor of the *Hull Advertiser* and a leading reformer, pointed out, this was a disease of the poorest in the town. Its most devastating impact was in the Old Town and the new slums to the north and west, particularly on either side of Hessle Road.[16]

When Dr Sutherland, of the General Board of Health, visited the town in July he made a series of recommendations to the poor law guardians to reduce disease, but when he returned in September his instructions had been completely ignored, and the epidemic was regarded by the guardians as 'a divine judgement utterly beyond human aid, and against which no means of life could be of any avail'. The muck garths were particularly condemned. He wrote scathingly: 'in the whole course of a pretty extensive experience, it has never been my lot to be brought into contact with a state of things altogether so abominable, or considering the present state of public health, so dangerous'.[17]

The public health debate following the cholera outbreak divided the town and the council. E.F. Collins had no doubt that the outbreak demonstrated the need for radical reform, including slum clearance. As the cholera death rate began to fall again, at the end of September 1849, Collins wrote in his paper:

> Cholera is a physical evil to be combated by physical remedies. To combat it, or rather to prevent its approach ... we must clear out such places as Stewart's Yard, Broad Entry, and Narrow Entry, where the people are weekly poisoned with foul smells and nauseous impurities as patent to the senses of all men as Hull itself.[18]

Collins drew attention to the appalling state of the housing most badly affected by cholera. In the St Paul's district of Sculcoates many of the poorest families lived in a single room. In Flagged Square 70 people lived in four small houses and in Howard's Row on Sutton Bank (north of Drypool) there were 20 four-roomed houses with nearly 300 people living in them, mostly Irish. In the north-west suburbs, occupied by impoverished cotton-spinners, up to 12 persons occupied a single room in the large houses in Mill Street. The smell in these houses was unbearable. The walls were black with dirt, and the courts and alleys contained such accumulations of filth that it was impossible to keep clean, despite heroic efforts by determined wives and mothers.[19]

In 1851, under the Public Health Act passed three years earlier, the town council became the local board of health, but reformers were outnumbered by those who wished to avoid expenditure, backed by the majority of the ratepayers. The reformers were led by doctors, most notably Sir Henry Cooper, and businessmen, including the town's two largest shipbuilders, and by Collins of the *Advertiser*, but they were unable to persuade the ratepayers to dig deeper into their pockets in the interests of public health. In 1854 a draft bill proposed to raise the money needed by ending the practice of derating houses let for less than £6 a year but, following an extremely noisy and angry public meeting in May, the final Act was much watered down, and simply gave the local board the power to provide cemeteries and introduce building regulations.

Although the reformers persuaded a majority on the local board to support a new sewage system, which would take the town's sewage into the Humber, the final scheme in 1862 was a low-cost version, lacking the pumps needed at high tide. The victory of the ratepaying interests on the local board had been assured when Charles Todd, a leading opponent of the 1854 bill, became clerk to the board in 1859. He boasted in 1862 that in the previous three years he had managed to reduce the rates from 2s. to 1s. 6d. and had turned the board's debt of £8,500 into a surplus of over £8,000.[20]

The 1850s and 1860s did see some improvements in public health, none more important than a greatly improved water supply. The cholera outbreak had caused the council to question the wisdom of extracting water from the river Hull, leading to a proposal of local plumber and glazier William Warden to carry out an experimental boring at Anlaby to perhaps increase the ancient spring's output. Warden's prediction of success proved justified, and in 1862 the installation of pumping machinery was completed. During the next 40 years the area of supply was constantly increased

87 *Pearson Park, c.1900, from a postcard sent in 1906.*

and by 1905 the pumps at Anlaby were providing high-quality spring water to over 25 square miles, and to a population of 254,000, saving countless lives.[21]

Another achievement was the town's first public park, People's Park, later Pearson Park, which opened on Beverley Road in 1860. Forty-two acres of land were given to the board by the mayor, Alderman Zachariah Pearson, which the board then had landscaped. It also opened a municipal cemetery in 1862, next to the privately owned General Cemetery, and widened a number of roads in the Old Town.[22]

88 *Pearson Park today, little changed in a hundred years.*

When the local board was wound up in 1876, with its responsibilities passed to the town council, many felt disappointed about how little had been achieved. Sewage still drained slowly, unpumped, towards the Humber and, more dangerous still, vast muck garths were still piled up by the 'night soil men' before being sold to farmers. According to local historian James J. Sheahan, writing in 1865, 18 contractors, employing about 400 men and boys, were collecting about 100 tons of night-soil every day, and 10 years later little had changed.[23]

Another insanitary, but very common, practice was to use refuse in foundations for building sites, particularly for cheap working-class houses. A report on the town in 1882 found that:

> All the nondescript putrescible organic matter that is to be found in the market, stall, and shop sweepings, kitchen refuse, street scrapings, and dust heaps of a great seaport town (conspicuously fish-heads and bad oranges) have gone to form the ground on which many of the back streets of Hull are built.[24]

The death rate in the town in the 1870s – 24 per 1,000 of the population – was only a little lower than in the cholera years of the 1840s, when it had averaged 27.5, and it was feared that the large numbers of immigrants now passing through the town could only increase the danger of epidemics.

In the second half of 1881 the town was indeed struck by another major epidemic, although there was no reason to blame those on their way to America. Scarlet fever that year killed 689, almost all babies and young children. Local doctors insisted on a government inquiry into the town's sanitary arrangements, and this was duly held the following year. This time, mindful of the general concern felt in the town, the council had no choice but to act on the recommendations, in spite of the cost. Consequently, pumps were fitted to the outfalls of the drainage system in 1883-4; a new fever hospital was built – something Dr Sutherland had recommended more than 30 years before; a refuse destructor was built in 1882, bringing an end to the practice of using household waste in house foundations; and the post of medical officer of health became a full-time appointment.

The epidemic also prompted the formation of a new Sanitary Association, led by the Revd Joseph Malet Lambert and the editor of the *Eastern Morning News*, William Hunt. In 1883 they launched their own inquiry into the housing of the poor. They found the worst conditions in the oldest parts of the town, where most of the houses were still being let in single rooms, but squalor and vice were found throughout the poorer areas. William Hunt, like Collins before him, saw his newspaper as a means of carrying the message of reform. He told his readers that the streets off Hessle Road were comparable 'with the foulest slums in Constantinople', and that in the slums the town sewage overflowed from decrepit privies, lying in the courts and yards in great puddles. The houses were filthy, broken windows were found stuffed with rags to keep out the rain and cold, and in some homes the inhabitants had no furniture at all and slept instead on straw. Pig-keeping was common, and in many courts the inadequate space was shared with pigs, cows, horses and poultry, as well as innumerable cats and dogs. Although it was omitted from their final report, the investigators also found evidence of widespread abuse of women and children, of prostitution and incest. Their report, as quoted in the *Eastern Morning News*, referred only to 'the most repulsive forms of vice' which they found the poor 'constantly subject to'. An improvement in living conditions, they concluded, had to be achieved before there could be hope of 'any general moral or religious improvement'.[25]

Members of the Sanitary Association also drew attention to the gradual increase in infant deaths from infantile diarrhoea. During the 1870s the average number of deaths per year from this illness was 237, with most of the victims under a year old. In the first decade of the 20th century the mortality rate averaged 311 per year and was still rising. The worst pre-war year was 1911, when 608 young children died. By 1900 the sanitary committee had undertaken a detailed investigation, suspecting a link between the prevalence of the disease in Hull and the prevalence of privies. In 1900 there were virtually no water closets at all in the working-class areas of the town but nearly 50,000 houses were using privies. The sanitary committee discovered those towns which had converted privies to water closets were the least likely to suffer from high rates of infantile diarrhoea. The sanitary committee recommended that Hull do the same, starting with the worst slums, the 11,000 or so back-to-backs. A private Act of Parliament would be needed to impose the conversions and to undertake the considerable expenditure required, but when the proposal was put to a poll of ratepayers in 1902 it was rejected, and the mortality rate for infantile diarrhoea continued to rise.

By 1914, therefore, the housing of the working classes of Hull was little better than in the 1830s and 1840s. The privy was still ubiquitous and the labours of the night-soil men still essential. Many thousands still lived in single rooms or tiny houses, in many cases without proper ventilation, in dark courts and yards. The quality of drinking water had improved but there were few other changes. A local Act of Parliament in 1903 allowed the council to ban the building of new houses without water closets, but this, plus the demolition of 779 exceptionally unhealthy houses, was the only progress made in the last years before the First World War. Without government subsidies there could be no hope of Hull following the example of Liverpool and Birmingham and building cheap, good quality houses for the poor. Municipal housing, like the removal of privies, would have to wait until the 1920s.[26]

Prostitution, pauperism and the New Poor Law

Throughout the 19th century a great many families lived constantly on the edge of dependence on poor law handouts, always hungry and in debt, and plunged into penury whenever the main breadwinner was laid off, or killed or maimed, as was not infrequently the case for the families of fishermen. For casually employed dock workers and seasonally employed seamen there were many months with little or no money coming into the house. To make matters worse, there was unusually little work available for women in Hull. Being a port, the town was rife with brothels (306 by 1869) and prostitutes, many actually not local girls but immigrants from Germany brought in by criminals. Juvenile prostitution was particularly common and in 1885 the town's chief constable was forced to resign and leave the country when he was discovered to be a patron of very young prostitutes. Two areas were particularly notorious, the streets around Paragon Station and the courts and alleys close to the fish docks, south of Hessle Road. In the 1880s Paragon Street was said to be a parade of prostitutes from 11 in the morning, with the numbers increasing during the day.[27]

The utter misery of so many poor families was little understood by the better off, and the poor law authorities often saw their problems as the consequence of their own moral failings, laziness and heavy drinking. The petty meanness of the New Poor Law was, however, a little less apparent in Hull in the 1830s and 1840s because the local body for some years remained independent of the Poor Law Board in London. Not all the town was included in the Hull Union; the new northern and eastern suburbs came instead under the Sculcoates Union, formed in 1837, for which a new workhouse was built in 1842-4 on Beverley Road. The Hull Union continued to use the old workhouse on Whitefriargate until 1852, when a new and larger workhouse was opened on Anlaby Road, on the outskirts of town.

The move to the new building marked the beginning of the end for the Hull guardians' independence. The London Board now insisted that conditions in the workhouse should be made 'less eligible' to reduce costs. Consequently, some of the little 'luxuries' began to disappear. The guardians were told, for instance, that they could not celebrate Hull Fair by giving their paupers plum pudding and the pauper children pennies. The regular tea and tobacco allowance also had to be cut out, as did weekend leave for the elderly.[28]

The London Board was horrified to learn that a very high proportion of both Unions' expenditure was on outdoor relief, something the Poor Law Commissioners were keen to get rid of altogether. The necessity of this form of relief in a town like Hull, where so many working people were employed in casual and seasonal work, was spelt out by the Sculcoates guardians in a petition they sent to the London Board in 1842:

> the general trade of [this] port is very fluctuating and uncertain. And one week a merchant … may have employment for many hands (when he has a ship arrives [*sic*]) and then may be many weeks or months before he could find employment for them, so that the labouring poor … have but few of them any certain master, the great bulk of them subsisting by day's work done first for one person and then another … and another large portion consists of the sailors who can only get employment during those months in which the northern ports of the continent are not frozen up.

The London Board could not suggest any viable alternative, and seasonal outdoor relief was allowed to continue in Hull. On New Year's Day, 1876, it was reported that in the previous week 841 paupers in the Hull Union had received indoor relief and 2,841 outdoor relief.

The Sculcoates workhouse at first accommodated only 500 people but in 1889 extensions were added to take in over eight hundred. By 1914 conditions had become rather more humane. One notorious rule abolished by this time was that all men and women, including elderly married couples, had to be accommodated separately.[29]

Churches, chapels and schools

The failure of the Anglican Church to reach the working classes had been made apparent by the religious census in 1834, and the church-building during the rest of the century attempted to address this. A description of a normal non-church-going Sunday in the Mill Street area in 1849 was given in the *Hull Advertiser*:

> The streets are full of the lodgers lounging about and going backwards and forwards for drink, the children running almost wild, and very frequently fights and thorough Irish rows occurring, apparently to the delight of the crowds of spectators.[30]

Up to 1844 only one of the new Anglican churches built in the town, St James's, in St James's Square in Myton, was built in the heart of a working-class area. Three more such churches followed, however, in the mid-1840s. The first was St Mark's, consecrated in 1844 to serve the notorious Groves area, for the immigrant cotton workers. In the following year St Stephen's was opened close to the equally notorious Mill Street and then, in 1846, St Paul's was completed and consecrated on the corner of St Paul and Cannon Street, another very unhealthy and overcrowded industrial area.[31]

89 *St Stephen's Church, opened 1845; an imposing Gothic church designed by Hull's leading architect, H.F. Lockwood. The church was badly damaged by aerial bombing in the Second World War and demolished in 1955. Its name survives in the recently opened shopping centre built on the site of the church.*

90 *St John's, Newland today; built in 1833, it is one of very few Hull churches still surviving from the early 19th century.*

By the time of the 1851 religious census the number of sittings in Anglican churches had reached almost 13,000, about 40 per cent more than in 1834, but the population of the town was nearly 85,000 now. Most of the new churches were not assigned their own parishes, but remained under the patronage of the vicar of Holy Trinity, the Revd J.H. Bromby, who strongly opposed the break up of his enormous parish and hindered the growth in church building quite considerably. The churches without parishes lacked funding and there was little further church building until after Bromby's retirement in 1867, by which time he was 96 years old after 70 years of service. When the Archbishop of York conducted his visitation in 1865 the Revd Bromby was unsurprisingly described as 'incapacitated for active service', and this was one of the reasons for the weakness of the Church of England in the town. It was also stated that at least five more churches were needed but there were barely funds for one.[32]

Bromby's retirement in 1867 was an opportunity for the Anglican Church to begin a new phase in its relationship with the town, and to address its failure to maintain its hold on the people. Holy Trinity Church was closed for restoration, and did not re-open until 1869, and partly to mark this event the Archbishop of York presided over a conference in October 1869 to discuss how the church might reach out to more people. While the town's population had risen from about 80,000 to over 120,000 in the previous 20 years, the number of churches had only risen from eleven to thirteen. Nonconformist chapels, on the other hand, had increased from 24 to 36, 'most of them very large'. And while Anglican clergy had opened new elementary schools, many of which were reaching working-class children, none had shown much interest in the living conditions of the poor.

From 1870 the pace of church-building quickened. Four new churches were opened between 1870 and 1874: St Matthew's on Anlaby Road, St Barnabas's on Hessle Road, St Jude's in Spring Bank and St Thomas's in Campbell Street; and eight more would follow in the next 30 years. A few clergy showed more interest in how the church could help working-class families, and the outstanding example was the vicar of St John's, Newland, the Revd Joseph Malet Lambert. He was appointed to the vicarage in 1881 and remained until 1912. From the outset he showed a considerable interest in the welfare of the poor. He quickly became one of the most active members of the Hull School Board, and later its chairman; he took a leading part in the Hull Sanitary Association, and regularly wrote articles on working-class housing for the *Eastern Morning News.*[33]

The national religious census carried out in 1851 showed that the approximate 2:1 advantage enjoyed by the nonconformist churches (in terms of numbers attending a service) revealed in 1834 had been maintained. Attendances on Census Sunday, 30 March 1851, at nonconformist services totalled 24,392, while only 12,229 attended the various Anglican services.[34]

Nonconformists continued to outstrip Anglicans throughout the 19th century, right up to the First World War. An anonymous survey published in 1881 claimed that in the previous 30 years the numbers attending Church of England services had risen by only 12 per cent, whereas Wesleyan Methodist numbers had risen by 54 per cent and Primitive Methodist numbers by 75 per cent. Some of the smaller Methodist branches lost support in the second half of the century, as did the Baptists and the Independents. For the Wesleyans and Primitive Methodists, however, the second half of the century was their period of greatest expansion. Nearly thirty Wesleyan and about twenty Primitive chapels and halls were either built or taken over between 1851

91   *The Great Thornton Street Wesleyan Chapel, completed 1842, from an engraving by L. Tallis. When it was built, this was the largest and most impressive of the Wesleyan Methodist chapels in the town. It was unfortunately destroyed by a fire in 1907.*

92 *The Methodist Central Hall, Prospect Street, today.*

and 1901, with six more added before 1914. Each of these two dominations was quick to react to any new evangelising initiative on the part of the other. A new Wesleyan chapel opening in a new locality would be quickly followed by a new Primitive chapel, and vice versa, even if there was insufficient money. In 1920, as a result of so much competitive building, only 13 of the 38 Primitive chapels built in the previous 100 years had been paid for.[35]

Both denominations built extensively in the expanding suburbs but in the first years of the 20th century – when the support for both churches was beginning to decline – the Wesleyans also built four large chapels in the older, central district, in the hope of winning back those who did not like the suburban chapels. In 1902 the Methodist Central Hall was built on Prospect Street and in 1905 Queen's Hall was built on Alfred Gelder Street, near the site of the old George Yard chapel. Thornton Hall was built in 1909 on the site of the Great Thornton Street chapel, destroyed by fire two years earlier; and in 1910 King's Hall was built on Fountain Road, on the site of an earlier, much smaller, mission chapel. All four could each accommodate over 2,000 people.

The superior numbers of Methodists over Anglicans is also indicated by the School Board elections from the 1880s, where Anglican candidates received far fewer votes than the Methodist candidates, and also by the strength of the temperance movement in the town. William Hunt, the editor of the *Eastern Morning News*, used his paper to promote temperance propaganda, and temperance hotels flourished in the 1880s and 1890s. In 1891 there were 19, with the largest being 'The Cobden', which stood on Charles Street. All 19 were owned by a

93 *Trafalgar Street church, Beverley Road, today. This church was originally a Baptist church, opened in 1906, following the union of the George Street and Trafalgar Street Baptist churches in 1903. In 1938 it became a nondenominational church.*

Methodist-run company, the 'Hull People's Public House Company'. The Wesleyans had enjoyed the support of wealthy businessmen throughout the 19th century. Two of the most successful entrepreneurs of the late 19th and early 20th centuries, the flour magnate Joseph Rank and T.R. Ferens, Liberal MP for East Hull from 1906 to 1918 and chairman of Reckitt and Sons Ltd, were both active Wesleyan Methodists.[36]

The Primitive Methodists remained a working-class church and never numbered prominent businessmen in their ranks. The same could be said of the Salvation Army, which opened its first meeting places in the town in 1881, with Temperance Hall in Mytongate and the Ice House Citadel in Cambridge Street. The rapid growth in the number of its meeting places is testimony to its success in some of the poorest parts of the town. In 1882 it opened its central hall and headquarters in Westmoreland Street, accommodating 1,800, and in the same year opened The Temple on Church Street. More meeting places opened in the next 30 years, in some cases replacing earlier ones, and in 1914 there were half a dozen Salvation Army centres scattered across the town.[37]

The Roman Catholic Church also flourished after an influx of Irish immigrants in the 1830s and 1840s, seeking work mainly in the cotton-spinning factories, boosted congregations before the 1851 census, when 1,050 attended the morning service and 600 in the evening. In 1851 there was only one Roman Catholic church in the town, the St Charles Borromeo, built in 1829 on Jarratt Street, replacing a little chapel built about thirty years before on North Street. The first Roman Catholic chapel in the town opened in about 1778 in Posterngate, but was destroyed two years later in an anti-Catholic riot inspired by the Gordon Riots in London. The strong evangelical nature of Protestantism in Hull in the 19th century tended to perpetuate anti-Catholic feeling, but as the Roman Catholic population of the town continued to increase, partly as a result of Irish immigration, so did the number of Roman Catholic churches, and three more opened by 1914. Also, a convent was opened by the Sisters of Mercy on Anlaby Road in 1857, and two more followed in 1899 and 1904.[38]

Denominational rivalry was already apparent in the provision of elementary education in the 1820s and 1830s. In 1851 more than 5,000 children were attending publicly provided day schools, most of these promoted by either Anglican clergy or nonconformist ministers. The former had been the first to provide day schools, and four church schools, affiliated to the National Society, already existed in 1837. Eight more followed before 1860, assisted by government grants available from 1833. For energetic evangelical Protestants like the Revd John Deck at St Stephen's, there could be nothing more important than ensuring that as many children as possible could read the Bible. Thus, in 1840 he opened the St Stephen's National School for the boys of this poor working-class area, followed by a separate girl's school in 1856. East of the river, a school was opened in 1840 to accompany the new church of St Mark's in the Groves area, and in 1842 a day school opened for St James's, just off Hessle Road, with a new building provided shortly afterwards. In 1846 there were 474 pupils enrolled, making it the largest school in the town. In 1852 the curate at St Mary's in Sculcoates, T.S. Bonnin, opened a new parish school on Bank Side, and the following year the first of the 'new churches', St John the Evangelist, which opened in 1792, finally acquired a day school by taking over the Savings' Bank School. Up to this time it had only had an infants' school. A new National school opened on Humber Street in 1857 and in 1859 another National school was opened in the industrial Trippett area. In 1864 the National school at Drypool, opened in 1828, was rebuilt and expanded to meet the demands of a much enlarged population, but there were to be no further church schools built until after the introduction of the 1870 Education Act, which both Anglicans and nonconformists alike saw as a challenge to denominational education.[39]

The great achievements of the Church of England in day school provision could not be matched by even the Wesleyan Methodists, although they proved to be the most active of all the Protestant nonconformists. Until 1837 the Wesleyans had only provided Sunday Schools, and nonconformist families either patronised the nondenominational British Schools or one of the many private schools. However, in 1837 it was decided to convert the Mason Street Sunday School into a day school, and shortly after this the school was replaced by the much larger South Myton School, one of the largest day schools in Hull, with accommodation for over 600 by 1870. Financial difficulties were a major obstacle. Small Wesleyan day schools were also attached to the chapels in Scott Street and George Yard, but both enjoyed only a brief existence. The Congregationalists also opened a day school in 1867, next to their chapel in Albion Street, but this also had to close, and the poverty of most parents who attended the various Primitive Methodist chapels precluded day school provision. The Roman Catholics, however, were rather more successful. Their first school opened in 1829, when the new church of St Charles Borromeo was built, and it thrived. The school log books for the 1860s show that school dinners were being provided, there was a gymnasium, and the children were sometimes treated to education by magic lantern. By this time, two further Catholic schools had been opened: in 1856 St Mary's had been built to serve the area east of the river Hull, and in 1859 the nuns of the new convent on Anlaby road opened a school for infants and girls.[40]

Church and chapel provision of education was soon to be supplemented, and eventually overtaken, by secular Board schools provided from a local educational rate. The Education Act of 1870 was introduced to 'fill the gaps' left by the denominations, and in Hull the gaps were very large indeed. About half the town's children of school age were still not attending any school at all; those that did attended on average for only 2½ years, and consequently the average school-leaving age was only 10½ years old. Voluntary organisations could not keep pace with the expansion of the town's population, where the poverty of many families ensured that as long as attendance was not compulsory they would continue to send their children to work as soon as possible.

94 *The former Blundell Street School as it appears today. Opened in 1878, it was one of the first schools built by the Hull School Board. It is now a sad picture of dereliction; boarded up and awaiting demolition.*

The Hull School Board was set up in 1871 and the first new school buildings opened in 1874, providing almost 2,600 extra places; another six Board schools had opened before the end of 1878. By 1886 the Board was providing over 21,000 places in 21 schools, some of which were former voluntary schools it had taken over, and by 1897 it had 37 schools, with over 31,000 places between them. By the end of the century the School Board had replaced the denominations as the principal provider of elementary education. In 1903, when the School Board was closed down and its schools handed over to the Education Committee of the city council, it was responsible for 41 schools, containing more than 39,000 places, though there were still 22 voluntary schools with about 12,600 places.[41]

In many towns School Boards had quickly improved the quality and quantity of schools, but this was not the case in Hull. Keeping running costs to a minimum meant Hull's education rate was lower than in any comparable city and standards were well below the national average. The curriculum was restricted to grant-earning subjects, salaries were kept low and pupil-teachers were used extensively, with only one certified teacher – assisted by pupil-teachers – for every 250 pupils. Moreover, the Board only opened three 'higher-grade' schools, offering a secondary education in practical and scientific subjects: the Central Higher Grade School in Brunswick Avenue in 1891, the Craven Street School in 1893, and the Boulevard School in 1895. All three schools were well-equipped with modern laboratories but woefully short of well-qualified graduate staff. The architectural

95 *The former Brunswick House Board School today. It opened in 1890-1 as the first of the Higher Grade Board schools. Today it is the home of the offices of the Children's and Young People's Services.*

quality of the Board school buildings, however, has received much praise. Pevsner and Neave described those which still survive as 'some of the best Victorian buildings in Hull'. The earliest, built in the 1870s, such as Lincoln Street and Blundell Street, were built in the Gothic style, with pointed windows, turrets and towers; those built a little later, in the 1880s, such as Buckingham Street and Newington Primary, were given a Queen Anne style, while the first of the Higher Grade Schools, Brunswick House, has a Jacobean front and William and Mary side elevation.[42]

Middle-class parents could afford rather better than the Board schools, but a high-class secondary education provided by academic teachers was not to be found at the ancient grammar school. This, already in decline in the early 1830s, closed completely from 1836 to 1838, and when it reopened it was an unambitious school of about 50 to 60 boys, teaching English and 'commercial' subjects with no pretensions to high academic achievement. Parents who wanted more for their children (or, at least, for their sons), including preparation for a place at one of the ancient universities, had to look elsewhere. To meet this need a group of local businessmen in 1836 launched a scheme for a Hull and East Riding Proprietary School, to be financed as a private company, raising £5,000 initial capital in 200 £25 shares. It was intended to be a non-sectarian boys' school, but for many Anglican Tories this was unacceptable, and a rival body was set up to promote a second school based on strictly Anglican teaching. Two

96 *The former Kingston College, built 1837; now Kingston Youth Centre.*
The college was originally considerably larger than this.

high-quality boys' schools were therefore established, Hull College, nonconformist and Whig, on Spring Bank, and Kingston College, Anglican and Tory, in Beverley Road. Both flourished at first, recruiting academic staff and sending a number of local boys to Cambridge. There was, however, considerable apathy towards education among the Hull business community and neither school survived the 1840s depression. Hull College closed in 1845 and Kingston College followed two years later, and it would be more than 20 years before another similar initiative was launched.[43]

In 1867 local businessman Robert Jameson launched a new proprietary college for boys as a limited liability company, the Hull and East Riding College. Like its predecessors, it struggled in the face of public apathy. Not all the shares could be sold and it was plagued by financial difficulties. In 1893 it closed down when a well-endowed rival school, Hymers' College, opened. But during its short life high standards were achieved, the Cambridge 'local' examinations were introduced into Hull, and for 20 years it was the town's leading school. In the 1880s, under its principal Francis Bond, the numbers on roll rose to 190 and it established a reputation for excellence, particularly in science teaching. In nine years its boys won 30 university scholarships and exhibitions.

The college's survival was helped by the continuing sad state of the grammar school. The Tudor schoolroom in which the school was housed was in a ruinous state by the 1870s, and in 1878 it was obliged to move into the Congregational Church schoolroom in Baker Street, where the number of pupils fell to as low as forty. In 1885 there

97 *Hymers' College, Hymers' Avenue, today.*

was even talk of handing it over to the School Board. Its revival came in the 1890s, following a move to new premises in Leicester Street and the appointment, in 1893, of an energetic and able headmaster, J.E. Forty. Under his leadership the curriculum and finances of the school were reorganised and the numbers of boys enrolled rose to 250 by 1900. After the First World War the school regained its reputation for academic excellence. In 1914 the independent, though rate-aided, Hymers' College, was still the best secondary school for boys in the city, and today it remains an extremely highly regarded, and high-achieving, independent school, now co-educational.[44]

For middle-class girls only small private schools offered secondary education for most of the 19th century, and some of these concentrated only on teaching social accomplishments. However, at least one particularly academic private school for girls, run by the Bremner sisters in Anlaby Road, offered to prepare girls for the Cambridge 'Locals', and in the 1880s Miss C.S. Bremner campaigned successfully to open the town's first public secondary school for girls. Hull High School for Girls was opened in 1890, financed by the locally supported Church Schools Company, and Miss E.H. Cochrane was appointed the first headmistress.[45]

For some of the town's more conservative inhabitants this was a controversial and unwelcome development. Far greater controversy, however, was created by the government's decision in 1902 to give church schools financial support from the rates. Nonconformists were horrified, and some would not pay the education rate unless the law was changed. The Hull and District Passive Resistance League was formed and in September 1904 passive resisters were brought before the magistrates for non-payment. The most determined were sentenced to a short spell in Hedon Road gaol; among them the secretary to the League, the Revd W. Boswell, and fellow nonconformist the Revd W.R. Wilkinson. While in prison their supporters gathered outside to sing hymns and on their release they were greeted as heroes. Denominational rivalry was clearly still very much alive in Hull.[46]

While religious divisions could still stir up such passion, those who argued for better education found themselves unable to muster much enthusiasm. Perhaps the greatest failing was in publicly funded elementary and secondary education, where class sizes remained enormous and the schools badly underfunded, even after the 1902 Education Act transferred responsibility to the city council. But Hull was also far behind in the provision of technical and commercial education. This had been first highlighted in 1884 by the report of the Royal Commission on Technical Instruction. A School of Art had been opened in the town in 1861, teaching applied art and industrial design, but Hull had no technical college, and when the commission's report prompted an appeal for funds to help open a college it raised only £266. In 1890, government funds were made available to local councils for this purpose and in 1895 the corporation finally opened a Municipal Technical School. Funds could not be found for a specialist building and in 1898 it moved into the far from convenient premises of the Sailors'

98   *The former College of Art, Anlaby Street; built in 1904, it has been described as 'the best of the city's Edwardian buildings'.*

Orphans Homes in Park Street, where it remained for the next 60 years. It offered courses in engineering, chemical industries and commerce, and there was also a detached School for Fishermen, teaching seamanship, in Hessle Road. In 1912 it had over 1,800 students, but the courses were mainly short, not to degree standard, and taught principally by part-time teachers in evening classes. A government report in 1913 described the premises in Park Street as ill-equipped and overcrowded, and concluded the college needed more and better qualified staff, more advanced courses and more cooperation with local industry. The Art School, situated in the Royal Institution building in Albion Street, fared rather better. When acquired by the corporation in 1903 it was in urgent need of improvement, and a striking new Italianate building was designed for it on Anlaby Road, to which it moved in 1905.[47]

Hull was also behind most other large towns in the provision of teacher-training. In 1905, however, the Roman Catholic Church opened a college for girls, Endsleigh Training College, in Beverley Road. The corporation opened its own municipal teacher-training college, for men and women, in September 1913 in a semi-rural location on Cottingham Road, with nine staff and 126 students. It had been hoped to have 100 male students and 50 female, but candidates, especially men, proved hard to find, and the college later specialised in training only women.[48]

Leisure

For a great many people beer and gin continued to offer the principal means of escape from life's hardships, but not without a social cost. When the local stipendiary magistrate, Thomas Travis, read a paper on crime and social life in Hull to the Holy Trinity Church conference in 1869, he painted a grim picture of heavy drinking, violence and prostitution. There were, he reported, 309 gin-shops and 287 beerhouses in the town. Opium and laudanum-taking were also very prevalent in the 1850s, especially among women, and at this time pipe smoking was almost as common among women as among men.[49]

More innocent fun was to be had at the Hull Fair, held annually in September and much enjoyed by all social classes, and at the theatres and music halls, both of which flourished in the town in the second half of the century, in spite of occasional denunciations from the town's more puritanical clergy. A theatre had been in existence in the town since the first half of the 18th century, and in the 1830s the Theatre Royal, built in 1810 to accommodate 1,700 people, still stood on Humber Street. In 1847 the Queen's Theatre opened on Paragon Street, with accommodation for 3,000 and a huge stage, 90 feet deep, on which military spectacles could be mounted. The Theatre Royal was destroyed by fire in 1859 but in 1864 the site was bought by the newly formed Hull Theatre and Concert Company and a new Theatre Royal, holding 2,300, was built the following year. Just five years later, this theatre was also destroyed by fire and in the same year the Queen's Theatre was closed and partially demolished. But Hull was not to be without a theatre for long, for yet another Theatre Royal – the fourth in the town – was built on the site of the Queen's Theatre in 1871, and this would survive until 1909. In 1897 the Grand Opera House and Theatre was built on George Street, and another theatre, the Alexandra, also opened nearby, on Charlotte Street, in 1902.[50]

Hull's first music hall opened in the Mechanics' Institute in 1862, when concerts were held in its saloon to accompany a waxworks exhibition. These proved so popular that in 1864 a former Methodist chapel in Porter Street was purchased and converted into the Alhambra Palace Music Hall, and a third music hall, the New Palace Theatre of Varieties, opened on Anlaby Road in 1897. 'Musical and variety entertainments' continued to be held at all three sites until just before the First World War, but in 1913 the Bijou Music Hall (formerly known as the Empire) at the Mechanics Institute had to be closed down in a dangerously derelict condition, and in the same year the

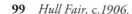

99 *Hull Fair, c.1906.*

100 *The former Regent Cinema, Anlaby Road; it was built in 1910 in just seven weeks. The towers were added later.*

Hippodrome (as the Alhambra Palace was known from 1905) was converted into a cinema. Partly because of the competition of 'moving pictures', the great days of the music hall had already passed by the beginning of the First World War, but in 1912 the old building of the former Theatre Royal was reopened as the Tivoli Music Hall, and the Theatre of Varieties would continue until 1939.[51]

Circuses had been coming regularly to Hull from the late 18th century and an equestrian troupe had appeared at the Theatre Royal in 1824. In 1864, a permanent site was acquired by Charles Hengler, on the Anlaby Road, on which he erected his Grand Cirque Varieté, a circular wooden building holding 2,500, with tiers of boxes, stalls, a pit and a gallery. A variety of entertainment was offered, mainly equestrian and acrobatic, but also minstrel shows, pantomimes and scenic spectacles, and popular religious meetings were also occasionally held. In 1898 it was rebuilt in brick and concrete but in 1910 it had to close, unable to compete with the cinema. Indeed, the building reopened later the same year as a cinema.[52]

The popularity of the cinema in the last years before the First World War was quite remarkable. Short bioscope films were first shown at Hull Fair at the end of the 19th century and by 1905 the Hippodrome Music Hall regularly included bioscopes in its programmes. In 1910 the Palace, the Empire, and the Alexandra were all licensed to show films, and in the next four years numerous existing halls were converted and new cinemas built. Twenty-one licenses were issued between 1912 and 1915 and a total of 29 cinemas or public halls were regularly showing films by 1914.[53]

The only other entertainments to claim such mass appeal were football and rugby. Rugby was brought to the town by a former York school boy, Anthony Bradley, who had

101 *The former Tower Cinema, also on Anlaby Road, opened in 1914. This was always a rather more prestigious building, as the ornately decorated classical front denotes.*

been at Rugby School. After settling in Hull, he established the town's first rugby team in 1865. The nucleus of the team consisted of Bradley and the five sons of the Revd Scott, the vicar of St Mary's. Bradley and his friends proved effective missionaries for the game, and more local teams were soon formed, including one known as Hull White Star, which quickly merged with Bradley's team to form Hull FC, as it is still known today. The team did not acquire a permanent home until 1895, when it moved into the Hull Athletic Club ground at the Boulevard, on Airlie Street, from which it gained its nickname, 'Airlie Birds'. By this time the Hull & District League had been long established and the game had a very considerable following. When Hull FC played their first match at the Boulevard a crowd of 8,000 came to watch. Hull's other principal team today, Hull Kingston Rovers, or Hull KR, 'the Robins', was formed in 1882 by a group of apprentice boilermakers in the Hessle Road area as Kingston Amateurs, playing at first on waste ground on Albert Street. The following year they joined the Hull & District League and two years later changed their name to Hull Kingston Rovers. Like Hull FC they lacked a permanent ground until 1896, when they established themselves at a ground on Craven Street, off the Holderness Road. In 1895 Hull FC was one of the founder members of the Northern Football Union, formed by 22 northern clubs breaking away from the Rugby Football Union. Hull KR joined the Northern Football Union two years later and in September 1899 played the first home derby in the NFU with Hull FC. They won 8-2 and 14,000 came to watch.[54]

The popularity of rugby football in Hull and the surrounding district made it harder for soccer to become established. The latter game was being played in the area in the 1890s, when the best team, Anlaby Soccer Club, shared the Craven Street ground with Hull Kingston Rovers, and large crowds could be expected at matches. Enthusiasm truly 'took off' in 1904 when Hull City Association FC was formed, which joined the Football League in the autumn of 1905. During the 1904-5 season it could only play 'friendlies' but its first match against a Football League club, Notts County, was watched by a crowd of six thousand. Differences with its rugby-playing landlords caused it to move home before the beginning of the 1905-6 season, to Anlaby Road cricket ground, but the success of the team in the Football League Second Division during the next few years ensured growing popularity for both the team and the game, and in 1910 Hull City came extremely close to winning promotion to the First Division, before losing out to Oldham Athletic.[55]

Cricket was first played in the area on an organised basis in the 1870s. The Hull Cricket Club was established in 1875, mainly to play local village teams. Just a few miles away, at Sutton-on-Hull, 22-a-side matches were being played in a field known as Church Mount, immediately to the east of St James's Church, in 1872, and other village teams may already have been established by this time. More teams were established in the next few years, including the Hull Zingari club, founded in 1896, but the game's popularity as a spectator sport was given a huge boost in 1899 when

County Championship matches were first played on 'The Circle' cricket ground on Anlaby Road. Large crowds flocked to see their Yorkshire heroes take on the best county teams from the rest of the country. One of the first to triumph on 'The Circle' was the great Yorkshire and England all-rounder, Wilfred Rhodes. In 1900 he took eight wickets in a single innings in a county match against Hampshire, for a mere 23 runs, a record which still stands today.

Other popular recreations at the beginning of the 20th century included cycling and swimming. The first 'penny-farthing' bicycles had appeared in the town in the 1860s and the development of the 'safety bicycle' in the 1880s prompted an enormous growth in the popularity of cycling, among both men and women. Cycling clubs were

formed and at weekends excursions of cyclists leaving Hull were a common sight. By 1891 there were 15 cycle dealers in the town, some of whom were also cycle makers. Swimming had been a popular past-time throughout the 19th century, and public swimming baths had opened on the bank of the Humber before 1805. At least three public baths were in existence in the 1830s, and when the new waterworks were opened at Stoneferry in 1845 public baths were included. A large, classically designed building was then built by the town council in Trippett Street in 1850, with individual baths for men and women, vapour baths, a women's plunge bath and a swimming bath for men only. They were closed in 1903 and the building later converted into a telephone exchange, but by this

102 *A moment of peace and calm, and a quiet chat, on the Holderness Road, c.1905.*

103 *A large crowd gather at Victoria Pier to enjoy the annual Regatta, c.1905.*

104 *The entrance to East Park from Holderness Road, in 1912.*

time other public baths had opened: on Madeley Street in 1885, and in Holderness Road in 1898 (the East Hull Baths). Before 1914 two more had opened: the Beverley Road Baths in 1905 and the Newington Baths on Albert Avenue in 1908.[56]

One very old past-time still popular in the 1880s was dog fighting. The police chose to turn a 'blind eye' to the fights, usually held on a Saturday night just off Beverley Road at Stepney. Information about a fight would be circulated by word-of-mouth. In a town with such strong Methodist roots, there were many ready to condemn all forms of gambling, as well as cruelty to animals. It was therefore not without controversy when horse racing was re-established in the town in 1888, when Hedon racecourse opened.

Those concerned with the moral health of the working classes welcomed the opening of public parks as a healthy alternative to the public house. Pearson Park was the first public park, opening in 1860, and in 1885 West Park opened on Anlaby Road, followed two years later by East Park on the Holderness Road. The latter was extended in 1913 by the completion of a large boating lake, and in 1911 the 50-acre Pickering Park was opened on Hessle Road, also with a large boating lake (today almost the only survival of the park's original layout). Free concerts given by bands in the parks in the summer were extremely popular but a very well-attended Sunday concert in 1888 provoked petitions against Sabbath desecration.[57]

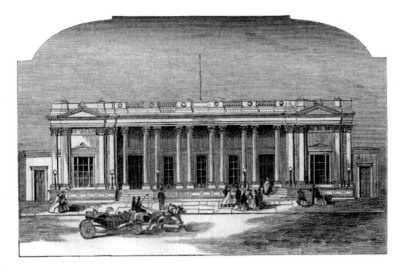

105 *The Royal Institution, Albion Street, opened 1854 and designed by Cuthbert Broderick.*

Victoria Pier also attracted many seeking a refreshing stroll. As the display board at the Victoria Pier explains today, 'Hull folk would wile away a pleasant afternoon on the pier admiring the river traffic and watching the arrival and departure of the Humber Ferry'. The city's official handbook in 1909 claimed, 'the air here is fresh and bracing. Every type of vessel is to be seen from this delightful promenade.'

The century before the First World War saw intellectual societies flourish as never before. The 'Hull Literary and Philosophical Society', established in 1822, proved very popular and had a membership of 457 by 1885. In 1837 it was meeting in the recently opened Assembly Rooms in Kingston Square, but in 1855 it moved into the newly built, and rather grand, Royal Institution on Albion Street. While the Society occupied the east end of the building, the subscription library, founded in 1775, used the west end. In 1879 a group of the society's members set up a separate Hull Literary Club, to promote research into local history and to publish local writers, and in 1880 the Hull Scientific and Field Naturalists' Club was established. Both groups, like the Literary and Philosophical Society, organised lectures and excursions and published an annual journal. In 1888 a Hull Geological Society was formed, in 1893 the East Riding Antiquarian Society, and in 1896 the Hull and District Philatelic Society. The museum of the Literary and Philosophical Society was also housed in the Royal Institution. In 1900 the society handed it over to the city council but the Royal Institution remained its home until the bombing of the Second World War, when the museum exhibits perished with the building that housed them.[58]

'We poor labouring men'

Lacking a large population of skilled artisans, trade unionism came rather late to Hull, except among boot- and shoemakers and the joiners working in the shipyards.

Consequently, Chartism had also had relatively little impact on the town. From the 1880s, however, 'New Unionism' (the establishing of trade unions among semi-skilled and unskilled workers) became a powerful force among the rapidly growing numbers of dock labourers, seamen, railway workers, shipbuilders and shipwrights. An outbreak of strikes in the summer of 1881, organised by shipwrights, tramway employees, marine firemen, seamen and dock labourers, helped to foster trade unionism. By 1886 the Hull Boilermakers' and Iron Shipbuilders' Society claimed to have 1,000 members, including 150 13-18 year-olds. In 1893 the Amalgamated Society of Engineers had 1,137 members in Hull, while trawlermen were organised in the National Federation of Fishermen; 800 bargemen and lighter-men were unionised, many in the Dockers' Union, which also claimed to have 1,500 members in the seed-crushing industry besides many hundreds of dockers; the Railway Workers' Union had 800 members and the Hull Seamen's Association 1,000 members.[59]

Trade unionism was encouraged by the success of the London dock strike in August 1889, and there were strikes in Hull that summer among engineers, shipwrights and seamen. During the next few years militancy among the Hull dockers seems to have increased, and in February 1893 dockers unloading three barges refused to continue work because one of the crew was not in the union. Their employer, Hull's most successful and wealthy shipowner, Charles Wilson, responded by re-joining the Shipping Federation (which he had left earlier because of its aggressive opposition to trade unionism) and announced he would now support the Federation's 'British Labour Exchange', which recruited 'free labour' to work in the docks and refused work to trade unionists not willing to work with 'free labour'. He also announced that his firm would not allow foremen or clerks to join any union. When the Exchange started operating, on 4 April, there was high unemployment in the town, and the union's bargaining position could hardly have been weaker. There were only two days work a week available for just 2,000 men and the situation was made worse by the Board of Guardians refusing to organise relief through public works, and the failure of the mayor's hardship fund, which raised only £255.

On 5 April the first 250 'free labourers' arrived from London, with another 500 the following day. Police from Leeds, Nottingham and London were brought in to protect them, and a detachment of 160 men from the Royal Scots and a troop of dragoons were needed to reinforce the police. The 'free labourers' and their protectors were repeatedly pelted with stones; the railway carriages carrying them to the docks had their windows smashed, and on at least one occasion the police had to make a baton charge to break up a crowd of 2,000 dockers who were stoning them. When a fire broke out in the Citadel timberyards on the night of 23 April it was widely seen as the work of desperate strikers. By this time the strike was clearly failing. Wilson and his fellow owners were bringing in free labour from across the country and even from Holland and Sweden; their clerks were being employed to empty ships, and unemployed men were queuing up to work as strike breakers. Moreover, the strikers and their families were starving, for their union lacked the funds needed for strike pay. On 19 May the union agreed a humiliating settlement, accepting that their members would in future work with non-members and that neither foremen nor gangers would be allowed to join the union from now on. Also, no union officials would be allowed on the docks. Militant unionism came to an abrupt end and there would be no further large-scale strikes until 1911, when London police were once more brought in to help break a dockers' strike, and violent clashes between police and strikers occurred again.[60]

A city at last, with the architecture to match

As part of the official celebrations of Queen Victoria's diamond jubilee, in 1897, a number of the country's larger towns, including Hull, were granted city status. The port had been for many years the third busiest in the country, behind only London and Liverpool, its population had exceeded 200,000 at the time of the last census in 1891, and the built-up area now stretched for two or three miles along the roads radiating from the old town centre. As well as the working-class suburbs, new areas of middle-class housing had also sprang up. The wealthier merchants had moved out to the villages west of the city early in the 19th century, and other middle-class families could be found in what Pevsner called the 'stuccoed villas and imposing terraces' built in the 1840s and 1850s along Anlaby Road, Spring Bank and Beverley Road, or in Pearson Park, which by the late 1860s was surrounded by grand villas. Also, from about 1870, the tall Victorian houses and tree-lined boulevards, which can still be seen, began to appear in the area known as 'The Avenues', just to the west of Pearson Park.[61]

Above: 106 *Tram on the Holderness Road, c.1905. The H on the rear of the tram shows that it is the Holderness Road tram.*

107 *The Avenues; houses on Salisbury Street, designed by George Gilbert Scott, jnr, 1877-9.*

Many now commuted by tram into the city centre, to the shops and offices still found in the Old Town, or a little to the west of it, towards Paragon Station. The first tramway opened in 1875, just 1½ miles of double track along Beverley Road, but others soon followed, and by the summer of 1877 horse-drawn trams could also be found on Spring Bank, Hessle Road, Holderness Road and Anlaby Road, and through the Old Town to Victoria Pier. In 1886 the first steam trams appeared, in Drypool, and in 1897 the corporation, which had acquired the trams in 1893, announced its plans for the electrification of the horse tramways. Electric trams started service in July 1899, first on Anlaby and Hessle Roads, and in 1900 on Holderness Road and Spring Bank. In 1909 the first motor bus service began, running from North Bridge to Stoneferry Green. Electrification greatly improved the speed of the trams and in their first six months of operation, on just two streets, they carried 4 million passengers. It also brought to an end a system that had grossly overworked both men and horses. The horse trams usually worked 14 hours a day with just one day off once a fortnight.[62]

The town's pride in its new city status was reflected in numerous grand public buildings erected in the first few years of the new century as part of a new city centre

108   *Tram on King Edward Street, c.1905. The statue of Sir William de la Pole can be seen in the foreground, standing at the King Edward/Jameson/Prospect Streets crossing. In the background is the Wilberforce Monument, and the domes of the Dock Office (now the Maritime Museum) can also be glimpsed in the distance.*

109 *The City Hall today;
completed in 1909.*

110 *The town hall,
built 1862-5, designed by
Cuthbert Brodrick; although
a fine example of Victorian
Gothic architecture it would
survive fewer than fifty years,
being replaced by Edwin
Cooper's guildhall in 1916.*

designed by the architect Alfred Gelder, the son of a farmer from North Cave and now a councillor and (in five successive years) mayor of Hull, who was knighted for his achievement in 1903. By 1900 most of the squalid buildings to the west of the Queen's Dock had been cleared away, and Queen Victoria Square was laid out in 1901-2, with a fine statue of the queen in the middle. Two wide new streets were laid out running from it, Alfred Gelder Street eastwards towards Drypool Bridge, and King Edward Street north-west, towards Spring Bank and Beverley Road. To the east of the square there already stood the impressive Docks Office, built in the late 1860s and today the Maritime Museum, and immediately to the west a new city hall was erected between 1903 and 1909 (and still stands today), designed by Joseph H. Hirst, the first city architect. This is an imposing example of Edwardian Baroque in stone ashlar, with an entrance flanked with Tuscan columns and crowned with a copper-covered dome; inside a grand staircase leads up to a large galleried concert hall.

Most grand of all was the new guildhall, erected between 1904 and 1916 and designed by the young Edwin Cooper. He was still only 30, and had won a competition to design an extension to the existing town hall, built in 1862. The original intention was to add law courts, a council chamber and offices along the new Alfred Gelder Street, but when these were completed, in 1911, it was decided to demolish the existing town hall and erect a new one, facing Lowgate, as grand as the new extension, and this was completed between 1913 and 1916. The total effect is extremely impressive. The elevation facing Alfred Gelder Street is 35 bays long and particularly grand, lacking only a fine square in front of it so that it can be viewed and appreciated properly.[63]

While Cooper's *tour de force* was being completed, other new buildings were also, in Pevsner's phrase, demonstrating 'this Edwardian spirit of improvement'. To the north, on Albion Street, a new Central Library was built between 1900 and 1901, in red brick with stone bands and dressings, and mention has already been made of the teacher-training college built between 1909 and 1913 on Cottingham Road. Meanwhile, to the east of the city, Sir James Reckitt, local industrialist and benefactor, was

111 *The new law courts, Alfred Gelder Street, c.1912.*

112 *The guildhall, designed by Edwin Cooper and completed in 1916.*

113   *The former General
Post Office, Lowgate.*

114   *Hull telephone box and
Victorian letter box, Salisbury
Street, today.*

having Hull Garden Village laid out, setting much higher
housing standards for future developers to follow. To the
west of the city new developments included Lee's Rest
Houses, built between 1914 and 1915, and Pickering
Park and Pickering Almshouses on Hessle Road, built
between 1909 and 1913. The former General Post Office,
built on Lowgate in 1908-9, is a monumental three-
storey building of Portland stone, built in Edwardian
Imperial style on the site of the medieval de la Pole
manor house.[64]

Perhaps the most well-known example of civic
initiative dating from this pre-war period is the city's
telephone system. The corporation was granted a licence
to operate a telephone system in 1902, and Hull can
still boast that it is the only city in the country not
under the British Telecom monopoly. The corporation
no longer runs the system – it was privatised in 1999
– but the very distinctive cream-coloured telephone
boxes, without the royal badge of GPO boxes, can still
be seen throughout the city.[65]

NINE

The Twentieth Century and Beyond

The First World War

The outbreak of war on 4 August 1914 was greeted in Hull, as in every British town, with enormous enthusiasm. Kitchener's poster was soon everywhere and patriotic war-fever united all classes. The little recruiting office at 22 Pryme Street could not cope with the numbers queuing up to enlist and from 6 September the corporation had to make rooms available in the City Hall. Soon there were military bands playing on the balcony, speeches were made in the square urging young men to do their duty, and recruiting posters hung from the walls. By the end of January 1915 more than 20,000 had enlisted. No self-respecting young man wanted to 'miss the fun', and for many the prospect of regular pay, three meals a day plus a uniform was attractive indeed, besides the thirst for adventure, opportunity for foreign travel, and the simple pressure of friends enlisting.[1]

Many of those who volunteered in the first few months could not only join up with their friends but also expect to fight alongside them in a 'Pals' battalion. Early in September 1914 the War Office had allowed men in Liverpool to enlist for battalions made up entirely of local men and were so overwhelmed that within a few weeks they had enough to form four battalions. Although a smaller town, Hull's 'finest' were keen to put together their own Pals' battalions, and very quickly formed the 10th, 11th, 12th, and 13th Battalions of the East Yorkshire regiment, known respectively as the 'Commercials', the 'Tradesmen', the 'Sportsmen and Athletes' and, with a little Yorkshire humour, 'T'others'. Each comprised 1,050 men. Uniforms did not arrive until November, and for a few weeks the new recruits trained and drilled at Wenlock Barracks in their civilian clothes, marching through the streets in their flat caps, boaters and trilbies. One new recruit even carried his umbrella and put it up when it started to rain, much to the annoyance of his officer. The 'Commercials', mainly middle class professionals, were regarded by the other recruits as a 'nobs' battalion. Ernest Land of the 11th later recalled: 'they used to snob you a bit, they was all clerks and teachers'.[2]

In 1915 another battalion was formed as a reserve, made up of men below the army's minimum height requirement and known as the 'Bantams'. Men who were too old for war service could join a 'rifle club' to help defend the country in the event of an invasion. The Hull Golf Club was particularly keen to promote this initiative and in July 1915, after months of campaigning, persuaded the government to give the idea official recognition, creating the East Yorkshire Volunteer Brigade.[3]

The true reality of the war's horrors, however, soon made themselves felt, first in the long lists of casualties and then, from June 1915, with the arrival of Zeppelin bombing. When the first attack came it was entirely unexpected and Hull was almost completely unprotected. On Sunday, 6 June 1915 Kapitänleutnant Mathy, commander of Zeppelin 'L9', was attempting to reach London but by the time he was over the English coast, at about 7.30 p.m., near Bridlington, it was clear that the wind would prevent him from carrying out his instructions. He therefore instead followed the line of the railway to Hull. He reached the city just before midnight. It was a clear night and the Zeppelin was visible from the ground, picked out by the Paull searchlights which tracked its progress across the city. The commander of the Humber Defences, Major General Ferrier, had given instructions at 9.30 p.m. that all lights in the city must be put out. As the airship approached the city it dropped flares to light up the docks before dropping its bombs. Hull had no anti-aircraft guns and the Zeppelin met no resistance except for the guns of H.M.S. *Adventure*, which was then being repaired in a Hull shipyard. It was not hit and passed slowly over the city, at about 3,000 feet, dropping its deadly cargo: 13 high-explosive shells and 50 incendiary bombs. The first cluster fell in Waller and Craven Streets, a densely packed area of working-class housing on the east side of the city, and a second cluster fell on Clarence and Church Streets, a similar area of working-class houses near the east bank of the river Hull, causing many fatal casualties and much damage. Another concentration of bombs then fell on the Old Town, hitting property in the market place, on Queen Street and High Street, causing fewer casualties but doing much damage, and one property took a direct hit and was completely destroyed, the large furniture store of Edwin Davis & Co., on South Church Side, just across the road from Holy Trinity Church. As the Zeppelin moved noisily across the city, heading westwards towards the Hessle Road area, it dropped its final cluster over the terraced houses of Campbell, Walker and Porter Streets, causing few additional casualties but again destroying many homes. Numerous fires broke out wherever the bombs fell, and the police, fire officers and members of the public were soon desperately trying to put them out and rescue those trapped beneath the rubble. The next day it was found that 40 houses and shops had

115　*The remains of Edwin Davis's shop in the market place
following the Zeppelin raid of 6 June 1915.*

been destroyed and 24 people killed. There were also numerous injuries and about 40 people had to be treated at dressing stations.[4]

But even as the last bombs fell, a second, very different, tragedy was unfolding. After the warning had been given of the Zeppelin's approach large crowds had gathered in the streets, and some were determined to take revenge for the bombing by attacking the property of those in the city thought to be of German origin. During the previous half-century many German émigrés had settled in the city, and although their only 'crime' was to have a German-sounding name, they now found themselves the objects of hatred. Any shops whose names suggested a German origin were regarded as fair game, and the numerous German-owned pork butchers' shops across the city were a particularly popular target. There had already been violent attacks on butchers' shops in Hessle Road and Charles Street just over three weeks before, after the sinking of the Cunard liner, the *Lusitania*, inflamed by the local press, especially the *Eastern Morning News*. The editorial of this newspaper had told its readers:

> The time has come when we must treat all Germans as our deadly foes. Too long we have been parleying with the enemy within the gate. We must begin our warfare at home. We have had too much of the German in England since the war began. We have husbanded spies. We have given liberty – not to say licence – to all sorts of conditions of Germans. There must be no more of it. We must look upon the Germans as people not to be trusted.

During the *Lusitania* riots the police had protected the shops' inhabitants and minimised the damage, but during the Zeppelin raid riots the police were too involved in fire-fighting and rescue work to intervene. Altogether, between midnight and 5 a.m. 18 properties were attacked, mainly in the Holderness Road, Caroline Street and Charles Street areas. Late in the following afternoon fresh attacks were launched on other properties across the city, the most serious being in New Cleveland Street, where a crowd of about 700 attacked a pork butcher's shop owned by a widow, Mrs Most, whose husband had been a naturalised German. Four policemen and six soldiers were sent to protect the property and its inhabitants, and while they rescued the terrified occupants they could do nothing to protect the property, or to stop the crowd from taking away virtually all of the family's possessions. Nine properties were attacked that evening, and further attacks began the next afternoon, carrying on until about midnight, when another 16 houses and shops had their windows smashed and, where the crowds were too large for the police to prevent it, some properties again suffered looting.[5]

Many of those who suffered were British citizens and some, like Mrs Most, had members of the family who were soon to join the armed forces. Both of Mrs Most's sons would serve on the Western Front; Private Most was killed and his brother wounded. Many of the victims of the riots left the city and never returned, and none received adequate compensation from the corporation for their losses. One family that stayed, the Hohenreins, whose butcher's shop on Waterworks Street had been established in the city as early as 1850, felt obliged – like the royal family – to change their name, and in July 1915 Charles Hohenrein became Charles Ross. Fortunately, there were no more serious anti-German riots in the city.[6]

Navigational errors prevented the city from suffering another attack two months later, when the same Zeppelin, with instructions to hit Hull, instead bombed Goole by mistake, but in March 1916 two other Zeppelins reached the city and Hull was still completely undefended. Searchlights could pick out the Zeppelins but there were no anti-aircraft guns to shoot them down. The blast from one or two of the bombs completely destroyed the glass roof of Paragon Station, and the flying glass caused a great many casualties. Altogether, 17 were killed in this latest raid and many others were badly injured. Both Zeppelins were again able to hover over the city, watched in horror by the helpless people below, some of whom were seen kneeling in prayer. The first airship stayed only for about ten minutes while it emptied its bomb bay, but the second ran into thick cloud and consequently stayed over the city for about an hour, hovering between 3,000 and 4,000 feet while it waited for its targets to become visible. One policeman came across an elderly widow sitting beside a grave in the cemetery, with her pet canary in a cage beside her. When he asked why she was not at home, taking shelter under the stairs, she explained that if she had to die she wanted to be close to her late husband when it happened.

The air-raid warning siren was always referred to in Hull as 'the buzzer' and it was frequently heard as Zeppelins passed overhead, but there were only three more occasions when the city was attacked. By August 1916, when the third raid occurred, the city was defended by anti-aircraft guns, which helped boost morale, although no Zeppelin was ever actually shot down over the city. During this raid, the mist over the Humber prevented the anti-aircraft gunners from seeing their targets, and the Zeppelins dropped more than 40 bombs, killing nine people. However, when a Zeppelin next attacked, in the early hours of the morning on 25 September 1917, a fighter plane was available to take off and chase it away from the city while the searchlights kept it in their beams. By this time Zeppelin attacks on the country were becoming less frequent as so many were now being either shot down or disabled. Hull suffered one of the last Zeppelin attacks of the war, however, in March 1918, when L63 managed to find Hull by following the railway from Hornsea, and succeeded in dropping six bombs on the city, killing one person. Very little was done to help civilians protect themselves from the raids. Many were too afraid to stay in their own houses when an alarm was sounded and preferred to gather in public parks, and some built their own shelters in their gardens.[7]

As more and more men joined the forces so the number of women employed increased, and from 1916, when conscription was introduced, their role became more critical than ever. Almost all local industries took on women to replace the enlisted men, including married women with children. Mrs Annie Ralph later recalled:

> When my husband joined up I was very poor, with two children to keep, a boy and a girl. I got a job with BOCM [British Oil and Cake Mills] in Wincolmlee. They used to give me half an hour to get the children up … The foremen were still working. They were quite good though one man was hostile to us women … We used to work from six in the morning till five at night and we got good wages. I really furnished my home from what I earned. It was heavy work, barrowing and loading lorries, but the atmosphere was friendly. Then I went on a machine, cleaning and purifying linseed oil. We used to wear clogs and overalls. It was a bit noisy but I enjoyed working there.[8]

At Rose, Down and Thompson's Foundry, 359 women were employed by the end of the war, comprising a third of the workforce, although at the beginning of 1914 there had been only three. Many women were employed in heavy and unpleasant work for long hours and low pay. Mrs Emma Keeitch, interviewed in 1985, recalled how, at the beginning of the war, she was employed at Moors' and Robson's brewery in Raywell Street:

> we used to push great big barrels of beer up onto the gantries and the man then flooded them all into a pipe. And there was bottle washing. The water for that was bitterly cold … We got eight shillings a week, seven in the morning till half past five at night, five days a week and seven to twelve on a Saturday.[9]

Large numbers of women were also employed on the local tramways, particularly as conductresses, and in the Women's Land Army. Women also served as nurses, joined the Army Auxiliary Corps, or did voluntary work. The Voluntary Aid Service headquarters were set up in Peel House, at 150 Spring Bank, and was run by a committee of ladies established by Lady Nunburnholme, whose husband, Lord Nunburnholme, was the Lord Lieutenant of the East Riding of Yorkshire and the prime mover behind the setting up of the Hull Pals' battalions. As well as organising fundraising events and collecting parcels for the troops, the committee also helped coordinate hospital accommodation for wounded soldiers, provided nurses for the hospitals, and ran a number of social centres both for the troops and their families, such as the Soldiers' and Sailors' Wives Club in Mason Street, the Paragon Station Rest Station and Canteen, and a Soldiers' Club at Beverley Road Baths. Hospitals set up especially for military use included the Royal Navy Hospital in Argyle Street, the Lady Sykes Hospital in the Metropole Assembly Hall in West Street, Reckitt's Hospital at the Reckitt factory, and the Brooklands Officers' Hospital on Cottingham Road.[10]

Hull's economy was badly affected by the war but before then the port had enjoyed a period of unprecedented prosperity. The tonnage of shipping which entered the port in 1913, 6,692,000, was a record. Coal exports reached a peak in 1913, when 4,519,000 tons were shipped out, a record never again surpassed. Wheat imports were also unprecedentedly high, reaching almost a million tons in 1912. In June 1914, just five weeks before the war broke out, King George V and Queen Mary paid a visit to the city to formally open the new docks named in honour of the king. The King George Dock was the largest and deepest dock yet built in the city, designed to maintain Hull's position as one of the country's major ports.[11]

Disruption came almost immediately. Many Hull ships were caught in German ports and others which had sailed for Russia and for other Baltic ports were unable to escape through the German patrols in the Kattegat. Much of Hull's trade before the war had been with Germany but this, of course, now ceased, and trade with Russia was also greatly reduced. Consequently wheat imports fell to less than 250,000 tons by 1918; oils and seeds imports fell similarly; and coal exports were down to only 1,300,000 tons by 1916. The total tonnage of shipping entering the port in foreign trade was by 1918 only a third of the immediate pre-war levels. Many Hull-owned ships were also sunk by enemy action. The port's largest shipowner, the Wilson Line, had lost 15 of its pre-war fleet of 79 ships by 1916, and in October that year had to accept a merger with Sir John Ellerman's company.[12]

The fishing industry also suffered considerably. The Admiralty requisitioned about three quarters of the port's entire fishing fleet and their crews for mine-sweeping and submarine detection work, about 300 ships, leaving only 93 trawlers to carry on fishing. Nearly a third of all the trawlers used as mine sweepers were sunk, sometimes with the loss of all their crew, and the proportion of losses among the fishing trawlers was even higher.[13]

116 *The Cenotaph and South African War Memorial, Paragon Square, c.1925.*

By the end of the war, about 70,000 men and women from Hull and the immediately surrounding area had served in the armed forces in one capacity or another, and the cost had been enormous. About 7,000 people from Hull were killed in the war, and at least 14,000 seriously wounded or disabled. Almost a whole generation of young men were wiped out and the lives of the survivors would never be the same again. In many streets, especially in the poorer parts of the city, street shrines had been put up during the war celebrating the heroism of those who had enlisted and commemorating the dead. A few could still be seen in the 1960s and 1970s, but most of these were swept away in the slum clearance programmes of those years, and today only two survive, one on Sharp Street, off Newland Avenue, and another at the entrance to Eton Street, off Hessle Road. Memorials to the dead can also be found below the east and south-east windows of Holy Trinity Church, but the city's principal memorial is the Cenotaph, erected in 1923-4 in Paragon Square and paid for by public subscription.[14]

When news of the Armistice reached Hull in November 1918 there was an overwhelming feeling of relief, mixed with grief: far too many were never coming back. But when the men who had survived did return, in 1919, there were street parties to celebrate, with lots of cake and lemonade for the children. 'God Bless Our Children' read one banner, across the Cumberland Street party, and on 19 July 1919 a grand fireworks display was held in East Park to celebrate 'Peace Night', following the recent official ending of the war, when representatives of the new German government had signed the Treaty of Versailles in Paris.

The 1920s and 1930s; a land fit for heroes?

Hull was by no means an unemployment 'black-spot' between the wars as it did not suffer the levels of unemployment found in the north-east towns or in South Wales, but in most years unemployment in Hull was above the national average, and as a consequence of this, especially in the 1920s and late 1930s, there was a net migration away from the town. This, together with a lower birth rate, ensured that the city grew only slowly between the wars. The census recorded a population of 295,017 in 1921 and 309,158 10 years later. The war prevented the holding of a census in 1941 but what figures are available suggest that migration had caused the population to fall, and the total was down to 295,172 in 1951. The birth rate had already fallen from 33.1 per thousand in 1901 to 28.5 in 1911; and it continued to fall in the succeeding decades, to 25.8 in 1921, 19.2 in 1931 and 17.5 in 1939.[15]

Unemployment was especially high among the dockers. Of the 10,320 dockers registered in 1924 just over 28 per cent were unemployed. During the next few years about 2,000 left the docks but in 1931 half the city's 8,420 dockers were out of work, and in 1934-5 a docker could not expect to have more than three and a half to four days work a week. Shipyard workers also suffered badly. The numbers employed fell by almost half between 1923 and 1937 and during the 1920s about a third were unemployed. The city's largest shipbuilder, Earle's, closed down in 1932 and its great crane, long a landmark for the city, was taken down and sold to a firm in Shanghai. But Hull was less badly hit than many other shipbuilding areas. Just over 2,000 men were still employed in the industry in 1937, mainly in ship repairing and in the construction of marine engines.[16]

For men facing years of unemployment, and for their families, the politicians' promises in 1918 to create 'a land fit for heroes' sounded hollow, but for those in work these were decades of rising living standards, better than their parents or grandparents had ever known. Although employment in the docks and shipyards contracted, other areas expanded considerably. The fishing industry, for instance, recovered rapidly from the war. By 1923 it was employing 3,350 men and 5,360 by 1937. Most of the trawlers lost during the war were quickly replaced by the local shipyards. Even before the end of 1915 Earle's had built 40 new trawlers and another 35 had been built by Hull's other shipbuilders.

By far the largest area of employment by 1937 was the distributive and retail sector.

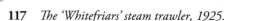

117 *The 'Whitefriars' steam trawler, 1925.*

It was the fastest growing part of the local economy, and in this respect Hull reflected a national trend. By 1923 it already employed over 11,000, more than any other sector, but during the next few years the numbers doubled to almost 23,000 employees. The building industry also grew rapidly, stimulated by the council's first – but very substantial – venture into house building. In 1923 it employed 3,360 and 6,600 by 1937. Other growth areas were in grain milling which employed 1,680 people in 1937, 70 per cent more than in 1923, and the gas, water and electricity industries, which between them grew at a similar rate and employed about 1,600 by 1937.[17]

The seed-crushing industry remained a very large employer, employing just over 9,000 people in 1937. This was one of Hull's 'might-have-been' industries. During the war there had been four large firms in this industry and one of them, British Oil and Cake Mills, had in 1917 begun the manufacture of margarine. This had seemed a very promising development but as butter became available again after the war the demand for margarine fell sharply. The firm then looked to boost profits by going into soap manufacturing, and in 1921 set up a new subsidiary, the British Soap Company, with a factory in Hull, and this proved a great success, but within four years it was selling enough soap to threaten the giant in the industry, Unilever, and consequently it was 'gobbled up' by the bigger firm. Soap production in Hull was then run down, and in 1933 it ceased altogether.[18]

There were a number of other success stories in these years. New industries were attracted to Hull as a major port. One such new firm was the Distillers Co. Ltd, who established a distillery at Salt End in 1925, manufacturing, among other products, industrial alcohol and acetone. The chocolate manufacturer Needler's had been established in the city before the First World War and now became an increasingly important employer, as did the National Radiator Company (later Ideal-Standard), which manufactured radiators and boilers; while two important drugs and surgical goods manufacturers, Smith and Nephew and Reckitt's, both expanded their workforce in the 1930s as a result of significant pharmaceutical breakthroughs. Smith and Nephew were one of the first pharmaceutical companies in the country to develop a drug to tackle strains of tuberculosis. Meanwhile, Reckitt's also developed a pharmaceutical division and produced an effective disinfectant which was harmless to the skin. This became famous as Dettol and would play a very important part in advances in hospital hygiene, especially in midwifery.[19]

Although there was a great deal of poverty, hardship and even hunger, particularly in the worst years of the Depression of 1929-31, life for many was cleaner and healthier, and quality of life for women, in particular, was improving. It was not only that women had won the vote at the end of the war; the fall in the birth rate was made possible by the introduction of effective birth control, while the infant death rate was also falling due to improvements in housing, one of the most important factors improving the quality of people's lives in these years.

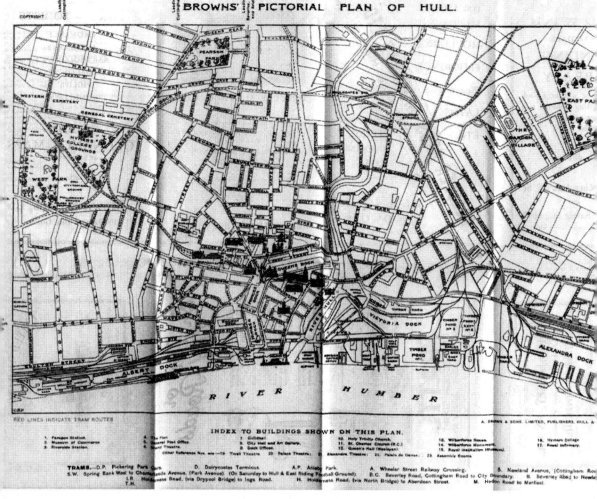

118 *Brown's Pictorial Plan of Hull, 1926,*
showing tram routes and major public buildings.

The Housing Act of 1920 initiated a revolutionary change in housing standards by offering substantial grants to local authorities and this measure, together with further Housing Acts in the 1920s and 1930s, made possible the first nationwide introduction of subsidised 'council housing'. Progress was at first slow but by the end of 1925 the first 1,000 cottage-style council houses had been built, and the private sector had built another 1,000 homes. During the next few years, between 1926 and 1928, there was a great spurt in council-house building, checked only by the onset of the Depression, and then in 1932 a second, shorter, spurt. Three large council house estates were created: in North Hull, to the north of Endike Lane; in West Hull, between Willerby Road and Priory Road; and in East Hull, to the east of Marfleet Lane. By 1935 the corporation was the landlord for about ten per cent of the population and had built 8,600 houses. The private sector had also built over 10,000 houses since the war.[20]

The improvements in the standards of housing were equally impressive. In the worst parts of the city there were as many as 130 houses to the acre but under the new housing regulations there could not be more than a dozen. The old earth closets were also rapidly disappearing in the 1920s, and by 1935 the last ones had gone, replaced by water closets. More and more houses were connected to the electricity supply; by 1932 there were 20,000 houses connected and 49,000 consumers, and during the next few years the numbers continued to increase. Large-scale slum clearance programmes began in the 1920s, spurred on by a survey published by the medical officer of health in 1925, which identified approximately 3,000 houses no longer fit for habitation, and a later survey, in 1930, added another 500 to the list. The first area to be cleared was New George Street, followed by the early Victorian slums of Mill Street, the Groves, Porter Street and Adelaide Street, and before the outbreak of the Second World War in 1939 a beginning had been made to replacing them with two ranges of five-storey blocks of flats. Not all the condemned houses had been removed by 1939, however, and there was still much replacement building needed.[21]

The clearance of Mill Street made possible the opening in 1931 of Ferensway, a wide thoroughfare running from Paragon Station to the junction of Spring Bank and Beverley Road, through a maze of slum streets and courts. The new road was named after one of the city's greatest benefactors, T.R. Ferens, the chairman of Reckitt and Sons and a former Liberal MP for East Hull, who had died the year before the road was opened. This name was an appropriate choice, not least because the original name was Quality Street. In the same year a new North Bridge was opened to the north of its predecessor, and this also helped speed the movement of traffic in this part of the city. Perhaps the most notable change in the city's appearance was the filling in of the basin of Queen's Dock, Hull's oldest dock, in 1935, and the conversion of the levelled area into a most attractive urban park, Queen's Gardens. Some regretted the lost opportunity to create an underground car park, but the landscaped gardens created so close to the city centre were soon a much appreciated amenity. The redevelopment of the area was completed by the removal of the Wilberforce Monument from its position in Queen Victoria Square, where it had stood since its erection in 1834-5, to the eastern end of the new Queen's Gardens, where it still stands today.[22]

One additional benefit of the making of Queen's Gardens was the removal of Monument Bridge, which

119   *The Wilberforce Memorial today, standing at the east end of Queen's Gardens, in front of Hull College.*

– when raised at peak times – had become an irritating obstacle to modern traffic, although, as John Markham remarked, it was 'a convenient excuse for late arrival at work'. By 1935, as new residential districts were created on the edge of the city, and as former villages such as Sutton-on-Hull and Marfleet became drawn into 'outer Hull', so increasing numbers of people commuted into the city centre every day. The majority, however, did not yet travel by car. During the 'rush hours' there were many cyclists and even greater numbers queued for a motor bus, trolley bus or tram. Hull's transport services were very good: cheap, reliable and plentiful. During the 1920s the number of trams continued to increase and a new tram depot was built in Cottingham Road. By 1927 there were 180 tram cars on 21 miles of track. In 1934, however, some tram routes were shortened to avoid duplication with motor bus services, and the first trolley buses began running in 1936, on 10 routes. In the next few years the number of trams and tram services was gradually reduced, replaced by either motor buses or trolley buses. The last tram was taken out of service in 1945.[23]

The quality of the city's schools also improved in the 1920s and 1930s, with more money being spent on education in the city than ever before. The new Director of Education for the city council, R.C. Moore, prepared a plan for the much needed improvement of Hull's schools in 1925-6. This aimed to reduce the size of classes, to increase and improve secondary school accommodation, to build new schools to meet the demands of the proposed new housing estates on the edge of the city, and to reorganise the city's schools along the lines recommended by the recent Hadow

120   *Queen's Dock in 1925, at this date still very busy with small ships and boats.*

121   *Queen's Gardens Lake today, with Hull College in the background.*

Report, including a distinct break in the education process at the age of eleven. Implementation of the plan began in 1926, initiating a new era of expansion and re-organisation. By 1939 the local education authority had built 14 schools for the new residential areas, either primary schools or schools with separate infant, junior and senior departments. The accommodation of the secondary schools was also much improved. In 1920 the girls of Newland High School (once the Brunswick Avenue Higher Grade Board School) moved into a new building built for them in 1914, in Cottingham Road, which had been commandeered for use as a military hospital during the war. In 1926 the junior section of the Municipal Technical College became the separate Riley High School, and two other secondary schools were created from former Board 'Higher Grade' schools, with improved accommodation and facilities: Craven Street School became the Malet Lambert High School, and the Boulevard School was transformed into

122 *Monument Bridge, 1925.*

Kingston High School. The Boys Grammar School, which had largely recovered from the long decline suffered in the previous century, was also given a new block in 1928 to reduce congestion, but plans for further improvements to the school's premises had to be shelved in 1939. Average class sizes were still high by comparison with post-Second World War standards, for in 1936 half of Hull's children were still in classes of 40 or more, but even this was a great improvement on the pre-1914 situation.[24]

Plans for the creation of a university college bore fruit in the 1920s, although not as successfully as might have been hoped. A carefully worked out proposal had been drawn up in 1906 but, partly because of the war, no action was taken until 1922, when T.R. Ferens bought an 18½-acre site on Cottingham Road, close to the Training College, and presented it to the corporation for this purpose. His intention was that the Technical College should be moved to this site, enabling it to become, with the Training College, the nucleus for a new university college. In 1925 he also gave the city £250,000 worth of Reckitt shares to further assist the process, and within a few months the project had finally taken off. A.E. Morgan was appointed principal in 1926, the

123 *The Cohen Building; built in 1928, this was, together with the Venn Building opposite, the original nucleus of the new University.*

University College was incorporated on 7 October 1927, and it opened its doors to its first students on 11 October 1928. Ferens' plans, however, were not realised, for Morgan had no intention of incorporating either the Technical College or the Training College into the new institution. Instead, the University College had only two faculties, of arts and pure science, and the only concession to local needs was to include courses on commerce and marine biology. The college suffered badly from lack of funds, growing only slowly in the 1930s, and up to 1939 never had more than about 200 students. Its adult education department, however, introduced in 1930, proved to be most successful, organising classes throughout the East Riding, and making the little college at least locally well-known.[25]

Although the Technical College remained at Park Street, it was able to expand and improve its facilities by detaching some of its departments. Thus the College of Commerce was founded in 1930, and in 1936 it took over the Boys' Central School in Brunswick Avenue. The Art School was also expanded, under a new principal, becoming the College of Art and Crafts in 1930, and offering a wider range of classes, including a five-year architecture course.[26]

The favourite source of entertainment was the cinema. Even before the outbreak of the First World War there had been almost thirty cinemas or other venues regularly showing films. Some of these subsequently closed but more opened during the war, when the cinema – and particularly Charlie Chaplin – became more popular than ever. Twelve more were opened between 1918 and 1938, by which time there were 36 cinemas altogether in the city, attended by many thousands of patrons a week, many of whom went almost every night. Mrs Thelma Symonds, who helped run a cinema during the First World War and in the interwar years, later recalled the era:

> the programme started off with a newsreel and then probably a short film – a comedy of some sort, and then the star film, which could be anything around an hour or an hour-fifteen minutes even. It was fitted with music – a musical score used to come with the film so the musicians had some idea of what to play, but when the talkies arrived life was very much easier because we could do without the musicians![27]

Some cinemas were literally fleapits, but much loved, especially by children, who could attend matinées on a Saturday afternoon for as little as 3d. or less. Others were almost as prestigious as their names suggested, such as the Regal, the Rex, the Regis, and the Royalty, all of which were opened in quick succession in 1934-5 by the same company. The 1930s was the great age of Hollywood, of Greta Garbo, Clark Gable, and Mae West. The first talkies arrived in 1929 and the same year three more cinemas opened, one of them the former Tivoli Music Hall, and the following year the Grand Theatre on George Street closed and reopened as a cinema.[28]

The public house also remained extremely popular, much to the dismay of the city's large numbers of teetotal chapel-goers. The pubs were, however, fewer in number than in the Victorian era. In 1901 there had been 452 pubs but many were swept away in the slum clearances of the 1920s and 1930s, and by 1935 there were only 288 left. But by the 1930s there were also about a hundred clubs licensed to sell alcohol and over 300 off-licences. Dancing was also extremely popular, perhaps encouraged by the movies, and made possible by the much greater personal freedom that girls – 'flappers' – now enjoyed. In 1903 there had only been 12 dance halls in the city; there were 73 by the late 1930s.[29]

The weekend started at lunchtime on Saturday, and for thousands of men and boys, dads and their sons, Saturday afternoon meant supporting either one's football or rugby team. Hull City Association Football Club, with its own ground on Anlaby Road, across the road from the cricket ground, had established a large and loyal following before the First World War, encouraged by the team's ability to usually finish in the top half of the Second Division. The years after the war, however, were both disappointing and frustrating. In seven seasons out of 11 the team finished in the bottom half of the division, and in 1930 they were relegated to the Third Division North. Yet 1930 also saw the team enjoy its greatest-ever achievement in the FA Cup, reaching the Semi-Finals against Arsenal. In the process the team beat Blackpool, Plymouth Argyle, Manchester City and Newcastle, before succumbing 1-0 to Arsenal in a replay at Aston Villa's ground.[30]

Support for the city's two professional rugby league teams, Hull FC and Hull KR, was divided largely on geographical lines. By 1918 Hull KR had long been established as the East Hull team, playing rugby at Craven Street since the 1890s, and it consolidated its fan base in this part of the city in 1922 when it moved its ground to Craven Park, at the east end of Holderness Road. Hull FC, on the other hand, had long been established at their ground on the Boulevard, in West Hull. The two were keen rivals, and no victory for either side was ever sweeter than one achieved against the other. In 1913 Hull FC paid Hunslet a record £600 for Billy Batten and the considerable salary of £14 per match, and Batten was the star of Hull's first ever Championship final victory, defeating Huddersfield 3-2 in 1920. Both teams enjoyed considerable success in the 1920s, but rather less in the 1930s, and in 1938 financial difficulties forced Hull KR to sell their ground at Craven Park to the Greyhound Racing Company, taking out a 21-year lease to enable them to continue playing there. The size of the crowd tended to vary with the opposition and the importance of the match, but in 1936 a record 28,788 turned up to the Boulevard for Hull's third round Challenge Cup match against Leeds.[31]

'The Circle' on Anlaby Road continued to be used as a first-class cricket ground throughout the interwar era and long after the Second World War. Among the greatest performances of this era were those of Maurice Leyland and Herbert Sutcliffe. In 1936 Leyland scored 263 for Yorkshire against Essex, and three years later Sutcliffe scored an unbeaten 234 against Leicestershire.

From the latter years of the 19th century large numbers of local companies and church groups organised their own sports teams, and the 1920s and 1930s were the heyday of such initiatives. Football and cricket were especially popular, but baseball was as well, and before the Second World War a number of Hull teams had established a reputation for excellence in this game. Many firms and churches also organised their own bands. The corporation tramway employees were not untypical in having their own band, plus their own cricket, football, tug-of-war, and swimming teams, as well as a hyacinth growers' society, which won numerous trophies in local competitions.

During the interwar years Hull became a lively and ambitious centre for the arts. Owing to the generosity of T.R. Ferens, a fine new art gallery was opened in 1927, built on the site of the redundant church of St John the Evangelist, which Ferens had bought for this purpose a few years earlier. Ferens himself was a keen art collector, as was Sir James Reckitt, and both men gave their personal collections to the new gallery. Their generosity ensured that the gallery charged no entry fee. Under its curator, Vincent Galloway, himself a highly regarded portrait painter, the gallery quickly gained a high reputation and acquired a particularly good collection of impressionist paintings.[32]

In spite of the Depression, and the popularity of the cinema, the 1930s were later seen as a 'golden age' for the theatre in Hull. In 1924 a group of talented local enthusiasts founded a repertory company, using the Lecture Hall in Kingston Square for its productions, but renaming it the Little Theatre. Under the leadership of the energetic and imaginative Peppino Santangelo, the company was able to overcome

124 *Ferens Art Gallery today.*

125 *The New Theatre today.*

financial difficulties and begin to flourish. In 1930 it was able to buy the theatre and in 1939 it acquired the Assembly Rooms, which were then converted into the New Theatre, which stands and flourishes to-day. Plays by Shakespeare and Shaw were regularly performed to full houses, and one of the actors who often took a leading role was a young James Mason. The move to the Assembly Rooms was the result of Santangelo's vision and determination, but even he was almost thwarted when war was declared before the conversion had been completed and the building work was stopped. His enthusiasm and force of character, however, ensured that by one means or another, the work was completed and the theatre enjoyed a triumphal opening on 16 October 1939.[33]

Those who enjoyed classical music were well served by orchestral concerts at the City Hall and by chamber music at the hall of the University College. The Palace Theatre on Anlaby Road – although normally a variety and comedy theatre – hosted the Carl Rosa Opera Company almost every year, with its varied repertoire of four or five operas. Choral singing was long established in the city, and had a high reputation, with two local choral societies, the Hull Vocal Society and the Hull Harmonic Society. In 1929 the two groups amalgamated to form the Hull Choral Union. Its annual Christmas performance of Handel's 'Messiah' in the City Hall remains popular to this day. Some members of the Choral Union also sang in the Hull Amateur Operatic Society, which put on a light opera at least once a year. Hull's own orchestra, the Hull Philharmonic, had been founded in 1881 at a meeting held at the *George Hotel* by a small group of mainly amateur musicians. By the 1920s and 1930s its reputation was such that it was able to attract guest conductors of the highest quality, including Sir Henry Wood, who came four times a year. Moreover, as is still the case, the orchestra did not restrict itself to well-known and popular classics; instead, its repertoire is constantly expanding with new works and composers.[34]

One of the most popular and famous celebrities of the 1930s was the daughter of a Hull fish merchant and a former pupil of Boulevard Municipal Secondary School, Amy Johnson. Her remarkable flying achievements, courage, good looks and mod-est charm made her an icon of the age. In 1930, less than a year after she had gained

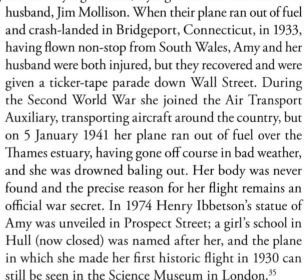

her pilot's licence, and still only 26, she flew solo in her De Haviland Gipsy Moth 11,000 miles to Australia, between 5 and 24 May. She was the first woman to achieve this, and gained international fame overnight as a result. Within just a few weeks her achievement was being celebrated in a popular song, 'Amy, Wonderful Amy', recorded by, among others, Jack Hylton and his orchestra. She had become both heroine and pin-up girl. During the next few years she set numerous other long-distance flying records, flying both solo and with her husband, Jim Mollison. When their plane ran out of fuel and crash-landed in Bridgeport, Connecticut, in 1933, having flown non-stop from South Wales, Amy and her husband were both injured, but they recovered and were given a ticker-tape parade down Wall Street. During the Second World War she joined the Air Transport Auxiliary, transporting aircraft around the country, but on 5 January 1941 her plane ran out of fuel over the Thames estuary, having gone off course in bad weather, and she was drowned baling out. Her body was never found and the precise reason for her flight remains an official war secret. In 1974 Henry Ibbetson's statue of Amy was unveiled in Prospect Street; a girl's school in Hull (now closed) was named after her, and the plane in which she made her first historic flight in 1930 can still be seen in the Science Museum in London.[35]

126   *Statue of Amy Johnson,*
outside the Prospect Centre.

The Second World War

During the Second World War Hull suffered the most terrible destruction by aerial bombing and it is impossible to describe adequately here the loss and heartbreak suffered, and the sheer courage and endurance shown by the people of Hull throughout these appalling years. The bare facts, however, can be easily stated. Hull suffered 82 raids during the six years of war and there were 815 alerts; 1,200 people were killed and 3,000 were injured; 86,715 houses, or more than 90 per cent of all Hull's houses, were either damaged or destroyed, and 152,000 people were made homeless. A much fuller account of Hull's ordeal during these years was written by the Assistant Editor of the *Hull Daily Mail*, Mr T. Geraghty, in 1951, entitled *A North-East Coast Town; Ordeal and Triumph*, and this has been repeatedly reprinted, most recently in 2002. Only a relatively brief account, drawn mainly from Mr Geraghty's work, can be attempted here.

The first preparations for a possible war were taken by the council as early as 1936, when it set up the Air-Raid Precautions Committee to 'think the unthinkable', and during the next two years plans emerged for the provision of shelters, the evacuation of the city's children and expectant mothers, the setting up of a Warden Service and Rescue and Decontamination Squads, and the implementation of blackouts. By the time this committee was developed into a government Emergency Committee, under councillors Leonard Speight and Leo Schultz, in March 1939, an enormous amount of work had already been done. There had already been blackout exercises, recruitment for the Warden Service, and dozens of training classes. The Hull Civil Defence Rescue Service, whose methods were to become a model for the rest of the country, had begun training in January 1939.[36]

The first bombs to fall on Hull came on the night of 19 June 1940, when incendiaries fell on East Hull, fortunately doing little damage but announcing the end of the 'Phoney War' for Hull. Just a fortnight later the city suffered its first daylight raid, the first launched by Germany on any English city, when a single aircraft managed to reach the city undetected and set fire to oil tanks at Saltend. So far there had been only slight damage and no fatal casualties, but late in August houses near the East Hull docks were hit and an Anderson shelter was damaged on Rustenburg Street, with six people killed and 10 seriously injured. In October 1940 there were many casualties (two fatal) and hundreds of houses damaged when two parachute mines fell at the end of Strathmore Avenue, near the river Hull, and in the following February another four people were killed when two 500lb bombs fell on Goddard Avenue. During February and March the number of alerts and raids increased; on 24 February 12 people were killed and 26 seriously injured when a row of terraced houses was hit on De la Pole Avenue, near the Alexandra Dock; three weeks later 38 people were killed and 79 injured when the Sissons paint works was hit in the Stoneferry area. On 18 March came the heaviest raid yet, on central and northern Hull, killing 92 people, injuring 70

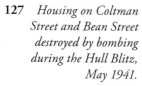

127 *Housing on Coltman Street and Bean Street destroyed by bombing during the Hull Blitz, May 1941.*

more and completely destroying 700 houses and an oil-extracting factory. On Monday, 31 March, yet another heavy raid, beginning at about nine o'clock, again caused terrible damage and numerous casualties. High explosives and landmines fell on almost every part of the city. The East Hull fire station was hit, along with the Control HQ, which was housed in the Shell-Mex building on Ferensway; roads were blocked by falling buildings, 500 houses were destroyed and another 2,000 damaged. Fifty-two people were killed and more than 70 seriously injured.[37]

More raids followed in April, including one in which a parachute mine scored a direct hit on a crowded public shelter on Ellis Street, killing all 50 adults and children sheltering inside. On the night of 7 May, shortly after 11 p.m., sirens announced what was to prove to be the most terrible raids of all. During the two successive nights of 7 and 8 May, every part of the city was hit, especially the city centre and areas close to the Victoria, Alexandra and King George Docks. On these two nights 420 people were killed and about 800 injured. Thousands of incendiaries were dropped and about 300 high-explosive bombs. The fire brigade had to deal with 800 fires, and hundreds of other fires were fought by other services and members of the public. The city centre was on fire, and enormous streaks of flame shot high into the night sky, visible from many miles away. Small shops and large stores were destroyed, the guildhall and the city hall were both badly damaged, and a great many offices, factories and warehouses were reduced to rubble. The Riverside Quay area was 'gutted from end to end', to quote Mr Geraghty, and 'timber stacks blazed sky high, sending sparks in vast circles to ignite other property'. In these two nights alone 50,000 houses suffered minor damage from blast, bomb or shrapnel, another 9,000 had doors and windows torn out of their frames, and 3,000 were completely destroyed. The corporation bus depot took a direct hit and was reduced to mere 'blackened walls and a tangled mass of iron', and the Prudential Buildings on King Edward Street were so badly damaged that the tower had to be demolished the next day for the public's safety. The heroic work of the casualty service and of local doctors and nurses was described by Mr Geraghty:

> The Casualty Service … took 550 casualties to first-aid posts or the hospitals, where magnificent work was done while the raids were on, sometimes in buildings bereft of roofs and windows and even on fire. Doctors attended people who were wounded and trapped by falling girders, women ambulance drivers drove through walls of fire to reach their destinations or convey their patients somewhere for treatment. There was no place of safety.

Although these two raids were the most deadly, the ordeal suffered by the people of Hull would continue for another four years, and there would be many more lives lost or blighted by injury and bereavement. On 2 June 1941 Hull suffered its 50th raid. There would probably have been no casualties on this day but for the 'all-clear' sounding too soon, and consequently 27 people died, moments after leaving their shelters. A heavier raid on 11 July killed another 21 people in central and south-west Hull, and injured 130 others; another 25 were killed and 50 injured just four days later in the north-west part of the city; and then, on 18 July, another extremely heavy raid took a very severe toll. East Hull and the Victoria Dock area were particularly targeted, and 140 people were killed, including families sheltering in the Franklin Street shelter, off Holderness Road. Altogether, 200 industrial buildings were damaged that night, including Rank's flour mill, which took a direct hit, the East Hull gas undertakings, Reckitt's factory and the General Post Office. About 7,000 houses were severely damaged and 1,500 were completely destroyed. After this there were half a dozen more raids before the end of the year, but none quite so deadly as this, and in the remaining years of the war the number of raids greatly diminished: just six in 1942, four in 1943, none at all in 1944 and two in 1945. The most bombed areas continued to be the working-class areas close to the docks, and the most deadly was the raid on 19 May 1942, when the area around the Fish Dock was badly hit. The biggest bomb ever dropped on Hull fell that night on Scarborough Street, a densely populated area close to the Fish Dock. Approximately 150 people were injured and 50 killed.[38]

The fortitude shown by so many of Hull's inhabitants in these years – together with an unconquerable sense of humour – was illustrated by a story told by Leo Schultz:

> After a night raid upon a working class district I accompanied the Regional Controller, General Sir William Bartholomew, on a visit to the damage. At one house which was completely destroyed, a woman, black with the soot that soiled everything after a raid, was searching among the rubble for the small household goods, the letters and the photographs which were all that remained of yesterday's home. The General asked her where her husband was and, quick as lightning, received the illuminating reply – 'In Libya – the coward!'[39]

The official image, that high morale and 'stiff upper lips' were universal, was, of course, not the whole truth. The Mass Observation surveys of the period showed that in many cities, including Hull, heavy German bombing did indeed shake morale, as might be expected, especially in those areas most likely to be hit.[40]

Moreover, there were those who took advantage of any opportunities for profiteering. A few members of the council had been suspected of such activity for some years before the war, and one, Councillor Digby Willoughby, had committed suicide in 1932 rather than face a government inquiry into his part in council land purchases. One man closely associated with him at that time, the builder and contractor R.G. Tarran, was also later accused of making excessive profits on government war contracts. However, Tarran was also the city's Chief Warden throughout the war, and sheriff in 1941, and he demonstrated great courage during many of the air raids. Fear of damaging morale during the war prevented the police from bringing charges, but in 1947 he and his fellow directors faced charges of false accounting and Tarran was very fortunate to escape a prison sentence.

He was found guilty and sentenced to nine months hard labour, but the verdict was reversed on appeal, on the grounds that he was unaware of the swindle.[41]

From post-war rebuilding to a new century

Hull could recover only slowly from the destruction of war, and for many years large sections of the city consisted merely of flattened bomb-sites, where wild flowers sprang up beside the footpaths carved out as useful short-cuts across the rubble by the town's commuters and shoppers. Long before the conflict had ended two of the country's most respected town planners, Sir Edwin Lutyens and Professor Abercrombie, were commissioned by the council to draw up a plan for post-war reconstruction, but this proved so ambitious and expensive that only a few of their ideas were implemented, and the council did not complete its own comprehensive plan until 1956. By this time, however, much had been achieved. Work on a new drainage system for east Hull, which was a vital prerequisite for later industrial and residential development, had begun before the end of 1945 and was completed by 1950, when a new scheme for west Hull was also begun. An ambitious rebuilding programme for the city centre began to take shape early in the 1950s. The first major department store to be rebuilt was Hammond's, which opened in June 1950, and in 1951 the Queen's House shops and offices project was begun. The destruction of so many of the city's houses meant that large numbers of 'pre-fabs' had to be built and the pre-war slum clearance programme was postponed until 1952. The rebuilding of the Riverside Quay was not completed until 1959, and delays in repairing wartime damage at the docks were partly to blame for the decline in the port's share of British overseas trade in the late 1940s and 1950s. As early as 1948 Manchester had replaced Hull as Britain's third largest port.[42]

A number of large council estates had been built on the edge of the city before the war, the rather unimaginatively named East Hull, North Hull and West Hull estates, but under the 1956 plan these were extended and new, even larger, estates were built, some of more than 100 acres. Consequently, during the 1950s and 1960s the built-up area of the city was extended in all directions, engulfing green fields, small villages and hamlets three or four miles from the city centre: to the east, the Greatfield estate; to the north-east the

128 *The Hull Royal Infirmary, Anlaby Road.*

129   *The Larkin Building and Graduate School, Hull University.*

Longhill estate, the Ings Road estate and Bilton Grange; to the north-west Orchard Park; and to the west Bricknell Avenue. As new houses were built, the worst of the Victorian slums could be demolished, but slum-clearance remained slow at first, and between 1952 and 1964 only about 3,500 houses were demolished.[43]

Numerous public buildings were erected in the 1960s, gradually changing the appearance of the city centre. A new Central Police Station was completed in 1959 on the north side of Queen's Gardens, and a new Customs House nearby in 1964. The College of Technology finally secured new and much more spacious accommodation when its nine-storey building was completed between 1960 and 1962, in a most prominent position to the east of Queen's Gardens, and in the same year the Central Library on Albion Street was given a new extension. The 14-storey Hull Royal Infirmary on Anlaby Road was begun in 1962 and completed in 1967, on the site once occupied by the Victorian workhouse. Further out of the centre, on Cottingham Road, the University College's achievement of full university status in 1954 was followed in the 1960s with a number of new buildings to accommodate the growing number of students. The chemistry building was completed in 1963, Middleton Hall and the Larkin Buildings were both built between 1965 and 1967, and the Wilberforce Buildings between 1968 and 1970. Pevsner and Neave found little of merit in most of Hull's new public buildings of the 1960s but the new university campus, they said, was an exception: 'one of the most pleasing university campuses in Britain, well maintained with plenty of grass and trees'.[44]

Slum clearance and council-house building continued apace throughout the 1970s, and whereas in 1945 there had been only about 10,500 council-built homes, by the 1990s there were over 50,000, or about half the entire housing stock of the city. The largest residential development was the Bransholme Estate, in north-east Hull, where over 10,000 homes were erected between 1968 and 1981, and today it has a population of over 30,000 and is the largest council estate in Yorkshire (and one of the largest in the UK).[45]

The rapid increase in car ownership in the 1960s and 1970s meant that, while those on lower incomes moved to the new council estates, more and more of the middle classes lived outside the city, commuting to work every morning by car. This, together with relatively high levels of unemployment, helped to reduce the size of the city's population in the second half of the century. In 1951 the population of the city stood at 295,172,

130   *The Marina.*

well below the peak census figure of 1931, when it had been 309,158, and during the next few decades it fell further, to 266,180 by 1991 and to 243,595 by 2001.[46]

The growing numbers of cars coming into the city every day prompted the corporation to introduce a number of transport improvements as early as 1948, when roundabouts were introduced to the outer circular road. The removal of the agricultural drains, as part of the post-war drainage improvements, not only shed the city of a notoriously smelly feature but also an obstruction to traffic. The Drypool Bridge was rebuilt in 1961, helping improve communications across the river Hull; flyovers were built to replace two level crossings in the 1960s, and other level crossings were removed altogether. A one-way traffic system was introduced in 1964 and in the same year the first multi-storey car park was built by the corporation in Osborne Street.[47]

However, the challenge of the motor car has been relentless and the corporation found itself obliged to consider radical road improvement schemes, and as a result the traditional layout of the city was changed enormously in the 1980s by the building of major dual-carriageways through the city. Freetown Way, completed in 1985, cut a swathe through the Georgian city to the north of the centre, running from the Spring Bank-Beverley Road junction to the North Bridge, and a much widened Castle Street was laid out to the south, crossing the river Hull by the new Myton Bridge, which opened in 1980, cutting the Old Town in half. Accessibility, both to the city centre and to the eastern docks, has improved but at a considerable cost. Pevsner and Neave reckoned these road schemes and associated clearances had done more damage to the city's architectural heritage than the Luftwaffe had managed in the Second World War. Much of Hull's Georgian heritage has been saved, however, and more recent developments have improved the city's appearance. The conversion of the former Humber Dock into a marina for leisure craft has been especially successful, and an ambitious pedestrianisation scheme has considerably improved the experience of shopping in the centre.[48]

Hull remains one of the country's largest and most important ports. The older, smaller docks (Prince's, Humber, Railway and Victoria) were closed between 1968 and 1970, but a new dock, the Queen Elizabeth, to the east of the city, opened in 1969 to enable the port to handle container traffic, and among the ships negotiating their entry into the port today are some of the world's largest 'super-ferries'. The roll-on, roll-off ferry service between Hull and Rotterdam began in 1965, with the completion of 'Ro-Ro' terminals at the King George Dock, followed shortly afterwards with a second service to Zeebrugge. Today the ferries handle over a million passengers every year. The Alexandra Dock was closed to commercial shipping in 1982 but such was the increase in demand for port facilities in the 1980s that it was reopened in 1991. The port has benefitted from the road improvements and by the opening of the Humber Bridge in 1981, although the potential benefit of the latter would probably be much greater still if the current tolls could be abolished. Now, further road improvements are badly needed, particularly to the A63, the principal route from the ports westwards through the city. A proposed scheme to both widen and lower the Castle Street section of the road would greatly improve access to and from the docks, while also greatly improving the appearance of the city by reconnecting the southern part of the historic 'Old Town'.[49]

The importance of the port to the city today can hardly be overstated. About 5,000 people are employed at the port and a further 18,000 jobs are directly dependent on the port's activities. In 2008-9 the port was handling approximately 13 million tonnes of cargo per year and this was expected to increase further in the following decade as a result of improved rail facilities. Many of the older industries established in the 19th century to process imported raw materials still survive and flourish, including the pharmaceutical firms Reckitt Benckiser and Smith and Nephew, and the millers Maizecor; and the port remains a major importer of timber from northern Europe – an ancient link long celebrated by an annual gift to the town of a very tall Christmas tree. An industrial estate has developed on land around Salt End, a mile and a half to the east of the King George and Queen Elizabeth Docks, and this has been developed by BP as an important centre for the storage and processing of oil, chemicals and spirit, all of which are discharged into pipes at the head of the Salt End jetties.[50]

The fishing industry, however, has almost completely gone; a victim of the last of the Icelandic 'Cod Wars' of 1975-6 and the EU's failure to agree an acceptable common fisheries policy. The last trawler to leave the principal fish dock, St Andrew's Dock, sailed in November 1975, and today very little survives of this once all-important industry of Hull. For the city's school children it is now part of Hull's history, celebrated in the Maritime Museum and in the museum ship, the *Arctic Corsair*, once part of the city's deep-sea fishing fleet but since 1999 a museum dedicated to the fishing industry. It is berthed in the river Hull between Drypool Bridge and Myton Bridge. In the 1950s and 1960s the fishing industry enjoyed rapid growth and high earnings, and employed almost 8,000 trawlermen, but by 2001 it employed barely two hundred. The industry had played a vital role in giving the city a unique identity as a port, famous or infamous for its 'three-day millionaires', as the trawlermen were called when they arrived home, collected their settling money and enjoyed themselves in the local pubs for a few intense days of holidaymaking before returning to the dangers and hardships of the sea. Not

131 *The* Arctic Corsair *Museum Ship, anchored in the river Hull.*

even the coal industry was as dangerous as deep-sea fishing in the northern waters. For three weeks or more at a time men had to live and work in the most difficult conditions, facing vicious winds and buffeting Arctic seas. In September 2010 a plaque was unveiled at St Andrew's Quay to commemorate the great many trawlermen from Hull who lost their lives at sea and the 'special relationship between the Hessle Road community and Hull's lost trawlermen'. In 1985, after a decade of neglect and growing dereliction, much of St Andrew's Dock was filled in, the fish meal factory was demolished – for so long the source of a smell the city's older residents will never forget – and the area began to be developed for retail and leisure use. On the nearby William Wright Dock, however, ship repair work continued for some years, and today it is the home of the purpose-built Fresh Fish Market, or Fishgate, and Hull remains an important centre for the marketing of fish and seafood, but even this is now threatened by European Union proposals for a ban on Icelandic mackerel imports.[51]

The death of the fishing industry meant unemployment levels in West Hull in the late 1970s and throughout the 1980s were depressingly high, and even in 2001 – after five years of impressive economic growth in the country as a whole – they still stood at 15 per cent, more than twice the level for the city as a whole (6.2 per cent) and far above the national average. The trawler owners received decommissioning money from the EU but the trawlermen received no redundancy payments at all and it would take more than 20 years of campaigning before the surviving trawlermen, only about 1,300 by then, won compensation from the government. In the meantime, many lives had been destroyed and many children had grown up knowing only severe poverty and deprivation.[52]

Hull's future must rely largely on the continuing development of the port and its related industries, on the development of new 'green' industries, on its position as a major retailing centre for a wide area, and on the growth of leisure and tourist industries. Hull is the largest urban area in the East Riding of Yorkshire and therefore a natural focus for retail shoppers. An important step towards exploiting this potential was taken in 1991 when the Prince's Quay Shopping Centre was opened, a much larger shopping area than the existing Prospect Centre on Prospect Street. The new centre was built on stilts over the old Prince's Dock (originally Junction Dock), which had closed more than twenty years earlier. With fountains now springing from the former dock, and outdoor cafés lining either side of the water, the shopping centre looks out onto an area once rather neglected but now one of the most pleasant parts of the city. In December 2007 the Vue Cinema, the first fully digital cinema in Europe, was opened as an additional attraction in the shopping centre.[53]

A second, even larger, shopping centre, St Stephen's, opened in September 2007 on Ferensway, which was in need of redevelopment. It was built on the site of the old bus station and is a most ambitious development, costing over £160 million and covering 52,000 square metres. The project includes a 24-hour superstore, shop units, another new cinema, a new home for the Hull Truck Theatre Company, a huge car park and a residential area. The old bus station has been replaced, adjacent to the centre, by a

new bus station which forms a 'Transport Interchange' with the Paragon railway station next door. As part of the general regeneration, the railway station has also been very attractively renovated to reveal its Victorian splendour. The process was completed in December 2010 by erecting a statue of the poet Philip Larkin in the concourse of the Interchange, as part of the 'Larkin 25' festival held that year, celebrating

132 *The much improved Prince's Quay area today, with the shopping centre to the left.*

133 *The St Stephen's Centre; the west entrance.*

the 25th anniversary of his death. Larkin is widely regarded as one of the greatest poets of the second half of the 20th century and he set many of his poems in the city, including 'Here' (an extract from which appears at the front of this book), 'The Whitsun Weddings' and 'Toads'. He lived in the city for 30 years, having taken the post of University librarian in 1955, a position he held until his death.[54]

One of the dangers of building so large a retailing centre, of course, is that the traditional shopping areas will lose customers and rapidly decline, and today many shops in Whitefriargate – until recently one of the city's principal shopping streets – do indeed stand empty. There is, however, every reason to hope that Hull's bold attempts to regenerate itself will succeed, not least because of the improvements being made in the city's leisure facilities, the development of the city's tourism, and by the encouragement of more people to live in the heart of the city. The success of this latter step is reflected in the decision to include residential areas in the St Stephen's centre, and one of the most important projects planned for the east bank of the river Hull – known as the 'Boom' – is a £100 million residential development which, when completed, will include over 600 luxury riverside apartments, together with shops, cafés, a hotel, and health and education facilities. In recent years more people have been choosing to live in the city centre, and a number of former warehouses beside the Old Harbour have been converted into flats. Developments such as the Boom project can only encourage this further. For the first time since the 1930s the population of the city is again growing, albeit slowly. In 2008 the population was approximately 258,700, 15,000 more than in 2001.[55]

Another part of the regeneration is the building of the Humber Quays development, giving the city more new office space and residential apartments. It is hoped that, after the current recession, the project will include another large hotel and a restaurant, next to the Humber, with fine views of the river.[56]

134   *Statue of Phil Larkin, striding to catch his train in the concourse of the Transport Interchange*

135   *One of a number of giant toads placed in various parts of the city as part of the 'Larkin 25' festival in 2010; this one is sitting outside the ARC building.*

welcome / ARC / visitors welcome

136 *The Humber Quays development.*

It was estimated in 2009 that Hull had about five million visitors every year, contributing about £210 million to the city's economy. One of the more recent, and most successful, attractions has been The Deep. This large underwater aquarium was opened in March 2002 and was built as one of the UK's National Lottery Millennium Commission projects. It has a very striking design, like the prow of a great ship, and it seems most appropriately sited, at Sammy's Point, where the river Hull flows into the Humber. It is hard to think of a more fitting attraction for the city than this, telling the story of the oceans and the creatures that live in them. In 2012 it was reported that more than three million people had visited.

The bicentenary of William Wilberforce's great achievement – the abolition of the Atlantic slave trade – in 2007 was a boost to the city's tourism industry, focusing international attention on the city, its most famous son, and the Wilberforce Museum, located in the house in which he was born. The house is of considerable interest in its own right,

137 *The Deep, beside the rivers Hull and Humber, as seen from the Victoria Pier.*

138   *The Maritime Museum, formerly the Dock Office, built 1868-71.*

but it is the Anti-Slavery exhibition which draws thousands of visitors to it every year. The Museum Quarter, which has been developed around Wilberforce House, on the city's

oldest street – High Street – is another of the city's more successful regeneration projects. Next door to the Wilberforce Museum is the Streetlife Museum of Transport; behind it can be found the *Arctic Corsair*, and beside the transport museum is the Hull and East Riding Museum, which tells the story of the region from prehistoric times up to the 17th century, and is perhaps most famous for containing the Hasholme Logboat, the largest surviving prehistoric boat in the country. A few minutes walk away, up one of the little medieval streets that link the

139   *The Spurn Lightship today.*

High Street to the market place, the 'Hands-on-History' exhibitions are situated in the Old Grammar School building, next to Holy Trinity Church. Here, in one of Hull's oldest secular buildings, many aspects of the city's social history are brought to life, and it is much used by school teachers and children. Other museums include the Spurn Lightship, the Yorkshire Water Museum, and the Maritime Museum; and just across the road from this last museum is the Ferens Art Gallery, whose permanent collection spans every artistic period from the medieval to the present day.

Hull City Hall remains the home of the long-established Hull Philharmonic Orchestra and the Hull Choral Union, and the Hallé Orchestra is a regular guest. The City Hall and the New Theatre are the city's principal venues for more popular entertainment: for tribute bands, musicals, pantomime, stand-up comedians and the World's Darts Championship. Serious, thought-provoking drama is found at the Hull Truck Company's new venue, on Ferensway. The new 440-seat theatre cost £14.5 million and opened in April 2009, but when Mike Bradwell founded the company in 1971 he did so because he could find no one to employ him, and half of those who answered his advertisement to form a company dropped out when they found they would have to move to Hull. When former teacher John Godber joined the company in 1984, as artistic director, it was 'broke' but had

140   *The Hull Truck Theatre and Albermarle Music Centre.*

enjoyed much critical acclaim for some of its productions. Godber was able to rescue its finances by writing a play with immediate appeal and resonance for Hull, about rugby football in the city, 'Up n Under'. This, and many more of John Godber's plays – particularly 'Teechers' and 'Bouncers' – have been an enormous success, and when the company moved from its theatre in Spring Street to its present venue it was only fitting to inaugurate the new era with another Godber play, 'Funny Turns'.[58]

Music of every type is alive and well in the city. As well as the Choral Union and Symphony Orchestra, Hull can also boast the largest professional chamber ensemble in the region, the Hull Sinfonietta, the Hull Philharmonic Youth Orchestra, the Hull Bach Choir, the Hull Male Voice Choir, the Arterian Singers, and two Gilbert & Sullivan societies. For those who appreciate brass bands there are two: the East Yorkshire Motor Services Band and the East Riding of Yorkshire Band. The annual Hull Jazz Festival takes place around the Marina at the beginning of August and is followed in early September by an International Sea Shanty Festival.[59]

Many very talented musicians from Hull have made careers for themselves in the world of pop, including Mick Ronson, who played with David Bowie in the 1960s and later recorded with Bob Dylan and Morrissey, and today is celebrated by a Mick Ronson Memorial Stage in Queen's Gardens. The Housemartins and Everything But the Girl were both from Hull, as were most of the members of Sade, whose album 'Diamond Life', released in 1984, was enormously successful, while Norman Cook of the Housemartins now performs as Fatboy Slim. Groups play at the *Springhead*, which has won awards as Live Music Pub of the Year, or the *Adelphi,* which has hosted bands including Stone Roses, Radiohead, and Green Day. Venues known to encourage local talent include the Ringside, the *Wellington Inn*, and the Tigers Lair. The Hull Arena, on Kingston Street, doubles as an ice skating/ice hockey arena (home of the Hull String Rays) and as a 2,000-seat concert hall which in recent years has hosted concerts by the Arctic Monkeys, Oasis, Morrissey and Robin Williams; bands also play at the City Hall, the KC Stadium and at the University.[60]

Hull has long been well known for its many pubs, bars and clubs, and for a drinking culture that tends towards late bars. Particularly popular venues inlcude the *Linnet and Lark*, the *Side Kicks Lounge*, and the *Lamp*. The expansion of the Univeristy in recent years – there are now about 18,000 students – has encouraged the creation of new wine bars and pubs close to the University and the Halls of Residence.[61]

The city's football team, Hull City AFC (the Tigers), has enjoyed a rollercoaster experience in the last few years. After an incredibly rapid rise from the lowest tier in the Football League between 2004 and 2008, the team were relegated from the Premier League in 2010 but returned to the top flight in 2013, under manager Steve Bruce, only to be relegated again at the end of the 2014/15 season, after some considerable FA Cup glory on the way and a first taste of European football as well. In 2014 the Tigers reached the final of the FA Cup for the first time in their history and only lost narrowly, in extra time, to Arsenal (by three goals to two, having taken a two-goal lead early in the game). Its first foray into Europe, a few months later, in the UEFA Europa League ended with an 'away goals' defeat agains Belgian team, Lokeren. The city's two rugby teams both play in the Super League; Hull FC (the Sharks) winning a place in 1997 and Hull KR (the Robins) in 2006, after winning the National League One Championship. Hull FC managed to finish second in 2006 but only eighth in 2015 and neither team can claim more than limited success in recent years. Hull FC reached the final of the Challenge Cup in 2013 but lost to Wigan 16-0, and in 2015 Hull KR also reached the final but only to suffer the humiliation of a record 50-0 defeat against Leeds.

Other sports enjoying increasing popularity include ice hockey and American football; and gambling on 'the dogs' returned to Hull in 2007 when greyhound racing was reinstated at the reopened Boulevard Stadium. Hull's oldest attraction, the ancient Hull Fair, is still held in October in West Park, on Walton Street, next door to the KC Stadium (now the home of both Hull City and Hull FC). One of the city's more recent attractions, the music and arts festival known as the Freedom Festival, has proved a great success. Indeed, it has been the considerable growth in cultural activites in recent years

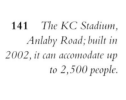

141 *The KC Stadium, Anlaby Road; built in 2002, it can accomodate up to 2,500 people.*

and the enthusiasm of the people of Hull that has led to the city winning the title 'City of Culture, 2017'. This has captured the imagination of a great number of people and the organisers promise a 'spectacular programme for 2017 that will deliver artistic excellence and events on a scale never before seen in the city.'

While there are many aspects of Hull's recent history to be proud of, there is another side which is far less attractive. Hull has not yet recovered completely from the collapse of the fishing industry in the 1970s, and unemployment was about twice the national average, at about 14.4 per cent in 2010. There are many families where two generations have grown up never having had a job, and those who are in work tend to be in low-wage jobs. In 2009 the average weekly pay in the city was calculated to be £407.70, £44.70 less than the regional average and £88.30 less than the national average. Consequently, Hull remains an area of considerable deprivation. Taking into account factors such as employment levels, average incomes, health, educational achievements, crime and housing, Hull was said to be the 11th most deprived area in the United Kingdom in 2007. In 2010 the proportion of the population dependent on state benefits was much higher in Hull than in most other cities (22.6 per cent of residents aged 16-64 compared to 16.0 per cent in Yorkshire and Humberside and 15.1 per cent in the country as a whole).[63]

Poverty and high levels of unemployment are closely associated with problems of health, low school achievement and crime. Average life expectancy in Hull in 2008 for men was 75 years and for women 79.5, about three years less than that of the country as a whole. Crime levels in the city have fallen in recent years, but are still worryingly high. In 2002-3 the overall crime rate in Hull was over twice the national figure; since then the gap has narrowed, but it is still significant. In 2009-10 there were 120.2 recorded crimes per 1,000 of the population of Hull; 83 per 1,000 in Yorkshire and Humberside and 79 per 1,000 in the United Kingdom. Vehicle crime and robberies were only just above the national avergae, but violent crime and burglaries were still well above.[64]

It is in those areas of the city where levels of crime, vanadalism, drug taking and deprivation are highest that one also finds state schools whose levels of academic achievement are well below national figures. In Hull, in recent years, the primary schools' results have been most encouraging, but at secondary level – in spite of considerable recent improvements – there are still huge problems. In 2008-9 only 37 per cent of the city's 16 year olds achieved five or more GCSEs, including mathematics and English language, at grade C or above. This was the second lowest rate in the country. This is not a new problem, as a survey in 2009 found that 18.2 per cent of adults in the city had no qualifications at all. The consequence is that many parents now choose to send their children to schools outside the city. In February 2011 it was reported that every day 2,000 pupils left Hull for East Riding schools. [65]

Many of the city's problems are associated with the large council estates built on the edges of the city between the 1950s and 1980s. Although when first built they represented a significant improvement in living standards, it was not long before complaints were being heard about their quality and particularly about severe condensation problems. Many residents also complained of the loss of neighbourliness, one of the few positive features of the older slums from which they had moved. The Bransholme and Orchard Park Estates have been particularly criticised as bleak and impersonal. Today, the complaints are more likely to be about under-age drinking, anti-social behaviour, burglary, vehicle crime, drug taking, and vandalism. Many houses on the Bransholme Estate are now boarded up, in particular the bungalows intended for the estate's older residents, and two streets have been demolished – Skilgate Close and Selworthy Close – leaving large empty spaces in the middle of the estate. The only secondary school on the Orchard Park Estate, the Sir Henry Cooper School, suffered a serious arson attack in February 2007 when a 12-year-old boy set fire to a block of classrooms and caused £50,000 worth of damage, destroying two classrooms, a computer room, the dining room and a staff room. [66]

Recent cuts in public expenditure have helped maintain high levels of unemployment and have had a damaging effect on the city's regeneration programme. It was announced in 2010, for instance, that the plans to build an ambitious extension to the Prince's Quay Shopping Centre, to be known as Quay West, were being cancelled. This was planned as a major investment, costing £300 million, to be completed in 2013. It would have added a further 60 shops, two new department stores and more leisure facilities. Following the cuts, the regeneration agency, Yorkshire Forward, was abolished. Plans to develop the waterfront Fruit Market were scrapped, together with the Castle Street redevelopment scheme, which had been aimed at relieving waterfront traffic congestion and improving access to the Marina. The later stages of the Humber Quays development have been postponed indefinitely, and the proposed hotel and restaurant are currently an abandoned building site. Plans drawn up in consultation with the residents of Orchard Park to demolish and rebuild hundreds of houses on the estate have also had to be abandoned.

The onset of the recession came barely a year after the city suffered its worst flooding for many decades. A magnificent 120ft-high surge barrier was built in 1980 to protect the city from the tidal surges of the Humber, and this is frequently in operation, being lowered between eight and ten times a year. But this could do nothing to save the city

142   *The Tidal Surge Barrier on the river Hull, built in 1980. The new footbridge linking the Old Town with the new developments east of the river can be seen in the foreground, and the Premier Inn tower – one of the first stages of this development – is in the background.*

when prolonged and torrential rain on 25 July 2007 flooded all the lowest-lying parts of the city. About 7,800 houses and over 1,000 businesses were soon underwater, and 90 of the city's 105 schools suffered damage. Altogether, about £100 million worth of damage was done, and in Hessle one man lost his life trying to clear a blocked drain. Some people were still not back in their homes three years later, including the residents of Northumberland Court sheltered housing, as the Grade-2 listed building made repair work exceptionally expensive.[68]

The future, however, is by no means bleak. Much regeneration work will go on and considerable progress has already been made to improve the city's appearance and preserve its heritage. Hull's architectural heritage is superb, well deserving the accolade of having its own *Pevsner Architectural Guide*. Moreover, as the authors of the *Guide* make clear, some of the most recent buildings are also some of the most interesting and innovative. The Deep aquarium is one such, but one might also mention the spectacular KC Stadium, opened in 2002; the History Centre, completed in 2009; the Albemarle Music Centre, with its vivid lavender-blue cone, completed in 2007; and the moveable ARC building (on the corner of Queen Street and Castle Street at the time of writing), which has won many awards for the originality of its design and its 'green' credentials. Some of the new schools built as part of a £400 million school-building programme, completed in 2014, are also extremely attractive, particularly the archbishop Sentamu Academy, the Winifred Holtby School Technology College, and the Sirius Academy.[69]

143   *The ARC building, Queen Street. ARC is the architecture centre for Hull and the Humber region. Its stated mission is to 'promote and foster the highest quality of sustainable design in architecture and public space'.*

There is every reason to hope that the city will soon be enjoying higher levels of employment and higher average incomes. In January 2011 the German engineering firm Siemens announced their intention of building a huge factory at the Alexandra Dock, to build up to 7,000 wind turbines for use on the North Sea. This has since been confirmed and is already bringing new jobs to the region, both employed directly by Siemens at the factory and by the numerous other companies needed to service so large an undertaking, in particular marine engineering firms. The development of 'green' industries on the Humber bank, both North and South, promise to be one of the most hopeful developments for the region in the first few decades of the 21st century.[70]

144   *The History Centre, Worship Street, opened in 2010, with one of the giant Larkin toads in the foreground.*

References

I   *The Medieval Town, 1160-1349*

1. M.H. Keen, *England in the Later Middle Ages* (1973), p.183; K.J. Allison (ed.), *The Victoria History of the Counties of England; Yorkshire, East Riding, I; the city of Kingston upon Hull* (1969), p.11
2. E.Gillett, and K.A. MacMahon, *A History of Hull* (1980), p.3; Allison, *op. cit.*, p.13; Chronicon De Melsa (Rolls Series), i, p.169
3. Allison, *op. cit.*, p.11; Chronicon de Melsa (Rolls Series), i, p.168; J. Bilson, 'Wyke upon Hull in 1293', *Transactions of the East Riding Antiquarian Society*, xxvi, pp.37-9; Environment Agency case study: 2007 Summer Floods (www.environment-agency. gov.uk)
4. Allison, *op. cit.*, p.13
5. *Ibid.*; Bilson, *op. cit.*, pp.41-2
6. Gillett and MacMahon, *op. cit.*, p.4; Allison, *op. cit.*, p.20; H. Calvert, *A History of Hull* (1978), pp.42-5, 50
7. J. Tickell, *History of the Town and County of Kingston upon Hull* (1798), p.10.
8. Gillett and MacMahon, *op. cit.*, p.4
9. E. Power, *The Wool Trade in English Medieval History* (1969), pp.54-5
10. Allison, *op. cit.*, p.16
11. Bilson, *op. cit.*, map opposite p.48
12. Gillett and MacMahon, *op. cit.*, pp.5-7
13. Allison, *op. cit.*, pp.19-21
14. *Ibid.*, p.21; Gillett and MacMahon, *op. cit.*, pp.7-8
15. Allison, *op. cit.*, pp.19, 72
16. *Ibid.*, pp.70-2; Hull Corporation Records, Bench Book (BB), 2, pp.184-91
17. Gillett and MacMahon, *op. cit.*, pp.15-16
18. *Ibid.*, pp.13-14; Power, *op. cit.*, pp.22, 54
19. Power, *op. cit.*, pp.114-16
20. *Ibid.*, pp.115, 119; Keen, *op. cit.*, pp.128, 162
21. Allison, *op. cit.*, pp.18, 71; Bilson, art. cit. map facing p.104
22. Gillett and MacMahon, *op. cit.*, p.24; N. Pevsner and D. Neave, *The Buildings of England: Yorkshire; York and the East Riding* (2nd edn, 1995), p.498; John Markham, *The Book of Hull* (1989), p.18
23. Allison, *op. cit.*, p.287; Pevsner and Neave, *op. cit.*, p.505
24. D. and S. Neave, *Hull* (2010), pp.46-7
25. Allison, *op. cit.*, p.334
26. *Ibid.*,
27. Allison, *op. cit.*, p.294; Pevsner and Neave, *op. cit.*, p.511
28. Calvert, *op. cit.*, p.106; Tickell, *op. cit.*, p.21
29. Gillett and MacMahon, *op. cit.*, pp.25-6
30. *Ibid.*, pp.26-7
31. *Ibid.*, pp.24-5; P. Ziegler, *The Black Death* (1991), p.147
32. Ziegler, *op. cit.*, pp.146-7
33. *Ibid.*, p.147
34. *Ibid.*
35. Gillett and MacMahon, *op. cit.*, p.38

II   *The Late Medieval Town*

1. Allison, *op. cit.*, pp.86-9; Gillett and MacMahon, *op. cit.*, pp.18-19, 79
2. Pevsner and Neave, *op. cit.*, pp.505-6
3. *Ibid.*; D. and S. Neave, *op. cit.*, p.42
4. Allison, *op. cit.*, pp.72-5

5. *Ibid.*, pp.82, 333; Keen, *op. cit.*, p.223
6. Gillett and MacMahon, *op. cit.*, p.36; J. Tickell, *op. cit.*, p.39
7. Gillett and MacMahon, *op. cit.*, p.36
8. This section is drawn mainly from Gillett and MacMahon, *op. cit.*, pp.39-44
9. *Ibid.*, pp.30-3, 39-44; Hull Corp. Rec., BB 3A, ff. 19, 86, 130
10. Allison, *op. cit.*, p.29; Gillett and MacMahon, *op. cit.*, pp.83-85
11. R.A. Griffiths, *The Reign of King Henry VI* (1998), pp.40, 233, 284-8, 336-7; G. Hadley, *A New and Complete History of the Town and County of Kingston-upon-Hull* (1788), pp.61-2
12. Allison, *op. cit.*, pp.24, 53; Gillett and MacMahon, *op. cit.*, pp.49-52
13. *Ibid.*, p.79; Allison, *op. cit.*, pp.86-9
14. Griffiths, *op. cit.*, pp.676-84; Suffolk's will was said to have included a request that 'his wretched body' should be buried in the Charterhouse at Hull (J.J. Sheahan, *History of the Town and Port of Kingston upon Hull*, 2nd edn, 1866, p.65)
15. Gillett and MacMahon, *op. cit.*, p.65; J.R. Lander, *The Wars of the Roses* (1990), pp.75-7
16. Gillett and MacMahon, *op. cit.*, pp.65-6
17. Quoted in Lander, *op. cit.*, p.81. The chronicle is usually referred to as 'Gregory's Chronicle'. However, William Gregory, the London alderman and chronicler to whom this refers, died in 1467 and his work was continued by an unknown author. See also Griffiths, *op. cit.*, pp.870, 880.
18. Gillett and MacMahon, *op. cit.*, p.66
19. *Ibid.*, pp.67-8
20. Lander, *op. cit.*, p.130; Allison p.26
21. Gillett and MacMahon, *op. cit.*, pp.68-9; Allison, *op. cit.*, p.26
22. Allison, *op. cit.*, p.26
23. *Ibid.*, pp.41, 86-7; J.R. Lander, *Government and Community; England 1450-1509* (1980), pp.19-20
24. Allison, *op. cit.*, pp.397-9
25. Sheahan claimed that 1, 580 people had died of the plague in 1478, and that this had followed two previous but less serious attacks in 1472 and 1476 (Sheahan, *op. cit.*, p.76)
26. Hull Corp. Rec. BB 3, ff. 23, 17
27. Gillett and MacMahon, *op. cit.*, p.38
28. *Ibid.*, p.58; Allison, *op. cit.*, p.75

III   *The Early Tudor Town, 1485-1558*

1. Allison, *op. cit.*, p.132; D. and S. Neave, *op. cit.*, p.40
2. Allison, *op. cit.*, p.132; Gillett and MacMahon, *op. cit.*, p.93
3. Allison, *op. cit.*, p.133
4. *Ibid.*, p.296; Pevsner and Neave, *op. cit.*, p.511
5. Quoted in Gillett and MacMahon, *op. cit.*, p.98
6. Sheahan, *op. cit.*, p.91
7. Gillett and MacMahon, *op. cit.*, p.98

8. Hull Corp. Rec., BB 4, f. 176
9. Christopher Haigh (ed.), *The English Reformation Revised* (1987), p.95; G.R. Elton, *Reform and Reformation, England 1509-1558* (1977), p.75
10. A.G. Dickens, *The English Reformation* (1967), p.58
11. *Ibid.*, pp.58-9; Gillett and MacMahon, *op. cit.*, pp.99-100
12. Allison, *op. cit.*, pp.90, 288, 295
13. R.B. Dobson (ed.), *The Church, Patronage and Politics in the Fifteenth Century* (1984), p.215
14. Quoted in Haigh, *op. cit.*, p.95
15. Tickell, *op. cit.*, p.160; Sheahan, *op. cit.*, p.80
16. Allison, pp.90-2
17. Sheahan, *op. cit.*, pp.84-7; Gillett and MacMahon, *op. cit.*, pp.100-1; Elton, *op. cit.*, pp.261-2; Tickell, *op. cit.*, pp.164-7
18. G.W.O. Woodward, *Dissolution of the Monasteries* (1966), p.83
19. Gillett and MacMahon, *op. cit.*, p.104
20. *Ibid.*; Woodward, *op. cit.*, p.136
21. Allison, *op. cit.*, p.341
22. Haigh, *op. cit.*, p.120; G. Hadley, *op. cit.*, pp.88-9; Susan Doran and Christopher Durston, *Princes, Pastors and People. The Church and Religion in England, 1529-1689* (1991), p.43
23. Elton, *op. cit.*, pp.339, 344-5, 348, 365-6, 380
24. Dickens, *op. cit.*, pp.323-4
25. *Ibid.*, pp.374-5
26. *Ibid.*, p.379
27. Gillett and MacMahon, *op. cit.*, pp.102-3
28. *Ibid.*, pp.103-4

IV   *Elizabethan Hull*

1. Gillett and MacMahon, *op. cit.*, p.111
2. Quoted in G.M. Trevelyan, *English Social History* (1967), p.204
3. Allison, *op. cit.*, pp.135-6
4. *Ibid.*, p.136
5. *Ibid.*, p.134; R. Davis, *Trade and Shipping of Hull, 1500-1700* (East Yorkshire Local History, Series no. 17), pp.7-9
6. Allison, *op. cit.*, pp.134-5
7. Gillett and MacMahon, *op. cit.*, pp.138-9
8. *Ibid.*, pp.139-40
9. *Ibid.*, pp.134, 140
10. Pevsner and Neave, *op. cit.*, p.507
11. Allison, *op. cit.*, p.142; Gillett and MacMahon, *op. cit.*, pp.106-7
12. Gillett and MacMahon, *op. cit.*, p.106
13. *Ibid.*, p.113
14. Allison, *op. cit.*, pp.411-12
15. Gillett and MacMahon, *op. cit.*, p.130
16. *Ibid.*, pp.147-8
17. Hull Corp. Rec. BB 4, ff. 245-6, 250
18. *Ibid.*, f. 302
19. Gillett and MacMahon, *op. cit.*, p.152
20. *Ibid.*, pp.153-4

21. Dickens, *op. cit.*, pp.324, 379; Allison, *op. cit.*, p.95
22. Hull Corp. Rec. BB 4, f. 50 ; Gillett and MacMahon, *op. cit.*, p.117
23. Hull Corp. Rec. BB 4, ff. 23, 30
24. *Ibid.*, f. 35
25. Gillett and MacMahon, *op. cit.*, p.119
26. Hull Corp. Rec. BB 4, f. 117; Gillett and MacMahon, *op. cit.*, pp.119-20
27. Hull Corp. Rec. BB 4, f. 283
28. *Ibid.*, f. 304
29. Gillett and MacMahon, *op. cit.*, pp.120-1
30. *Ibid.*, p.123
31. Allison, *op. cit.*, p.95
32. Gillett and MacMahon, *op. cit.*, pp.116-17
33. Allison, *op. cit.*, pp.95-6
34. Gillett and MacMahon, *op. cit.*, pp.122-3
35. *Ibid.*, pp.127-8
36. Allison, *op. cit.*, p.97; H. Aveling, *Post-Reformation Catholicism in East Yorkshire, 1558-1790* (East Yorkshire Local History Series, no. 11), pp.29-30, 65
37. Allison, *op. cit.*, pp.154-5
38. *Ibid.*, p.155
39. *Ibid.*, pp.160-2
40. *Ibid.*, pp.163, 439; Gillett and MacMahon, *op. cit.*, pp.125-6
41. Allison, *op. cit.*, pp.163, 341-5
42. *Ibid.*, p.348; J. Lawson, *A Town Grammar School Through Six Centuries*, pp.48-55

v *The Jacobean Town and the Civil War, 1603-1660*

1. Gillett and MacMahon, *op. cit.*, p.112
2. Allison, *op. cit.*, pp.155-7
3. Gillett and MacMahon, *op. cit.*, p.158
4. Allison, *op. cit.*, pp.136-8; Davis, *op. cit.*, pp.11, 22-3
5. Allison, *op. cit.*, pp.139-41, 147; D. and S. Neave, *op. cit.*, p.9
6. Martyn Bennett, *The English Civil War; A Historical Companion* (2004), p.119; B.N. Reckitt, *Charles I and Hull* (1952), pp.26-8; Tickell, *op. cit.*, p.716
7. Gillett and MacMahon, *op. cit.*, pp.158-9
8. *Ibid.*; Allison, *op. cit.*, pp.97-8; Hadley, *op. cit.*, p.118
9. Allison, *op. cit.*, p.100
10. *Ibid.*; A.M.W. Stirling, *The Hothams*, Vol. 1 (1918), p.32; Bennett, *op. cit.*, p.118-19, 223; Christopher Hill, *The Century of Revolution, 1603-1714* (1978), pp.96-7
11. Bennett, *op. cit.*, pp.172, 223; Hill, *op. cit.*, pp.103, 111
12. Allison, *op. cit.*, p.102; Reckitt, *op. cit.*, pp.17, 22-3
13. Allison, *op. cit.*, p.102; Reckitt, *op. cit.*, pp.25-6; Tickell, *op. cit.*, p.716
14. Reckitt, *op. cit.*, pp.26-7; C.V. Wedgwood, *The King's War* (1983), pp.87-8; Bennett, *op. cit.*, pp.118-19; Gillett and MacMahon, *op. cit.*, pp.168-9

15. Reckitt, *op. cit.*, pp.47-61; Gillett and MacMahon, *op. cit.*, pp.169-71
16. Allison, *op. cit.*, pp.103-4; Gillett and MacMahon, *op. cit.*, p.171
17. Hill, *op. cit.*, pp.115-16
18. Reckitt, *op. cit.*, pp.71 *sqq.*; Gillett and MacMahon, *op. cit.*, p.172; Bennett, *op. cit.*, p.119
19. Bennett, *op. cit.*, pp.29-30, 120; Allison, *op. cit.*, pp.104-5
20. John Shawe, *Memoirs of Master John Shawe* (1882), pp.157-8; Hadley, *op. cit.*, pp.186-92; Tickell, *op. cit.*, pp.481-7; Gillett and MacMahon, *op. cit.*, pp.172-4
21. Bennett, *op. cit.*, p.120; Allison, *op. cit.*, p.105; Gillett and MacMahon, *op. cit.*, pp.172-5; Reckitt, *op. cit.*, pp.93 *sqq.*; Hull Corp. Rec. BB5, ff 296, 599-600
22. Allison, *op. cit.*, pp.106-7; Bennett, *op. cit.*, p.221
23. Allison, *op. cit.*, pp.107-8; Shawe, *op. cit.*, pp.35-6, 38-40, 181-2
24. Shawe, *op. cit.*, pp.38-40; Gillett and MacMahon, *op. cit.*, p.177
25. Allison, *op. cit.*, pp.108-9, 311-12; Shawe, *op. cit.*, pp.42-5; Bennett, *op. cit.*, pp.185-6

vi *From Restoration to Glorious Revolution, 1660-1700*

1. Allison, *op. cit.*, pp.138-40; Charles Wilson, *England's Apprenticeship, 1603-1763* (1967), pp.42, 192
2. Wilson, *op. cit.*, p.40; Allison pp.140-1; T.S. Willan, *The English Coastal Trade 1600-1750* (1938), pp.69-72, 79-82, 87-9; Davis, *op. cit.*, pp.13-15
3. Allison, *op. cit.*, p.143
4. Ivan and Elizabeth Hall, *Georgian Hull* (1978), pp.8-9; Allison, *op. cit.*, pp.443-4
5. Allison, *op. cit.*, pp.157-8; Lawson, *op. cit.*, p.70
6. Allison, *op. cit.*, pp.163-4; Gillett and MacMahon, *op. cit.*, p.194
7. Hill, *op. cit.*, pp.171-2; Allison, *op. cit.*, p.109; Shawe, *op. cit.*, pp.43-4, 63, 65-71, 185
8. Allison, *op. cit.*, pp.311-12; Gillett and MacMahon, *op. cit.*, p.192; Hadley, *op. cit.*, p.350
9. Allison, *op. cit.*, p.312; J.P. Kenyon, *The Stuarts* (1966), pp.120-1; A.E. Trout, 'Nonconformity in Hull', *Congregational History Society Transactions*, ix, pp.11, 14-17; W. Whitaker, *Bowl Alley Lane Chapel*, pp.41, 45-6, 48, 51-3, 62, 75, 87-9
10. Allison, *op. cit.*, pp.111-12, 296; D. and S. Neave, *op. cit.*, p.48
11. Aveling, *op. cit.*, p.53
12. Gillett and MacMahon, *op. cit.*, p.189
13. *Ibid.*, p.181
14. *Ibid.*, pp.182-3; Maurice Ashley, *England in the Seventeenth Century* (1977), pp.141-2, 144, 163
15. Gillett and MacMahon, *op. cit.*, p.183; Allison, *op. cit.*, pp.113-4
16. Ashley, *op. cit.*, pp.142-4, 145-6
17. Allison, *op. cit.*, p.114
18. *Ibid.*, p.119
19. Ashley, *op. cit.*, pp.148-53

20. *Ibid.*, pp.167-8; Allison, *op. cit.*, p.114
21. Ashley, *op. cit.*, pp.171-2
22. *Ibid.*, pp.172-3; Allison, *op. cit.*, p.115; Kenyon, *op. cit.*, pp.151, 155
23. Gillett and MacMahon, *op. cit.*, p.184
24. *Ibid.*, p.185; Allison, *op. cit.*, pp.119-20; Hadley, *op. cit.*, pp.270-2
25. Allison, *op. cit.*, p.120
26. Ashley, *op. cit.*, pp.176-7; Gillett and MacMahon, *op. cit.*, p.185; Hadley, *op. cit.*, p.276; Allison, *op. cit.*, p.115
27. Tickell, *op. cit.*, p.583; Gillett and MacMahon, *op. cit.*, p.185; Allison, *op. cit.*, pp.120, 408; Sheahan, *op. cit.*, p.675

VII *The Georgian Town*

1. Most of the information concerning the development of Hull's trade in the Georgian period is drawn from the 'Hull 1700-1835' section of *The Victoria County History*, edited by K.J. Allison, pp.174-84
2. A map showing Hull's canal and navigable river communications is included in H. Calvert's *A History of Hull*, p.315
3. Gillett and MacMahon, *op. cit.*, pp.220-1; G.E. Cherry, *Urban Change and Planning* (1972), pp.232-3
4. Gillett and MacMahon, *op. cit.*, pp.222-4
5. Allison, *op. cit.*, pp.188-9; John Craggs, *Craggs' guide to Hull. A description, historical and topographical, of the town, county and vicinity of the town of Kingston upon Hull* (1817), p.1; Sheahan, *op. cit.*, pp.367-8; Tickell, *op. cit.*, p.872
6. Hadley, *op. cit.*, pp.319, 369; Gillett and MacMahon, *op. cit.*, pp.225-6
7. Allison, *op. cit.*, pp.391-2; R.G. Battle, *Directory of Hull* (1791), pp.65-8
8. Allison, *op. cit.*, pp.190-2
9. D. Defoe, *A Tour Through the Whole Island of Great Britain* (Everyman edn, 1928), ii, p.244
10. D. and S. Neave, *op. cit.*, pp.13, 123-4
11. Allison, *op. cit.*, pp.209, 449-51; the Georgian buildings to be seen on a walk through some of these streets of the 'Northern Suburb' are described and illustrated by D. and S. Neave in *Hull*, pp.121-31
12. Allison, *op. cit.*, p.209
13. *Ibid.*, pp.190-1
14. *Ibid.*, p.210
15. Hadley, *op. cit.*, p.303
16. Allison, *op. cit.*, pp.210-11, 349, 440
17. *Ibid.*, p.211; Tickell, *op. cit.*, p.777
18. Gillett and MacMahon, *op. cit.*, p.235
19. Allison, *op. cit.*, pp.210-11; *Hull Advertiser*, 3 May 1796
20. *Hull Advertiser*, 24 January 1800; 22 August 1800
21. Gillett and MacMahon, *op. cit.*, pp.238-40
22. *Ibid.*, p.238
23. *Hull Rockingham*, 12 February, 1812
24. Allison, *op. cit.*, p.233

25. Sheahan, *op. cit.*, p.204; Gillett and MacMahon, *op. cit.*, pp.255-6
26. Gillett and MacMahon, *op. cit.*, p.257
27. Allison, *op. cit.*, p.440
28. Tickell, *op. cit.*, pp.734-6
29. Allison, *op. cit.*, p.212
30. Markham, *op. cit.*, pp.70, 118, 119
31. Gillett and MacMahon, *op. cit.*, p.243; Allison, *op. cit.*, pp.411-12; Hadley, *op. cit.*, pp.320, 306
32. Gillett and MacMahon, *op. cit.*, p.211
33. Allison, *op. cit.*, p.209
34. *Ibid.*, pp.418-19. The theatre was described, however, in Craggs' *Directory* of 1835 as 'one of the … most handsome provincial theatres in the kingdom, unsurpassed in extent of stage or lightness of appearance'. By this time attempts to run a summer season had long been abandoned; the season ran only from November to February.
35. Allison, *op. cit.*, p.419
36. *Ibid.*, p.209
37. *Ibid.*, pp.420-1
38. *Ibid.*, p.423
39. *Ibid.*, p.315
40. Jane Garbutt, *Reminiscences of the Early Days of Primitive Methodism in Hull* (1886); Sheahan, *op. cit.*, pp.557-8
41. Allison, *op. cit.*, p.313
42. *Ibid.*, p.213; Gillett and MacMahon, *op. cit.*, pp.209, 212
43. Allison, *op. cit.*, pp.213, 293, 299, 310; Sheahan, *op. cit.*, pp.528-9
44. This part of the chapter is based mainly on the information given in the 'Education' section of the *Victoria County History*, pp.348-53, 363-4
45. Tickell, *op. cit.*, p.832
46. *Ibid.*, p.833
47. Hadley, *op. cit.*, pp.378-81; Craggs, *op. cit.*, pp.50-1
48. William White, *Directory of Hull* (1831), pp.lv–lvi; J. Greenwood, Picture of Hull (1835), p.112
49. Sheahan, *op. cit.*, pp.643-7
50. Lawson, *op. cit.*, pp.199-206
51. Gillett and MacMahon, *op. cit.*, p.253
52. *Ibid.*, p.252
53. Quoted in Allison, *op. cit.*, p.199
54. Gillett and MacMahon, *op. cit.*, p.251-2; Allison, *op. cit.*, pp.199-200; Norman McCord, *The Anti-Corn Law League 1838-1846* (1975), pp.56-8

VIII *Victorian and Edwardian Hull, 1837-1914*

1. Census of Population
2. Allison, *op. cit.*, pp.223-4; Robert Barnard, *Moors' and Robson's Breweries Ltd* (1996), p.3; Robert Barnard, *Barley, Mash and Yeast, a History of the Hull Brewery Co., 1782-1985* (1990)
3. Allison, *op. cit.*, pp.223, 256-7; W. White, *Directory of Hull* (1867), p.188; *Kelly's Directory of Hull* (1889), p.259 (1899), p.470 (1913), p.606

4. Allison, *op. cit.*, pp.225-6, 254-6; Sheahan, *op. cit.*, p.365; *Kelly's Directory of Hull* (1913), pp.541, 566; D. Wynn, *Murder and Crime, Kingston-upon-Hull* (2008), pp.8-9

5. Gillett and MacMahon, *op. cit.*, p.271-2; Pevsner and Neave, *op. cit.*, p.524; D. and S. Neave, *op. cit.*, p.134

6. Gillett and MacMahon, *op. cit.*, p.275-9; Markham, *op. cit.*, p.76

7. *Ibid.*, pp.351-3; Allison, *op. cit.*, pp.395-6

8. Allison, *op. cit.*, pp.227-31

9. Gillett and MacMahon, *op. cit.*, p.353-4

10. *Ibid.*, pp.354-5

11. Allison, *op. cit.*, pp.221-2, 246-50

12. *Ibid.*, pp.247-8

13. *Ibid.*, p.248

14. This section is based mainly on Allison, *op. cit.*, pp.231-8, 264-6; other sources used are shown below

15. Gillett and MacMahon, *op. cit.*, pp.257-8

16. *Ibid.*, pp.258-60; *Hull Advertiser*, 21 September 1849

17. Quoted in Allison, *op. cit.*, p.234

18. *Hull Advertiser*, 28 September 1849

19. Gillett and MacMahon, *op. cit.*, pp.286-7

20. Sheahan, *op. cit.*, pp.422-6

21. Gillett and MacMahon, *op. cit.*, pp.263-4

22. *Ibid.*, pp.268-9

23. Sheahan, *op. cit.*, p.385

24. Quoted in Allison, *op. cit.*, p.265

25. Gillett and MacMahon, *op. cit.*, pp.327-8; *Eastern Morning News*, 2 November 1883

26. Allison, *op. cit.*, p.266

27. Gillett and MacMahon, *op. cit.*, pp.286, 288, 313-14, 332-3

28. Allison, *op. cit.*, p.238

29. *Ibid.*, pp.238, 440; Sheahan, *op. cit.*, pp.618-19, 621; *Kelly's Directory* (1889), p.8

30. *Hull Advertiser*, 21 December 1849

31. Allison, *op. cit.*, p.239

32. *Ibid.*, pp.239-40; *Census of Religious Worship in England and Wales, 1851*, HO 129/24, p.cclix

33. Allison, *op. cit.*, pp.266-7

34. *Census of Religious Worship in England and Wales, 1851*, HO 129/24, pp.519-20

35. Allison, *op. cit.*, pp.316-17

36. *Ibid.*, pp.267-8, 317

37. *Ibid.*, pp.327-8

38. Tickell, *op. cit.*, p.825; Sheahan, *op. cit.*, pp.569, 572; Aveling, *op. cit.*, p.57

39. Allison, *op. cit.*, pp.351-2, 364, 367

40. *Ibid.*, p.352

41. *Ibid.*, pp.353-4

42. *Ibid.*; Pevsner and Neave, *op. cit.*, p.522; D. and S. Neave, *op. cit.*, p.18

43. Lawson, *op. cit.*, pp.199-206, 223-8; Allison, *op. cit.*, p.353

44. Lawson, *op. cit.*, pp.231 *sqq.*; Allison, *op. cit.*, pp.354-5

45. Sheahan, *op. cit.*, pp.643-7

46. Gillett and MacMahon, *op. cit.*, pp.339-40

47. Allison, *op. cit.*, pp.355-7, 358

48. *Ibid.*, p.359

49. *Eastern Counties Herald*, 21 October 1869

50. Allison, *op. cit.*, p.419; Sheahan, *op. cit.*, pp.668-71

51. Allison, *op. cit.*, p.419

52. *Ibid.*, p.420

53. *Ibid.*, pp.421-3

54. www. hullfc.com; www.hullkr.co.uk

55. www.hullcityafc.net

56. Gillett and MacMahon, *op. cit.*, pp.333-4; Allison, *op. cit.*, pp.381-2

57. Gillett and MacMahon, *op. cit.*, p.334; D. and S. Neave, *op. cit.*, pp.146-50, 170-1

58. Allison, *op. cit.*, pp.423-5

59. *Ibid.*, pp.250-9

60. *Ibid.*, pp.259-60; Gillett and MacMahon, *op. cit.*, pp.355-60

61. Pevsner and Neave, *op. cit.*, pp.552-6; D. and S. Neave, *op. cit.*, pp.154 -8

62. Gillett and MacMahon, *op. cit.*, pp.363-4

63. D. and S. Neave, *op. cit.*, pp.53-9, 60-70; Pevsner and Neave, *op. cit.*, pp.516-19

64. D. and S. Neave, *op. cit.*, pp.97-8, 125-6, 169, 170-1, 174-7

65. *Ibid.*, p.32

IX *The Twentieth Century and Beyond*

1. D. Bilton, *The Trench; the Full Story of the 1st Hull Pals* (2002), pp.14-15

2. *Ibid.*, pp.16-17

3. www. paul-gibson.com/hull-in-the-first-world-war

4. J. Markham (ed.), *Keep the Home Fires Burning; the Hull area in the First World War* (1988), pp.13-14; D.G. Woodhouse, *Anti-German Sentiment in Kingston upon Hull: the German Community and the First World War* (1990), pp.42-3; Gillett and MacMahon, *op. cit.*, pp.375-6

5. Woodhouse, *op. cit.*, pp.33-9, 44-54

6. *Ibid.*, pp.67-79; Markham (ed.), *Keep the Home Fires Burning*, p.45

7. Gillett and MacMahon, *op. cit.*, pp.376-7

8. Markham (ed.), *Keep the Home Fires Burning*, p.74

9. *Ibid.*, p.86

10. www. paul-gibson.com/hull-in-the-first-world-war

11. Markham, *Book of Hull*, p.96; Allison, *op. cit.*, p.270

12. Allison, *op. cit.*, pp.270-2; Gillett and MacMahon, *op. cit.*, p.377

13. Allison, *op. cit.*, p.272; Gillett and MacMahon, *op. cit.*, p.375

14. www. paul-gibson.com/hull-in-the-first-world-war

15. Allison, *op. cit.*, p.272; Gillett and MacMahon, *op. cit.*, p.380

16. Allison, *op. cit.*, p.274; Gillett and MacMahon, *op. cit.*, p.378

17. Allison, *op. cit.*, p.274

18. *Ibid.*

19. *Ibid.*, pp.274-5; Gillett and MacMahon, *op. cit.*, pp.388-9

20. Allison, *op. cit.*, pp.275-6; Gillett and MacMahon, *op. cit.*, pp.381-2

21. Allison, *op. cit.*, p.276; Gillett and MacMahon, *op. cit.*, p.382; Markham, *Book of Hull*, p.111

22. Allison, *op. cit.*, p.276; Markham, *Book of Hull*, p.112

23. Allison, *op. cit.*, p.381; Markham, *Book of Hull*, p.112

24. Allison, *op. cit.*, p.358; Markham, *Book of Hull*, p.113

25. Allison, *op. cit.*, pp.358-60; Markham, *Book of Hull*, p.113

26. Allison, *op. cit.*, p.360

27. Markham (ed.), *Keep the Home Fires Burning*, p.66

28. Allison, *op. cit.*, pp.421-3; Markham, *Book of Hull*, p.112

29. Gillett and MacMahon, *op. cit.*, p.383

30. www.hullcityafc.net/page/History

31. www.talkrugbyleague.co.uk; www.hullkr.co.uk

32. Allison, *op. cit.*, p.425; Gillett and MacMahon, *op. cit.*, p.393

33. Gillett and MacMahon, *op. cit.*, p.393; www.hullcc. gov.uk; www.yorkshire.com/HullTheatre

34. Gillett and MacMahon, *op. cit.*, pp.392-3; www.hullchoralunion.org

35. C.B. Smith, *Amy Johnson* (1967), chapters 17-21; Markham, *Book of Hull*, p.113; Gillett and MacMahon, *op. cit.*, p.395; www.bbc.co.uk/insideout/ yorkslincs; www.hullhistorycentre.org.uk

36. T. Geraghty, *A North East Coast Town: Ordeal and Triumph. The Story of Kingston upon Hull in the 1939-1945 Great War* (1951), p.9; Dickson, Tony, *Kingston upon Hull City Transport: a short history of 90 years service, 1899-1989* (Hull, 1990)

37. Geraghty, *op. cit.*, pp.9-13, 109-10

38. *Ibid.*, pp.13-22, 111-12

39. *Ibid.*, p.1

40. Gillett and MacMahon, *op. cit.*, p.402

41 *Ibid.*, pp.396-9

42. Markham, *Book of Hull*, p.119; Allison, *op. cit.*, pp.280-4

43. Allison, *op. cit.*, pp.280-2

44. Markham, *Book of Hull*, p.119; Pevsner and Neave, *op. cit.*, pp.523, 525-6

45. Pevsner and Neave, *op. cit.*, p.503

46. Census of Population

47. Allison, *op. cit.*, p.283

48. Pevsner and Neave, *op. cit.*, p.503; Markham, *Book of Hull*, p.120

49. Markham, *Book of Hull*, p.121; www.hullcc.gov.uk

50. www.riverhumber.com; www.hullmaritimealliance. com

51. www.hullwebs.co.uk; www.riverhumber.com; www. fishgate.co.uk; *Hull Daily Mail*, 13 October 2010; *Guardian*, 9 January 2002

52. *Guardian*, 9 January 2002

53. www.hullcc.gov.uk; D. and S. Neave, *op. cit.*, p.105

54. www.hullcc.gov.uk; D. and S. Neave, *op. cit.*, p.134-7

55. Hull Forward, 29 July 2005, www.hull.co.uk/news; *Hull Daily Mail*, 1 September 2009

56. D. and S. Neave, *op. cit.*, p.113; Hull Forward, 2007, www.hull.co.uk

57. D. and S. Neave, *op. cit.*, p.116-7; www.hullcc.gov.uk

58. www.hullchoralunion.org; www.hullcc.gov.uk; www. yorkshire.com/HullTheatre

59. www.hullcc.gov.uk

60. www.hullvibe.co.uk/venue; www.hullcc.gov.uk

61. www.hulllettingagents.co.uk

62. www.hullcityafc.net

63. www.hullcc.gov.uk

64. www.hullcc.gov.uk

65. www.hullcc.gov.uk; *Hull Daily Mail*, 2 February 2011

66. Markham, *Book of Hull*, p.120; www.hullcc.gov.uk

67. *Hull Daily Mail*, 9 June 2010, 30 October 2010; BBC News Online, 17 June 2010, 22 June 2010

68. BBC News Online, 25 June 2007, 13 July 2007, 22 July 2007; Environment Agency Case Study, 2007 Summer Floods: tackling surface water flooding in Hull (www.environment-agency.gov.uk)

69. D. and S. Neave, *op. cit.*, pp.116-17, 119-20, 128-9, 136-7, 167; Hull City Council leaflet, *Teach in Hull*

70. *Scunthorpe Telegraph*, 20 January 2011; www. humberbusiness.com/economy; www.skyscrapercity. com; www.yorkshire-forward.com

Select Bibliography

Details of websites used can be found in the References.

Primary Sources:

Hull Corporation Bench Book

Newspapers:

Eastern Counties Herald
Hull Advertiser
Hull Daily Mail
Hull Forward
Hull Rockingham

Directories:

Baines' Directory of Yorkshire, East Riding, 1823
Battle, R.G., *Battle's Directory of Hull*, 1791, 1803, 1806, 1810-11, 1817, 1822
Craggs, John, *A new triennial Directory and Guide of Kingston-upon-Hull, and the suburbs*, 1835
Kelly's Directory of the Port of Hull and Neighbourhood, 1885, 1889, 1892, 1893, 1899, 1913
Noble, Joseph, *The Directory of Kingston-upon-Hull*, 1838
Purdon, William, *The Directory of Kingston-upon-Hull*, 1839
Pigot's National and Commercial Directory, 1834
Universal British Directory, 1794
White, William, *White's Directory of Hull*, 1826, 1831, 1838, 1867

Secondary Sources:

Alderson, J., *A brief outline of the history and progress of the cholera at Hull* (1832)

Alec-Smith, R.A., *Kingston upon Hull: Views of Yesterday and Today* (1951)

Allison, K.J. (ed.), *The Victoria History of the Counties of England; Yorkshire, East Riding, I; the city of Kingston upon Hull* (1969)

Armstrong, P., *Excavations in Sewer Lane* (1977)

Armstrong, P., *Excavations in Scale Lane/Lowgate* (1980)

Armstrong, P. and Ayers, B., *Excavations in High Street and Blackfriargate* (1987)

Ayres, B., *Excavations at Chapel Lane Staith* (1979)

Barnard, Robert, *Barley, Mash and Yeast, a History of the Hull Brewery Co., 1782-1985* (1990)

Barnard, Robert, *Moors' and Robson's Breweries Ltd* (1996)

Bellamy, J.M., *The Trade and Shipping of Nineteenth Century Hull* (1971)

Bilson, J., 'Wyke Upon Hull' (*Transactions of the East Riding Antiquarian Society, xxvi*)

Bilton, David, *Hull Pals* (1999)

Bilton, David, *The Trench; the Full Story of the 1st Hull Pals* (2002)

Calvert, Hugh, *A History of Hull* (1978)

Chambers, William, *Kingston-upon-Hull, Vols 1, 2(i) and 2(ii)* (reprinted 1985)

Chapman, Ben and Mave, *Kingston upon Hull* (2006)

Cherry, Gordon E., *Urban Change and Planning* (1972)

Childs, W.A. (ed.), *The Customs Accounts of Hull, 1453-1490* (1986)

Cook, J., *The History of God's House of Hull, Commonly called the Charterhouse* (1882)

Coupland, R.S., *William Wilberforce*

Craggs, John, *Cragg's guide to Hull. A description, historical and topographical, of the town, county and vicinity of the town of Kingston upon Hull* (1817)

Davis, R., *The Trade and Shipping of Hull, 1500-1700* (1964)

Dickens, A.G., *The East Riding of Yorkshire with Hull and York* (1955)

Dickens, A.G., *The English Reformation* (1964)

Dickson, Tony, *Kingston upon Hull City Transport: a short history of 90 years service, 1899-1989* (Hull, 1990)

Doran, Susan and Durston, Christopher, *Princes, Pastors and People* (1991)

Drewery, R.F., *A select list of books on Hull and district* (1968)

Elton, Chris, *Hull City; A Complete Record 1904-1989* (1989)

Faull, Margaret L. and Stinson, Marie (eds) *Domesday Book, Yorkshire* (2 vols) (1986)

Fletcher, Anthony, *Tudor Rebellions* (1968)

Frost, Charles, *Notices relative to the Early History of the Town and Port of Hull* (1827)

Gawtress, W., *The Corporation of Hull* (1833)

Gawtress, W., *A Report of the Inquiry into the Existing State of the Corporation of Hull* (1834)

Geraghty, T., *A North East Coast Town: Ordeal and Triumph. The Story of Kingston upon Hull in the 1939 – 1945 Great War* (1951)

Gent, T., *History of Kingston-upon-Hull* (1735)

Giles, Midge, *Amy Johnson, Queen of the Air* (2003)

Gillett, Edward, and MacMahon, Kenneth A., *A History of Hull* (1980)

Good, Helen, *Kingston upon Hull Records: Letters, 1576-1585* (1997)

Good, Helen, *Kingston upon Hull Records: Bench Book 4, 1580-1585* (1997)

Good, Helen, *Kingston upon Hull Records: Bench Book 4, 1585-1590* (1998)

Good, Helen, *Kingston upon Hull Records:Letters, 1585-1587* (2000)

Good, Helen, *Elizabethan Hull Documents (University of Hull Diploma in Regional and Local History, Module 20172)*

Greenwood, *Picture of Hull* (1835)

Griffiths, R.A., *The Reign of King Henry VI* (1998)

Hadley, G., *A New and Complete History of the Town and County of Kingston upon Hull* (1788)

Haigh, Christopher (ed.), *The English Reformation Revised* (1987)

Hall, Ivan and Elizabeth, *Georgian Hull* (1978)

Hardy, Clive, *Hull at War* (1993)

Harper-Bill, Christopher, *The Pre-Reformation Church in England* (1989)

Horrox, R., *The Changing Plan of Hull, 1290-1650* (1978)

Horrox, R., *The De La Poles of Hull* (1983)

Horrox, R. (ed.), *Selected Rentals and Accounts of Medieval Hull, 1293-1528* (1983)

Jackson, G., *Hull in the Eighteenth Century* (1972)

Jackson, G., *The Trade and Shipping of Eighteenth-Century Hull* (1975)

Jordan, G.J., *The Story of Holy Trinity Church, Hull*

Keen, M.H., *England in the Later Middle Ages* (1973)

Lander, J.R., *Government and Community; England 1450-1509* (1980)

Lander, J.R., *The Wars of the Roses* (1990)

Laverack, E., *Documents relating to the Charterhouse of Kingston upon Hull* (1906)

Lawson, J., *A Town Grammar School through Six Centuries* (1963)

MacMahon, K.A., *The Beginnings of the East Yorkshire Railways* (revised edn, 1974)

MacMahon, K.A. (ed.), *An Index to the Hull Advertiser and Exchange Gazette, 1794-1825* (1955)

MacMahon, K.A., *Acts of Parliament and Proclamations Relating to the East Riding of Yorkshire and Kingston upon Hull, 1529-1800* (1961)

MacTurk, G.G., *A History of the Hull Railways* (1879; revised edn, 1970)

Markham, John (ed.), *Keep the Home Fires Burning; the Hull area in the First World War* (1988)

Markham, John, *Streets of Hull* (1987)

Markham, John, *The Book of Hull* (1989)

Neave, David and Susan, *Hull* (2010)

Neave, David, *The Dutch Connection* (1988)

Parry, D. (ed.), *The Meadley Index to the Hull Advertiser* (1987)

Pevsner, Nikolaus and Neave, David, *The Buildings of England: Yorkshire; York and the East Riding* (2nd edn, 1995)

Reckitt, B.N., *Charles the First and Hull* (1952)

Reckitt, B.N., *The History of Reckitt and Sons Limited* (1965)

Robinson, Robb, *Trawling; the Rise and Fall of the British Trawl Fishery* (1996)

Shawe, J., *Memoirs of Master John Shawe* (1882)

Sheahan, J.J., *A General and Concise History and Description of the Town and Port of Kingston-upon-Hull* (2nd edn, 1866)

Sheppard, T., *The Evolution of Kingston-upon-Hull* (1911)

Sibree, James, *Recollections of Hull during half a century* (1884)

Simpson, Henry, *History of the Hull Royal Infirmary* (1888)

Smith, Constance B., *Amy Johnson* (1967)

Stirling, A.M.W., *The Hothams*, vol. 1 (1918)

Storey, A., *Trinity House of Kingston-upon-Hull* (1967)

Symonds, John, *The Visitors' Descriptive Guide Book to Kingston-upon-Hull* (1867)

Tickell, J., *The History of the Town and County of Kingston-upon-Hull* (1798)

Tunstall, J., *The Fishermen* (1962)

Willan, T.S., *The English Coasting Trade 1600-1750*

Wildridge, T.T., *Old and New Hull* (1884)

Woodhouse, D.G., *Anti-German Sentiment in Kingston upon Hull: the German Community and the First World War* (1990)

Woodward, G.W.O., *Dissolution of the Monasteries* (1966)

Woolley, W., *A Collection of Statutes relating to Kingston-upon-Hull* (1830)

Wynn, Douglas, *Murder and Crime in Kingston upon Hull* (2006)

Ziegler, Philip, *The Black Death* (1991)

Index